WOMEN AT WORK

WOMEN AT WORK

including

THE LONG DAY

*The Story of a
New York Working Girl*

by Dorothy Richardson

&

INSIDE THE NEW YORK TELEPHONE COMPANY

by Elinor Langer

EDITED WITH AN INTRODUCTION
BY WILLIAM L. O'NEILL

*Chicago
Quadrangle Books
1972*

Library of Congress Catalog Card Number: 72–182506

International Standard Book Number:
Cloth 0–8129–0216–5
Paper 0–8129–6184–6

INTRODUCTION

AT first these two studies seem to have little in common. One concerns factory work at the turn of the century, the other white-collar work in the late 1960's. One deals with working-class women, the other with lower-middle-class women. One writer toiled of necessity, the other by choice, to gather material for an essay. Yet there are good reasons for reprinting them together. Each deals with occupations that were typical of their time. In 1900 most New York working girls were employed in unregulated stores and sweatshops. By 1969 clerical and bureaucratic positions were usual. These two reports suggest how far working women have come in the past seventy years. Yet they also show how much remains the same. Working girls in 1900 rarely earned enough to support a family. Most, in fact, did not make enough to live above the subsistence level. Even allowing for inflation, phone company women make more money for less work. But they cannot maintain a family on wages of $100 and $120 a week either. Then, as now, only a handful of employed women could support themselves, much less their dependents, in anything resembling comfort. Wages still reflect women's status as the most underpaid element of the work force.

The Long Day's origins are obscure. Nothing is known of Miss Richardson herself. In fact, when published, the book had no author's credit at all. It came out in 1905, but there is no way of telling how much earlier it had been written, nor during exactly which years the experiences described took place. Miss Richardson said that she came from a middle-class background, which is obvious, and that she recast her experiences for the sake of dramatic effect. That too hardly needs saying. Yet while we might welcome further information about the author, the book speaks perfectly well for itself. To my knowledge it is the best account of the life of an urban working girl seventy or seventy-five years ago. There were a number of worthwhile studies of working women made in those years.[1] Some trade-union women have

[1] See, for example, Katharine Anthony, *Mothers Who Must Earn* (New York, 1914); Louise M. Bosworth, *The Living Wage of Women Workers* (New York, 1911); Elizabeth Beardsley Butler, *Saleswomen in Mercantile Stores* (New York, 1912); Mary Van Kleeck, *Artificial Flower Makers* (New York, 1913); and *A Seasonal Industry: A Study of the Millinery Trade in New York* (New York, 1917). Most of these books were sponsored by the Russell Sage Foundation.

INTRODUCTION

written biographies which deal in passing with their early experiences as workers.[2] There were even a few books written by middle-class women who took jobs so as to report on them.[3] But *The Long Day* is unique in having been written by a middle-class woman who took unskilled jobs because she had to. Because of her experience Miss Richardson wrote on subjects that others ignored. No other book shows so well the effect of popular culture on working girls in this period. None demonstrates so clearly how useful it was to them. A few years later, when moving picture theaters became common, people started writing about the medium's harmful influence on working-class life.[4] But before films, middle-class writers and intellectuals were uninterested in popular culture, except as it threatened morals. Miss Richardson had the usual contempt for it, yet despite herself she shows us how singing popular ballads made work easier to bear, and how cheap romances occupied minds numbed by sweated labor. Miss Richardson is equally scornful of the

[2] See, for example, Mary Anderson, *Woman at Work* (Minneapolis, 1951); Alice Henry, *The Trade Union Woman* (New York, 1915); and Agnes Nestor, *Woman's Labor Leader* (Rockford, Ill., 1954).

[3] See, for example, Lillian Pettengill, *Toilers of the Home: The Record of a College Woman's Experience as a Domestic Servant* (New York, 1903).

[4] Jane Addams, *The Spirit of Youth and the City Streets* (New York, 1909) includes a pioneer attempt to show the negative consequences of movie-going. The poet Vachel Lindsay, on the other hand, loved films. His book *The Art of the Moving Picture* (New York, 1970) has recently been reissued.

INTRODUCTION

" pleasure clubs " that working-class girls and boys joined. She thinks them probably immoral, certainly sordid and pathetic. But again, there is something moving in the girls' almost desperate attempts at gaiety. Youth lasted but a short time in sweatshops. Why begrudge the young their brief moments of joy? Pleasure clubs had a serious purpose too. The only escape from sweated labor for most girls was marriage. And as so much of their life was spent in sexually segregated occupations, they had to meet boys where they could. Pleasure clubs filled, however poorly, a real need.

To modern readers what is probably weakest about *The Long Day* is Miss Richardson's continual moralizing. She seems to have had fewer ethnic and religious prejudices than was usual for WASPs then. But she shared their intense concern with looks. Dress and speech were how she identified and pigeonholed strangers. Her own morale gave way, she tells us, only when she was no longer able to keep up appearances. Worse still, she had no sympathy for the unfortunates who succumbed to vice. Apart from one story gotten secondhand, she gives us only a single case history to show the moral hazards of city life. This concerns an utterly pathetic creature called Henrietta. Mentally unstable, half-starved, given to liquor and narcotics (the " infamous nostrums of the malpractitioner "), a woman of easy virtue, Henrietta is meant to horrify us. Yet the girl was no prostitute. She still worked, though she was not paid enough to live on.

INTRODUCTION

Her "gentleman-friend" or friends were the only bright spots in her life. They provided her margin of survival—thin as it was. Miss Richardson makes all these facts plain. Yet the knowledge of them inspires no compassion on her part.

Indeed, her treatment of prostitution is the most unsatisfying part of the book. She admitted that she knew more about it than convention allowed her to relate, more's the pity. Prostitution was then at its peak, partly because of the many single male immigrants in large cities, partly because of moral norms that denied men access to respectable women of their own class. Women in turn became prostitutes mainly, it appears, out of want. At the time, radicals always said that prostitution was a consequence of the maldistribution of wealth. Though a cliché, this was probably true. In 1912 Pittsburgh moral reformers made a study of houses of prostitution and found that of 506 inmates nearly all had previously worked at jobs paying less than $10, and usually less than $5, a week, whereas they made from $10 to $25 a week as prostitutes. One does not, therefore, have to strain too hard to explain the incidence of prostitution among working-class women. Yet Miss Richardson can account for it only by saying that women became prostitutes after failing as wage-earners. They disliked working because they didn't know how to work. Her whole book refutes this quaint notion. Most jobs open to girls then were unskilled, and no amount of liking to work would make them more rewarding.

INTRODUCTION

She herself rose from poverty through luck, but especially
because she was better educated than most girls, hence able
to go to night school and learn a skill.

Much of *The Long Day's* fascination derives precisely from
this contradiction between rich observations and impoverished conclusions. Miss Richardson tells in detail how the
girls looked and spoke, how little they made, and what they
did to live. She appreciates the need for trade unions. She
even recognizes sometimes the extent to which women are
exploited as women, and not just as workers—most notably
in laundries where the work is so brutal that only blacks
and women will do it. Mostly though, she falls back on
character as the great molder of destiny. When girls write
obscenely on the walls of what she admits is a dormitory run
as a combination police state and racket, this is the " frightful
testimony of their innate depravity." She cannot explain
why the flowermakers were a " better " class of girls than
the boxmakers. In fact, the question does not occur to her.
People have a better character because they have a better
character.

Thus, while *The Long Day* is about the most telling exhibit
of life as a working girl that we have, it is as important for
its defects as its virtues. It shows us that most working girls
had little grasp of what dominated their lives. It shows us
that most middle-class people, even experienced ones like

INTRODUCTION

Dorothy Richardson, were equally blind. *The Long Day* is
the best place to begin studying the condition of working
women in, or just before, the Progressive era that I know of.
But to understand what was happening one must go on to
the formal studies made then, especially by the Russell Sage
Foundation, and beyond them to the first-person accounts of
labor leaders, radicals, and social workers who knew there
was more to poverty than wrong thinking.

In Elinor Langer's two pieces on the New York Telephone
Company we confront a sensibility entirely different from
Dorothy Richardson's. Miss Richardson describes conditions
as foreign to us as if in another country. But her views on
them embodied the conventional wisdom of her time. Since
so much of it has survived, one may be irritated, though
hardly surprised, by her prejudices. Miss Langer, on the
other hand, is perhaps a radical, certainly an environmental-
ist. She does not think people create themselves, rather that
they are what life has made them. Thus she tries to understand the shaping influences on phone company workers.
And she likes them personally. Of course, Elinor Langer
could afford to. She worked from choice. Her job had no
effect on her self-image. Dorothy Richardson, on the other
hand, felt degraded by what she did, as by the associations
imposed on her. Her mental health—self-respect as she called
it—depended on keeping apart from most of her co-workers.

INTRODUCTION

Then too, as a native-born WASP of bourgeois origins she had little in common but poverty with them. Elinor Langer's fellow workers were women whose background she knew, whose tastes she could at least understand and may once have shared. American girls are now socialized together as they were not in the nineteenth century. Most go to identical high schools, dress and speak alike, and absorb the same popular culture. A middle-class girl today forced to become self-supporting would not be brutally separated from everything familiar to her as was Dorothy Richardson. To experience real culture shock as she did, one would have to move to a ghetto or become a migrant worker, which in the ordinary course of events would never happen.

This is not to slight Elinor Langer's accomplishment. If it was easy for her to join the phone company and get along with her colleagues, analyzing the experience was surely difficult. Though better equipped than Miss Richardson to comprehend her situation, she was dealing with a far more complex situation. *The Long Day* concerns women who were in fact wage slaves, victims of a primitive and brutalizing industrial system. Phone company workers, on the other hand, are more satisfied than not. Their working conditions are good. Their jobs, if often pointless, require special training. They belong to a relatively sophisticated element of a much more technically advanced economy. Most important,

INTRODUCTION

perhaps, this is an economy of abundance rather than scarcity. In *The Long Day* girls worked to live. Phone company employees work to live better. Their paychecks go frequently to luxuries rather than staples. And their work itself, which consists mainly of selling more expensive services to people who are already well served, perfectly reflects the logic of an affluent society. Their job is to stimulate demand where none exists. Where there are no needs there must, at least, be wants. Dorothy Richardson and her fellows could not buy the goods they made. Phone company workers can and do. In the past, overproduction led to unemployment, in the present to overconsumption. Factory girls were enslaved by work; phone company women are slaves to pleasure—of a sort.

So we see again that *Brave New World* is the truly prophetic statement of our age. Broadly speaking, there are three important visions of the future. One school, which includes Marxists, technocrats, and utopian novelists, holds that change is mainly in the direction of a rationalized society. Its adherents believe that applied intelligence will do away with inequity and want and humanely fulfill our vital needs. Another school, of which Orwell's *1984* is the classic expression, anticipates a super police state, to whose demands humanity will be bent. A third, and much smaller group of futurists, take their cues from Huxley and argue that post-industrial society is moving toward a totalitarian state based on the pleasure principle.[5] Recent developments have made this seem the most likely vision. Society becomes ever larger, more complex and bureaucratic. The individual is less and less able to influence, much less resist it. On the other hand, affluence promotes bohemianism and the pleasure principle, not only among hippies and youngsters but in the population at large. The middle classes still prefer weekend camping trips to drug trips, though the latter are not unknown. The pleasure principle advances all the same. Work, once seen as an end in itself, is now to many simply the means by which they buy life's real ends—leisure, travel, consumer goods, and such. We have a long way to go before reaching *Brave New World*. For most people there is still an unfavorable balance between work and pleasure. But the line of development seems clear enough.

The phone company is especially interesting, then, because it foreshadows, however dimly, coming events. Its customer service workers are oppressed and exploited, though in subtle ways compared with the old industrial system. They recognize this somewhat, but most apparently accept

[5] A more contemporary description of this prospect (which uses Huxley's very phrase, " brave new world ") is Clark Kerr, *et al.*, *Industrialism and Industrial Man* (Cambridge, Mass., 1960). It predicts the withering away of parliamentary democracy leading to a " new slavery," together with rising levels of individual diversity and bohemian license which amount to a " new freedom."

INTRODUCTION

both the company's rules and the ideology which justifies them. This willingness to identify with the system is a peculiarly middle-class trait. Life makes working-class people cynical about their jobs. They have few illusions, but few are required of them. What they do does not commonly demand conviction. But where service is the chief product, as with the phone company, belief is required. So the phone company recruits lower-middle-class women who have the bourgeois need to identify with their employers, yet are not sufficiently educated or experienced to be critical of them. In the future more and more jobs will be like this, and, as the working class keeps declining, there will be more and more properly conditioned people to fill them.

The phone company is the future in miniature—bureaucratic, authoritarian, paternalistic, subtle. It puts the workers' strengths and weaknesses alike to its own uses. Their liking for one another leads them to help each other out, so performance levels can be set higher than if they worked alone. Supervisors are drawn from the work force, so the regard they are held in by former colleagues is extended to management. "Niceness" eases frictions and muffles hostility. Though labor and management have quite different interests, all are bound together by a common ethic and code of conduct. There is no class-consciousness. Far from being alienated, phone company women are essentially satisfied with their lives. Their complaints—excessive pressure, low wages, inadequate fringe benefits—are of a sort the company can respond to over time without making any basic changes. All this is likely to drive radicals to despair, as Elinor Langer's conclusion indicates. Where Dorothy Richardson could offer suggestions, however futile and irrelevant, Miss Langer can only hope dimly and with little conviction that phone company women are not so unaware as they seem.

At the very least these two reports illustrate what everyone must agree is the most valid complaint of liberated women. Women have always done society's dirty work, at first mainly in the home, now increasingly outside it. It is an old cliché that industrialization freed women. Yet in fact only a small proportion of working women have been employed by industry as such. At the turn of the century more were in sweatshops than in real factories, and bad though the sweatshops were, this was lucky for them, as factories were even worse. Perhaps the largest employers of women (and children) operatives were textile mills whose hands had a life expectancy only two-thirds that of the general population. Jobs for women, then as now, were not usually industrial. Now, even more than then, women labor in shops, stores, and offices as clerical, sales, and service workers. Their work is not a direct result of industrialization, but rather because business and government expanded with it.

Women have always been shut out of highly paid skilled jobs in industry. What they do may be useful and necessary

INTRODUCTION

(over a third of the work force is female); still, they are concentrated in marginal areas devoted to consumption and distribution rather than to production. And it is production workers who have gained most from unionization and rising productivity. Hence women are discriminated against as workers in several ways. They are confined to poorly paid occupations, and even within them paid less than men of similar, or even inferior, qualifications. In the federal government the greatest concentration of women workers is in civil service grades 3 and 4, while for men it is grades 11 and 12. Women workers are on the average better educated than men, but make about 60 per cent of the median wages of employed males. The State of Wisconsin pays its women employees with college degrees less than men with high school diplomas. Nationally, a woman chemist with a Ph.D. averages less income than a male chemist with a bachelor's degree. If women had no other problems these inequities alone would justify feminism.

A further difficulty, which feminists are particularly alive to, stems from the demographic changes affecting women in this century. In Dorothy Richardson's day the typical working woman was twenty-six years old and single. In 1920 she was twenty-eight and still single. Now she is forty-one and married. In 1900 most women were not and never would be gainfully employed. Now 80 per cent of all women work at some time in their lives, and both the proportion who work and the number of years they do so is still rising. Society makes no allowance for this, though it is the single greatest change affecting family life to have taken place in the past fifty years. Many countries protect their working mothers by absorbing some or all the costs of childbirth, guaranteeing employed women maternity leaves, sometimes with pay, and most commonly by giving child allowances to every family. Sweden, besides doing more for women and children than any country, also allows government employees with dependent children to work part-time.

But in America, unless a woman is on welfare she gets virtually no help. Hence some women must work who otherwise would not, and then are penalized for doing so. This is hard on working mothers, many of whom must become wage-earners (10 per cent of all heads of families are working women), and harder still on children. Over three million working women have children under six years of age at home, yet there are licensed day-care facilities for only about 200,000 children. A 1958 survey discovered 400,000 children under twelve for whom no provisions at all had been made. Society demands that women work, but when they do they and their children must suffer. No other developed Western nation has such vicious, irrational, and self-defeating policies toward working women. Yet American women are continually reminded of the unique blessings national affluence has bestowed on them. Who needs to ask why some have

INTRODUCTION

become radical feminists? The wonder is that most have not.

Taken together, then, these two pieces must inspire mixed feelings. On one level enormous progress has been made. Phone company women are incomparably better off than the factory girls Miss Richardson described. At the same time, workers, especially women workers, are still exploited, even if less brutally. They do not have much more influence over what happens to them than before, and perhaps even less social awareness. And they are locked into a monopolistic system based on excess profits through excess consumption. Many of the worst features of traditional capitalism have vanished, but without realizing the hopes of radicals and visionaries who imagined that material progress and ethical gains would go together. Few guessed that rising incomes and improved working conditions would make people easier to manipulate. Fewer still thought the pleasure principle would spread so broadly. Social change has been very rapid indeed over the past quarter of a century. Yet the chief result seems to be that the brave new world is now nearer than we think.

William L. O'Neill

THE LONG DAY

The Story of a
New York Working Girl

by Dorothy Richardson

(1905)

CONTENTS

CHAPTER   PAGE

  I In which I Arrive in New York   3

  II In which I Start Out in Quest of Work   16

  III I Try "Light" Housekeeping in a Fourteenth-street Lodging-house   27

  IV Wherein Fate Brings Me Good Fortune in One Hand and Disaster in the Other   44

  V In which I am "Learned" by Phœbe in the Art of Box-making   58

  VI In which Phœbe and Mrs. Smith Hold Forth upon Music and Literature . .   75

  VII In which I Acquire a Story-book Name and Make the Acquaintance of Miss Henrietta Manners   92

  VIII Wherein I Walk through Dark and Devious Ways with Henrietta Manners .   108

  IX Introducing Henrietta's "Special Gentleman-friend"   123

  X In which I Find Myself a Homeless Wanderer in the Night   142

  XI I Become an "Inmate" of a Home for Working Girls   151

CONTENTS

CHAPTER   PAGE

XII IN WHICH I SPEND A HAPPY FOUR WEEKS MAKING ARTIFICIAL FLOWERS 180

XIII THREE "LADY-FRIENDS," AND THE ADVENTURES THAT BEFALL THEM 197

XIV IN WHICH A TRAGIC FATE OVERTAKES MY "LADY-FRIENDS" 215

XV I BECOME A "SHAKER" IN A STEAM-LAUNDRY 229

XVI IN WHICH IT IS PROVED TO ME THAT THE DARKEST HOUR COMES JUST BEFORE THE DAWN 249

EPILOGUE 266

THE LONG DAY

I

THE rain was falling in great gray blobs upon the skylight of the little room in which I opened my eyes on that February morning whence dates the chronological beginning of this autobiography. The jangle of a bell had awakened me, and its harsh, discordant echoes were still trembling upon the chill gloom of the daybreak. Lying there, I wondered whether I had really heard a bell ringing, or had only dreamed it. Everything about me was so strange, so painfully new. Never before had I waked to find myself in that dreary, windowless little room, and never before had I lain in that narrow, unfriendly bed.

Staring hard at the streaming skylight, I tried to think, to recall some one of the circumstances that

3

might possibly account for my having entered that
room and for my having laid me down on that cot.
When? and how? and why? How inexplicable it
all was in those first dazed moments after that rude
awakening! And then, as the fantasies of a dream
gradually assume a certain vague order in the waking recollection, there came to me a confused consciousness of the events of the preceding twenty-
four hours—the long journey and the weariness of
it; the interminable frieze of flying landscape, with
its dreary, snow-covered stretches blurred with black
towns; the shriek of the locomotive as it plunged
through the darkness; the tolling of ferry-bells, and
then, at last, the slow sailing over a black river toward
and into a giant city that hung splendid upon the
purple night, turret upon turret, and tower upon
tower, their myriad lights burning side by side with
the stars, a city such as the prophets saw in visions,
a city such as dreamy childhood conjures up in the
muster of summer clouds at sunset.

Suddenly out of this chaotic recollection of un-
earthly splendors came the memory, sharp and pinch-
ing, of a new-made grave on a wind-swept hill in
western Pennsylvania. With equal suddenness, too,
the fugue of thundering locomotives, and shrieking
whistles, and sad, sweet tollings of ferry-bells massed

itself into the clangorous music of a terrifying mon-ody—" WORK OR STARVE, WORK OR STARVE ! "

And then I remembered ! An unskilled, friendless, almost penniless girl of eighteen, utterly alone in the world, I was a stranger in a strange city which I had not yet so much as seen by daylight. I was a waif and a stray in the mighty city of New York. Here I had come to live and to toil—out of the placid monotony of a country town into the storm and stress of the wide, wide, workaday world. Very wide awake now, I jumped out of bed upon the cold oil-cloth and touched a match to the pile of paper and kindling-wood in the small stove. There was a little puddle of water in the middle of the floor under the skylight, and the drip in falling had brushed against the sleeve of my shirt-waist and soaked into the soles of my only pair of shoes. I dressed as quickly as the cold and my sodden gar-ments permitted. On the washstand I found a small tin ewer and a small tin basin to match, and I dabbed myself gingerly in the cold, stale water.

Another jangle of the harsh bell, and I went down dark stairs to the basement and to breakfast, won-dering if I should be able to recognize Miss Jamison; for I had caught but a glimpse of my new landlady on my arrival the previous midnight. Wrapped in a faded French flannel kimono, her face smeared with cold cream, her hair done up in curling " kids," she had met and arranged terms with me on the landing in front of her bedroom door as the housemaid conducted me aloft. Making due allowance for the youth-and-beauty-destroying effects of the kimono, curling " kids," and cold cream, and substituting in their stead a snug corset, an undulated pompadour, and a powdered countenance, respectively, I knew about what to look for in the daylight Miss Jamison. A short, plump, blonde lady in the middle forties, I predicted to myself. The secretary of the Young Women's Christian Association, to which I had written some weeks before for information as to respectable and cheap boarding-houses, had responded with a number of names and addresses, among them that of Miss Elmira Jamison, " a lady of very high Christian ideals."

Miss Jamison was no disappointment. She fulfilled perfectly all my preconceived notions of what she would look like when properly attired. Spying me the moment I got inside the dining-room door, she immediately pounced upon me and hurried me off to a seat, when a girl in a dirty white apron began to unload off a tray a clatter of small dishes under my nose, while another servant tossed a wet, warm napkin upon my plate. My breakfast consisted of heterogeneous little dabs of things in the collection of dishes, and which I ate with not the greatest relish in the world.

There were several score of breakfasters in the two big rooms, which seemed to occupy the entire basement floor. They ate at little tables set uncomfortably close together. Gradually my general observations narrowed down to the people at my own table. I noticed a young man opposite who wore eye-glasses and a carefully brushed beard; an old lady, with a cataract in her left eye, who sat at the far end of the table; a little fidgety, stupid-looking, and very ugly woman who sat next the bearded young man; and a young girl, with dancing, roguish black eyes, who sat beside me. The bearded young man talked at a great rate, and judging from the cackling laughter of the fidgety woman and the intensely interested expression of the cataracted lady, the subject was one of absorbing interest.

Gradually I discovered that the topic of discourse was none other than our common hostess and landlady; and gradually, too, I found myself listening to the history of Miss Elmira Jamison's career as a purveyor of bed and board to impecunious and homeless mortals.

7

WOMEN AT WORK

Five years ago Miss Jamison had come into this shabby though eminently respectable neighborhood, and opened a small boarding-house in a neighboring street. She had come from some up-State country town, and her bureaus and bedsteads were barely enough to furnish the small, old-fashioned house which she took for a term of years. Miss Jamison was a genius—a genius of the type peculiar to the age in which we live. She was n't the " slob " that she looked. The epithet is not mine, but that of the young gentleman to whom I am indebted for this information. No, indeed; Miss Jamison was anything but a " slob," as one soon found out who had occasion to deal with her very long. A shrewd, exacting, penny-for-penny and dollar-for-dollar business woman was concealed under the mask of her good-natured face and air of motherly solicitude. Miss Jamison, at the very start-out of her career, was inspired to call her little " snide " boarding-house after the founder of the particular creed professed by the congregation of the neighboring church. The result was that " The Calvin " immediately became filled with homeless Presbyterians, or the homeless friends and acquaintances of Presbyterians. They not only filled her house, but they overflowed, and to preserve the overflow Miss Jamison rented the adjoining house.

8

THE LONG DAY

Miss Jamison was now a successful boarding-house keeper on a scale large enough to have satisfied the aspirations of a less clever woman. But she longed for other denominations to feed and house. Of the assortment that offered themselves, she chose the Methodists next, and soon had several flourishing houses running under the pious appellation " Wesley," which name, memorialized in large black letters on a brass sign, soon became a veritable magnet to board-seeking Methodism.

The third and last venture of the energetic lady, and the one from which she was to derive her largest percentage of revenue, was the establishment of the place of which I had so recently become an inmate. Of all three of Miss Jamison's boarding-houses, this was the largest and withal the cheapest and most democratic: in which characteristics it but partook of the nature of the particular sort of church-going public it wished to attract, which was none other than the heterodox element which flocked in vast numbers to All People's church. The All People's edifice was a big, unsightly brick building. It had been originally designed for a roller-skating rink.

All People's, as the church was colloquially named, was one of the most popular places of worship in the city. Every Sunday, both at morning and even-

ing services, the big rink was packed to the doors
with people who were attracted quite as much by the
good music as they were by the popular preaching of
the very popular divine. A large percentage of this
great congregation was recruited from the transient
element of population which lives in lodgings and
boarding-houses. From its democracy and lack of
all ceremony, it was a church which appealed particularly to those who were without ties or affilia-
tions. Into this sanctuary the lonely young man
(or girl) of a church-going temperament was almost
sure to drift sooner or later if his probationary period of strangerhood happened to fall in this section
of the city.

The clever Miss Jamison put a sign bearing the
legend, " All People's," on each of the doors of six
houses, opposite the church, which she acquired one
by one as her business increased. The homeless and
lonely who came to All People's for spiritual refresh-
ment, or to gratify their curiosity, remained to
patronize Miss Jamison's " special Sunday " thirty-
five-cent table d'hôte, served in the basement of one
house; or bought a meal-ticket for four dollars,
which entitled them to twenty-one meals served in
the basement of another of the houses; or for the
sum of five dollars and upward insured themselves

the privilege of a week's lodging and three meals a day served in still another of the basements.

Such is the history of Miss Jamison as detailed at the breakfast-table that Sunday morning.

I went out for a walk late in the afternoon, and wandered about, homesick and lonely. When I returned dinner was over and the dining-room almost deserted, only a few remaining to gossip over their dessert and coffee. At my table all had gone save the young girl with the dark eyes, who, I felt instinctively, was a very nice and agreeable girl. As I approached the table, she raised her eyes from the book she was reading and gave me a diffident little bow, when, seeing I was so glad to respond to it, she immediately smiled in a friendly way.

From the glimpse I had caught of her during the morning meal, I had thought her very pretty in a smart, stiffly starched, mannish-looking shirt-waist. That night she looked even prettier, clad in a close-fitting cloth gown of dark wine-color. I noticed, too, as I sat down beside her, that she was an unusually big woman.

" How do you like the boarding-house by this time? " she asked, with an encouraging smile, to which I responded as approvingly as I could in the remembrance of the cheerless hall bedroom far above,

and in the presence of the unappetizing dinner
spread before me.

" Well, I think it 's rotten, if you 'll excuse my
French," laughed Miss Plympton, as she cut a
square of butter off the common dish and passed it
to me. "And I guess you think so, too, only you 're
too polite to roast the grub like the rest of us do.
But you 'll get over that in time. I was just the
same way when I first begun living in boarding-
houses, but I 've got bravely over that now.

" I 've been here just a little over a week myself,"
she went on in her frank and engaging manner. I
saw you this morning, and I just knew how you felt.
I thought I 'd die of homesickness when I came.
Not a soul spoke to me for four days. Not that
anybody would want to particularly get acquainted
with these cattle, only I 'm one of the sort that has
got to have somebody to speak to. So this morning
I said to myself, when I saw you, that I 'd put on
nerve and up and speak to you even if you did turn
me down. And that 's why I waited for you to-
night."

I responded that I was glad she had been so informal; absence of formality being the meaning I
interpreted from her slang, which was much more
up-to-date and much more vigorous than that to

which I had been accustomed in the speech of a small
country village. As I ate, we talked. We talked
a little about a great many things in which we were
not at all interested, and a very great deal about
ourselves and the hazards of fortune which had
brought our lives together and crossed them thus at
Miss Jamison's supper-table,—subjects into which
we entered with all the zest and happy egotism of
youth. Of this egotism I had the greater preponderance, probably because of my three or four years'
less experience of life. Before we rose from the
table I had told Miss Plympton the story of my life
as it had been lived thus far.

Of her own story, all I knew was that she was a
Westerner, that she had worked a while in Chicago,
and had come to New York on a mission similar to
my own—to look for a job. We went together to
her room, which was as small and shabby as my own,
and a few minutes later we were sitting round the
little Jenny Lind stove, listening to the pleasant
crackle of the freshly kindled fire. Both were
silent for a few minutes. Then my new friend
spoke.

" What does that put you in mind of ? " she asked
slowly.

" You mean the crackle of the kindling-wood and

the snap of the coal as the flames begin to lick it? " I asked.

" U-m-m, yes; the crackle of the wood and the snap of the coal," said the girl in a dreamy tone.

" Home! " I cried, quick as a flash. " It makes me think of home—of the home I used to have," and my eyes blurred.

" Here, too! Home! " she replied softly. " Funny, is n't it, that we have so many ideas exactly alike? But I suppose that 's because we were both brought up in the country."

" In the country! " I exclaimed in surprise. " I thought you were from Chicago."

" Oh, no; I 'm from the country. I did n't go to Chicago till I was twenty. I lived all my life on a farm in Iowa, till I went up to get a job in Chicago after my father died and I was all alone in the world. We lived in the very wildest part of the State—in the part they call the ' Big Woods.' Oh, I know all about frontier life. And there 's hardly any kind of ' roughing it ' that I have n't done. I was born to it."

She laughed, opening the stove door, for the elbow of the pipe was now red-hot and threatening conflagration to the thin board partition behind, which divided the little room from that of the next lodger.

THE LONG DAY

A loud thump upon the board partition startled us. We listened for a few moments,—at first with alarm,—and then realized that the noise was only the protest of a sleepy boarder.

Presently, as we continued to talk, the banging of a shoe-heel on the wall grew more insistent. We heard doors opening along the hall, and a high, raucous voice invoked quiet in none too polite phrase. So I said, " Good night," in a whisper and tiptoed to my own door.

Thus began my acquaintance with Minnie Plympton—an acquaintance which, ripening later into a warm friendship, was to have an incalculable influence upon my life.

II

WHEN I woke up the next morning it was to find a weight of homesickness lying heavy upon my heart—homesickness for something which, alas! no longer existed save in memory. Then I remembered the girl on the floor below, and soon I was dressing with a light heart, eager to hurry down to breakfast. I was somewhat disappointed to find that she had eaten her breakfast and gone. I went out upon the stoop, hailed a newsboy, and sought my skylight bedroom.

It was with a hope born of youth and inexperience that I now gave systematic attention to " HELP WANTED—Female." I will confess that at first I was ambitious to do only what I chose to esteem " ladylike " employment. I had taught one winter in the village school back home, and my pride and intelligence naturally prompted me to a desire to do something in which I could use my head, my tongue, my

16

wits—anything, in fact, rather than my hands. The advertisements I answered all held out inducements of genteel or semi-genteel nature—ladies' companions; young women to read aloud to blind gentlemen and to invalids; assistants in doctors' and dentists' offices, and for the reception-room of photograph galleries. All of them requested answers in " own handwriting, by mail only." I replied to scores of such with no success.

There was also another kind of illusive advertisement which I answered in prodigal numbers in the greenness of these early days. These were those deceitfully worded requests for " bright, intelligent ladies—no canvassing." And not less prodigal were the returns I got. They came in avalanches by every mail, from patent-medicine concerns, subscription-book publishers, novelty manufacturers—all in search of canvassers to peddle their trash.

I might have saved much superfluous effort, and saved myself many postage-stamps, had I been fortunate enough to have had the advice of Miss Plympton throughout this first week. But Miss Plympton had gone away for several days. I had not seen her since we had parted on Sunday night; but Monday evening, when I went to the table, I found a hasty note saying she had gone out of town to see about a job, and would see me later. That was all. I found myself longing for her more and more as the week wore away.

Meanwhile, however, I did not allow the sentiment of an interrupted acquaintance to interfere with my quest for a job, nor did I sit idle in Miss Jamison's boarding-house waiting for replies. I had only a few dollars in the world, and on the other side of those few dollars I saw starvation staring me in the face unless I found work very soon. I planned my search for work as systematically as I might have conducted a house-cleaning. As soon as each day's grist of " wants " was sifted and a certain quota disposed of by letter, I set out to make personal applications to such as required it. This I found to be an even more discouraging business than the epistolary process, as it was bitterly cold and the streets were filled with slush and snow. The distances were interminable, and each day found my little hoard dwindling away with frightful rapidity into innumerable car-fares and frequent cups of coffee at wayside lunch-counters. I traveled over miles and miles of territory, by trolley-car, by elevated train and ferry-boat, to Brooklyn, to Harlem, to Jersey City and Newark, only to reach my destination cold and hungry, and to be interviewed by a seedy man with a patent stove-lifter, a shirt-waist belt, a contrivance for holding up a lady's train, or a new-fangled mop—anything, everything that a persistent agent might sell to the spendthrift wife of an American workingman.

By the end of the week I was obliged to hunt for another boarding-house as well as continue the search for work. My little bedroom under the sky-light, and three meals per day of none too plentiful and wretchedly cooked food, required the deposit of five dollars a week in advance. With but a few dollars left in my purse, and the prospect of work still far off, nothing in the world seemed so desirable as that I might be able to pass the remainder of my days in Miss Jamison's house, and that I might be able to breakfast indefinitely in her dark basement dining-room.

Sunday morning came around again. I had been a week in the city, and was apparently no nearer to earning a livelihood than the day I started out. I had gained a little experience, but it had been at the cost of nearly five precious dollars, all spent in street-car fare and postage-stamps; of miles and miles of walking through muddy, slushy streets; and at the sacrifice of my noon lunch, which I could have had done up for me at the boarding-house without extra charge, but which my silly vanity did not allow me to carry around under my arm.

Sunday morning again, and still no Miss Plympton. She was under discussion when I reached the breakfast-table. The lady with the cataract and her friend were speaking of how well she always dressed, and one of them wondered how she managed to do it, since she had no visible means of support. Dr. Perkins did n't seem to relish the turn the conversation had taken, and suddenly he fell completely out of it. But the gossips clacked on regardless, until they were brought to a standstill by a peremptory exclamation from the end of the table.

" Excuse me," spoke up the doctor, dryly, " but I 'll have to ask you to change the subject. You are talking about a young lady of whom you know absolutely nothing ! "

The scandal-mongers finished breakfast in silence and soon shuffled away in their bedroom slippers.

" Old cats ! " said the doctor, energetically. " Boarding-house life breeds them. A boarding-house is no place for anybody. It perverts all the natural instincts, mental, moral, and physical. You 'd hardly believe it, but I 've lived in boarding-houses so long that I can't digest really wholesome food any more."

THE LONG DAY

When at last we rose to go, he handed me a card
upon which I later read this astonishing inscription
in heavy black type: " PAINLESS PERKINS "; and,
in smaller type underneath, the information that the
extracting or filling of molars; crown and bridge
work; or the fitting of artificial teeth, would be done
by Painless Perkins in a " Particularly Pleasing
Way," and that he was " Predisposed to Popular
Prices."

With no books to read, and no advertisements to
answer, and no friend with whom to gossip, the day
stretched before me a weary, dreary waste, when I
happened to think of the church across the way,
something of the history of which I had heard from
Painless Perkins. And so I joined the crowd of
strangers who were pouring into the doors of " All
People's " to the music of a sweet-toned bell.

I was there early, but the auditorium was packed,
and I was ushered to a camp-chair in the aisle. The
crowd was not suggestive of fashionable New York,
though there were present many fine-looking, well-
groomed men and women. But nearly everybody
was neatly and decently if not well dressed. Many
of the faces looked as sad and lonely as I felt. They
appeared to be strangers—homeless wanderers who
had come here to church not so much for worship

as to come in touch with human beings. I was too tired, too discouraged even to hear what the earnest-voiced preacher said. The two girls sitting directly in front of me listened intently, as they passed a little bag of peppermints back and forth, and I envied them the friendship which that furtive bag of peppermints betokened. If I had had any prospect of getting a job the following week, I too could have listened to the preacher. As it was, my ears were attuned only to the terrifying refrain which had haunted me all week: "WORK OR STARVE, WORK OR STARVE!" After a while I tried to rouse myself and to take in the sermon which was holding the great congregation breathless. It was about the Good Samaritan. I heard a few sentences. Then the preacher's voice was lost once more in that insistent refrain.

Dinner at noon and supper in the evening in the dark house across the street, and still my friend was absent. The scandal-mongers were as busy as ever, for Painless Perkins was away.

Monday morning I made my way eastward on foot, across Union Square. The snow had been falling all night and was still sifting down in big, flowery flakes. The trees under their soft, feathery burdens looked like those that grow only in a child's picture-book. The slat-benches were covered with soft white blankets that were as yet undisturbed, for the habitual bench tramp was not abroad so early in the morning.

I was up extraordinarily early, as I started out on a double search. The first item on my list— "Board and room, good neighborhood, $3.00 "— took me south across Fourteenth Street, choked and congested with the morning traffic. The pavements were filled with hurrying crowds—factory-hands, mill-girls, mechanics—the vanguard of the great labor army. I hunted for Mrs. McGinniss's residence in a street which pays little attention to the formality of numbers. An interview with a milk-cart driver brought the discouraging news that I might find it somewhere between First and Second avenues, and I hurried on down the street, which stretched away and dipped in the far distance under the framework of the elevated railroad. The stoop-line on either side presented an interminable vista of small, squalid shops, meat-markets, and saloons.

Wedged between a paper-box factory and a black-smith's shop I found Mrs. McGinniss's number. It was a five-story red-brick tenement, like all the others that rise above the stoop-line of this poverty-stricken street. A soiled scrap of paper pasted beneath the button informed possible visitors that Mrs. McGinniss lived on the fifth floor, that her bell was out of order, and that one should " Push Guggenheim's."

The Guggenheims responded with a click from above. I ascended a flight of dark stairs, at the top of which there was ranged an ambuscade of numerous small Guggenheims who had gushed out in their underdrawers and petticoats. Their mother, in curl-papers, gave explicit directions for my guidance upward.

" Is this where Mrs. McGinniss lives? " I inquired of the dropsical slattern who responded to my rap.

" I 'm her."

Mrs. McGinniss's manner was aggressive. Conscious of her bare, sodden arms and dripping gingham apron, she evidently supposed I had mistaken her for a laundress instead of the lady of her own house, and she showed her resentment by chilly reticence.

" I don't run no boarding-house, and I don't take just any trash that come along, either."

I agreed that these were excellent qualities in a landlady, and then, somewhat mollified, she led the way through a steamy passage into a stuffy bedroom. It had one window, looking out into an air-shaft filled with lines of fluttering garments and a network of fire-escapes. A slat-bed, a bureau, a washstand with a noseless pitcher, and a much-spotted Brussels carpet completed the furnishings, and out of all exuded ancient odors of boiled cabbage and soap-suds.

" There 's one thing, though, I won't stand for, and that 's cigarettes. I 've had the last girl in my house that smokes cigarettes I 'm going to have. Look at that nice carpet! Look at it! All burned full of holes where that trollop throwed her matches."

I hurried away, with a polite promise to consider the McGinniss accommodations.

The abode of Mrs. Cunningham was but a few blocks away. Mrs. Cunningham did not live in a flat, but in the comparative gentility of " up-stairs rooms " over a gaudy undertaking establishment. She proved to be an Irish lady with a gin-laden breath. Her eyes were blue and bleared, and looked in kindly fashion through a pair of large-rimmed and much-mended spectacles, from which one of the glasses had totally disappeared. She was affable, and responded to my questions with almost maudlin tenderness, calling me " dearie " throughout the interview. Her little parlor was hung with chromo reproductions of great religious paintings, and the close atmosphere was redolent of the heavy perfume of lilies and stale tuberoses. Remarking the unusual prodigality of flowers, the good lady explained that the undertaker beneath was in the habit of showing his esteem by the daily tender of such funeral decorations as had served their purpose. Mrs. Cunningham's accommodations at four dollars per week were beyond my purse, however; but, as she was willing to talk all day, my exit was made with difficulty.

The remainder of that day and a good part of the days that followed were spent in interviewing all manner of landladies, most of whom, like Mrs. McGinniss's bell, were disordered physically or mentally. Heartsick, I decided by Saturday to take blind chances with the janitress of a Fourteenth-street lodging-house. She had a cleft palate, and all I could understand of her mutilated talk was that the room would be one dollar a week with " light-housekeeping " privileges thrown in. I had either to pay Miss Jamison another five dollars that next morning or take chances here. I took the hazard, paid the necessary one dollar to the more or less inarticulate woman, and went back to Miss Jamison's to get my baggage and to eat the one dinner that was still due me—not forgetting to leave a little note for the still absent Minnie Plympton, giving her my new address.

III

I TRY "LIGHT" HOUSEKEEPING IN A FOURTEENTH-
STREET LODGING-HOUSE

BEDTIME found me thoroughly settled in
my new quarters, and myself in quite an
optimistic frame of mind as I drew close
to the most fearfully and wonderfully mutilated little cook-stove that ever cheered the heart of a lonely
Fourteenth-street "light housekeeper." In the red-
hot glow of its presence, and with the inspiring example of courage and fortitude which it presented,
how could I have felt otherwise than optimistic?
It was such a tiny mite of a stove, and it seemed
to have had such a world of misfortune and bad
luck! There was something whimsically, almost
pathetically, human about it. This, it so pleased
my fancy to believe, was because of the sufferings
it had borne. Its little body cracked and warped
and rust-eaten, the isinglass lights in its door long
since punched out by the ruthless poker, the door
itself swung to on the broken hinge by a twisted

nail—a brave, bright, merry little cripple of a stove, standing on short wooden legs. I made the interesting discovery that it was a stove of the feminine persuasion; "Little Lottie" was the name which I spelled out in the broken letters that it wore across its glowing heart. And straightway Little Lottie became more human than ever—poor Little Lottie, the one solitary bright and cheerful object within these four smoke-grimed walls which I had elected to make my home.

Home! The tears started at the mere recollection of the word. The firelight that flickered through the broken door showed an ironical contrast between the home that now was and that which once had been, and to which I looked back with such loving thoughts that night. A narrow wooden bedstead, as battered and crippled as Little Lottie, but without the latter's air of sympathy and companionship; a tremulous kitchen table; a long box set on end and curtained off with a bit of faded calico, a single chair with a mended leg—these rude conveniences comprised my total list of housekeeping effects, not forgetting, of course, the dish-pan, the stubby broom, and the coal-scuttle, along with the scanty assortment of thick, chipped dishes and the pots and pans on the shelf behind the calico curtain. There was no bureau, only a waved bit of looking-glass over the sink in the corner. My wardrobe was strung along the row of nails behind the door, a modest array of petticoats and skirts and shirt-waists, with a winter coat and a felt sailor-hat. Beneath them, set at right angles to the corner, was the little old-fashioned swell-top trunk, which precaution prompted me to drag before the door. It had been my mother's trunk, and this was the first journey it had made since it carried her bridal finery to and from the Philadelphia Centennial. In the quiet, uneventful years that followed it had reposed in a big, roomy old garret, undisturbed save at the annual spring house-cleaning, or when we children played " The Mistletoe Bough " and hid in it the skeleton which had descended to us as a relic of our grandfather's student days.

What a change for the little old trunk and what a change for me the last twelve months had brought about! After the door had been further barricaded by piling the chair on top of the trunk, and the coalscuttle on top of the chair, I blew out the evil-smelling lamp and crept with fear and trembling into a most inhospitable-looking bed. It received my slight weight with a groan, and creaked dismally every time I stirred. Through the thin mattress I could feel the slats, that seemed hard bands of pain across my tired body.

From where I was lying I could look straight into Little Lottie's heart, now a steady, glowing mass of coals. Little Lottie invited me to retrospection. How different it all was in reality from what I had imagined it would be! In the story-books it is always so alluring—this coming to a great city to seek one's fortune. A year ago I had been teaching in a little school-house among my Pennsylvania hills, and I recalled now, very vividly, how I used to love, on just such cold winter nights as this, when the wind whistled at every keyhole of the farm-house where I boarded during the school year, to pull my rocking-chair into the chimney-corner and read magazine stories about girls who lived in hall bed-rooms on little or nothing a week; and of what good times they had, or seemed to have, with never being quite certain where the next meal was to come from, or whether it was to come at all.

I was wakened by the rattle of dishes, the clatter of pots and pans, and the rancid odor of frying bacon, bespeaking the fact that somebody's breakfast was under way in the next room to mine. I stepped across the bare, cold floor to the window, and, rolling up the sagging black-muslin blind, looked out upon the world. Bleak and unbeautiful was the prospect that presented itself through the interstices of the spiral fire-escape—a narrow vista strung with clothes-lines and buttressed all about with the rear walls of high, gaunt, tottering tenements, the dirty windows of which were filled with frowzy-headed women and children. Something interesting was going on below, for in a moment every window was thrown up, and a score of heads leaned far out. I followed suit.

In the sloppy, slush-filled courtyard below two untidy women were engaged in coarse vituperation that shortly led to blows. The window next to mine was quickly raised, and I drew back to escape being included in the category of curious spectators to this disgraceful scene—but too late.

" What 's the row? " a voice asked with friendly familiarity. It was the girl who had been frying the bacon, and she still held a greasy knife in her hand. I answered that I did not know. She was very young, hardly more than sixteen. She had a coarse, bold, stupid face, topped by a heavy black pompadour that completely concealed any forehead she might be supposed to possess. She was decidedly an ill-looking girl; but the young fellow in his shirtsleeves who now stuck his head out of the window alongside of hers was infinitely more so. He had a weak face, covered with pimples, and the bridge of his nose was broken; but, despite these manifest facial defects, and notwithstanding the squalor of his surroundings, a very high collar and a red necktie gave him the unmistakable air of the cheap dandy. Again I gave a civil evasion to the girl's trivial question, and as I did so her companion, looking over her frowzy pompadour, stared at me with insolent familiarity. I jerked my head in hurriedly, and, shutting the window, turned my attention to Little Lottie. It was not long before my tea-kettle was singing merrily. I was about to sit down to the first meal in my new abode, when an insinuating rat-tat sounded on the door. I opened it to find the ill-looking young fellow leaning languidly against the door-jamb, a cigarette between his teeth.

" What do you wish? " I asked, in my most matter-of-fact manner.

He puffed some smoke in my face, then took the cigarette from his mouth and looked at me, evidently at a loss for an answer.

" The girl in there wants to know if you 'll loan her one of your plates," he replied at last.

" I am sorry," I said, with freezing politeness —

THE LONG DAY

" I am very sorry, but I have only one plate, and I 'll need that myself," and I closed the door.

After breakfast I walked up to First Avenue to lay in my provisions for the day—a loaf of bread, a quart of potatoes, a quarter of a pound of butter, and two cents' worth of milk. Never in my life before had I bought anything on the Sabbath day, and never before had I seen a place of business open for trade on that day. My people had not been sternly religious people, and, theoretically, I did n't think I was doing anything wicked; yet I felt, as I gave my order to the groceryman, as though I were violating every sacred tradition of birth and breeding. After that I tried to do all necessary marketing the day before, and if I needed anything on Sunday I made myself go without it.

Returning with my unholy provisions tucked under my arm and a broken-nosed blue pitcher deftly concealed under my protecting cape, I made my first daylight inventory of that block of Fourteenth Street where I lived. On each corner stood a gaudy saloon, surmounted by a Raines law hotel. It seemed to have been at one time the abode of fashion, for though both ends of the block were supported by business buildings, the entire middle presented a solid front of brownstone, broken at intervals by long flights of steps leading to handsome, though long-neglected black-walnut doors. The basements were given over to trade.

On the stairs I was brought face to face again with my sinister-looking young man. I looked straight ahead, so as to avoid his eyes. But I found the way blocked, as he stretched his arms from banister to wall.

"What 's the matter with you?" he began coaxingly. "Say, I 'll take you to the theater, if you want to go. What do you say to ' The Jolly Grass Widows ' to-morrow night?"

Thoroughly frightened, I responded to the unwarranted invitation by retreating two steps down the stairs, whereupon the young ruffian jumped down and grasped the arm in which I held my packages. I don't know what nerved me up to such a heroic defense, but in the twinkling of an eye he fell sprawling down the stairs, followed by the flying remnants of my landlady's milk-pitcher. Then I ran up the remaining two flights as fast as my feet would carry me, and landed in the midst of an altercation between the inarticulate landlady and my girl neighbor. In passing, I could make out enough of the wrangle to understand that the latter was being ordered out of the house.

THE LONG DAY

When quietness had been restored, there was a tap at my door. I demanded the name of my visitor in as brave a voice as I could command. " Mrs. Pringle," returned the broken voice of the landlady. I saw, when I opened the door, that she wanted to talk to me. I also saw, what I had not noticed in my hasty interview the night before, that she was superior to most of the women of her class. She had been grimy and unkempt the night before, after her long week's work of sweeping and cleaning and coal-carrying; but to-day, in her clean wrapper and smooth gray hair, there was a pathetic Sabbath-day air of cleanliness about her spare, bent figure. Somehow, I felt that she would not be so very angry when I explained about the pitcher, and I invited her in with genuine cordiality.

She listened in silence to my story, her knotted hands folded upon her starched gingham apron.

" That 's all right! " she replied, a smile lighting up her tired face. " I 'm just glad you broke the pitcher over that vile fellow's head."

" You know him, then? " I suggested.

She shook her head. " No, I don't know him, but I know the bad lot he belongs to. I 've just warned this girl in here to leave as soon as she can pack her things. I gave her back her rent-money. She only come day afore yesterday, and I supposed she was an honest working-girl or I 'd never have took her. She pretended to me she was a skirt-hand, and it turns out she 's nothin' but a common trollop. And I hated to turn her out, too, even if she did talk back to me something awful. She can't be more 'n sixteen; but, somehow or t' other, when a girl like that goes to be bad, there ain't no use trying to reason 'em out of it. You come from the country, don't you?"

There was a kindly curiosity mirrored in the dim, sunken eyes which surveyed me steadily, a lingering accent of repressed tenderness in her voice, and I did not deem it beneath my dignity to tell this decent, motherly soul my little story.

She listened attentively. "I knowed you were a well-brought-up young woman the moment I laid eyes on you," she began, the maimed words falling gently from her lips, despite the high, cracked voice in which they were spoken. "And I knowed you was from the country, too; so I did. You don't mind, honey, do you, if I speak sort of plain with you, being as I 'm an old woman and you just a slip of a girl? Do you, now?"

I replied that she might speak just as plainly as she liked with me and I would take no offense, and then she smiled approvingly upon me and drew her little checked breakfast-shawl closer about her sunken bosom.

"I like to hear you say that," she went on, "because so many girls won't listen to a word of advice —least of all when it comes from an old woman that they thinks don't know as much as they does. They don't relish being told how careful they ought to be about the people they get acquainted with. Now I 'm talking to you just as if you was one of my own. You may think you are wise, and all that,— and you are a bright sort of girl, I 'll give you credit for that, only this is such a wicked city. A young girl like you, with no folks of her own to go to when she 's discouraged and blue, 'll find plenty and to spare that 'll be willing to lead her off. This is a bad neighborhood you 're in, and you got to be mighty careful about yourself. Forewarned is forearmed, as you 've heard tell before; and I have saw so many young girls go wrong that I felt could have been saved if somebody had just up and talked straight at them in the beginning, like I 'm talking here to you. I had a girl here in this house two years agone. A pretty girl she was, and she was from the country too. Somewheres up in Connecticut she come from. She was a nice, innocent girl too, so

she was, when she come here to rent a room. This
very room you 've got was the one she had. Just
as quiet and modest and respectful spoken to her
elders as you are, she was. She worked down in St.
Mark's Place. She was a cap-maker and got four
dollars a week. She started out to live honest, for
she 'd been brought up decent. Her father, she told
me when she come here, was a blacksmith in some of
them little country towns up there. She thought
she could make lots of money to come down here to
work, and that she could have a fine time; and I
guess she was terrible disappointed when she found
just how things really was. She hankered for fine
clothes and to go to theaters, and there was n't any
chanst for neither on four dollars a week. By and by,
though, she did get to going out some with a young
fellow that worked where she did. He was a nice,
decent young fellow, and I 'll warrant you she could
have married him if she had acted wise and sensible;
and he 'd like as not have made her a good provider.
I don't blame the men out and out, as some folks
do; and I say that when a young fellow sees that a
girl 'll let him act free with her, he just says to
himself she 'll let other fellows act free with her, and
then he don't want to marry her, no difference how
much he might have thought of her to begin with.

That 's what, I think, started this girl going wrong.
At first he 'd just bring her to the door when they 'd
be out to the the*a*ter, but by and by she got to taking him up to her room. Now it 's none of my business to interfere with people's comings and goings
in this house, being as I 'm only the janitress. I
have my orders from the boss—who 's a real nice
sort of man—to only rent rooms to respectable people, and to put anybody out where I knows there 's
bad conduct going on. He 's strong on morals, the
boss is. He used to be a saloon-keeper, and the Salvation Army converted him; and then he sold out
and went into this business. He has this place, and
then he has a boarding-house on Second Avenue.
These Germans are awful kind men, when they are
kind, and Mr. Schneider has did a lot of good. If
any of his tenants get sick and can't pay their rent,
or if they get out of work, he don't bounce them into
the street, but he just tells them to stay on and pay
him when they get caught up; and would you believe it that he never loses a cent, either! "

Here the woman stopped for breath, which gave
me an opportunity to turn the channel of her talk
back to the girl from Connecticut.

"Well, I did n't have no right to tell the girl
that she must n't take her gentleman friend to her

room, because there ain't no law again it in any
light-housekeeping rooms. The people who live here
are all working-people and earn their livings; and
they 've got a right to do as they please so they 're
quiet and respectable. But I took it on myself to
kind of let the girl understand that her beau would
think more of her if she just dropped him at the
front door. A man 'll always pick a spunky, independent girl that sort of keeps him at a stand-off
every time, anyway. She looked sort of miffed
when I said this, and then I said that she could set
up with him any time she wanted in my sitting-
room in the basement, what is real comfortable furnished and pretty-looking—and which you too is
perfectly welcome to bring any gentleman company
to any time you 've a mind.

" Well, she looked at me sort of scornful, and answered me real peart-like, and said she guessed she
could take care of herself. She tossed her head in
a pretty taking way she had, and walked down-
stairs, as though I had turribly insulted her; so
what could I do? "

Again she paused, panting for breath in short,
wheezy gasps.

" And what became of her at last? " I asked.

" What became of her! " she echoed. " What

becomes of all of 'em? " and she jerked her head
significantly in the vague direction of the street.
" She left soon after that, though I never said another word to her, but just kept on bidding her the
time of day, as if nothing had ever passed between
us. I felt turrible about her leaving, too; and I tried
to persuade her she was making a mistake by leaving a house that she knowed was decent and where
she could manage to live within her means. Oh,
you don't know how I felt for days and weeks after
she went. I knew how good she was when she come
to this house, and I kept thinking how my Annie
might have been just as foolish and heedless if she 'd
been throwed amongst strangers and had the same
temptations. I don't know where she went exactly.
She did n't give me much satisfaction about it, and
I never seen her again, till one morning this winter,
when I went out to bring in my ash-cans, I run right
into her. It was real early in the morning, just getting daylight. I always get up at five o'clock winter and summer, because I 'm used to it; and then
I 've got to, so 's to get the work done, for I can't
work fast with my rheumatics. It was hardly light
enough yet for me to recognize her right away, and
she did look so forlorn and pitiful-like walking there
so early in the morning in the snow. It had snowed

in the night, and it was the first we 'd had this season. She did n't see me at first. She was walking slow,—real slow and lingering-like,—like them poor things do. I was standing at the top of the stairs in the areaway, and her face was turned across the street, as if she was expecting somebody. I tried to speak to her, but sometimes something catches me when I 'm strong moved and I can't sound a word for several moments. And that 's the way I was struck that morning. I started to run after her; then I thought better of it, and sort of guessed she 'd turn around at the corner and come back. So I went to the cans and made believe to be turrible interested in them, and when I looked up, sure enough she had started back again, and I had caught her eye.

" Thinking of Annie, I bade her the time of day real friendly-like, just as though everything was all right, and I asked her to come in and have a bite of breakfast. I 'd left the coffee on the stove, and had fried myself a nice mess of onions. She looked sort of half shamed and half grateful, and had started to come with me, when all of a sudden she stopped and said she guessed she could n't that morning. Then she strolled off again. I picked up my ash-cans and started down-stairs, but I was n't half-way down when I saw her hurrying along the other side of the street with a man I 'd seen come round the corner by Skelly's saloon while we was talking together. And I never saw her again."

An expression of pathos, infinitely sweet and tender, had crept into the woman's thin, worn face— an expression in strange, almost ludicrous, contrast to the high, cracked voice in which the tale had been delivered. I gazed at the bent old creature with something like reverence for the nobility which I now could read so plainly in every line of her face— the nobility which can attach itself only to decency of life and thought and action. In my brief interview with her in the twilight of the evening before I had heard only the ridiculous jargon of a woman without a palate, and I had seen only an old crone with a soot-smeared face. But now the maimed voice echoed in my ears like the sound of the little old melodeon with the broken strings—which had been my mother's.

" I must be going now," she said, rising with an effort. " You 'll come down and see me sometimes, won't you, honey? I like young people. They sort of cheer me up when I feel down. Come down this afternoon, if you have n't got any place to go. Come down and I 'll lend you some books."

I thanked her, and promised I would.

WHEREIN FATE BRINGS ME GOOD FORTUNE IN ONE
HAND AND DISASTER IN THE OTHER

MONDAY morning—a cheerless, bleak Monday morning, with the rain falling upon the slush-filled streets. I ate a hurried breakfast of bread and butter and black coffee, locked my door, and started out with renewed vigor to look for a job. I had learned by this time to use a little discrimination in answering advertisements; and from now on I paid attention to such prospective employers only as stated the nature of their business and gave a street number.

I had also learned another important thing, and that was that I could not afford to be too particular about the nature of my job, as I watched my small capital diminish day by day, despite my frugality. I would have been glad, now, to get work at anything that promised the chance of a meager livelihood. Anything to get a foothold. The chief obstacle seemed to be my inexperience. I could obtain plenty of work which in time promised to pay me five dollars a week, but in the two or three months' time necessary to acquire dexterity I should have starved to death, for I had not money to carry me over this critical period.

Work was plenty enough. It nearly always is so. The question was not how to get a job, but how to live by such jobs as I could get. The low wages offered to green hands—two and a half to three dollars a week—might do for the girl who lived at home; but I had to pay room-rent and car-fare and to buy food. So, as long as my small capital could be made to hold out I continued my search for something that would pay at least five dollars a week to begin with.

On Monday night I was no nearer to being a bread-winner than when I had started out for the first time from Miss Jamison's boarding-house. I climbed the bare stairs at nightfall, and as I fumbled at the keyhole I could hear the click of a typewriter in the room next to mine. My room was quite dark, but there was a patch of dim white on the floor that sent a thrill of gladness all over me. I lighted the lamp and tore open the precious envelop before taking off my gloves or hat. It was a note from Minnie Plympton, saying she had got employment as demonstrator for a cereal-food company, and was making a tour of the small New England cities. The letter was dated at Bangor, Maine, and she asked me to write her at Portland, where she expected to be all week; and which I did, at considerable length, after I had cooked and eaten my supper.

Bread and butter and black coffee for breakfast, and potato-soup and bread and butter for supper, with plain bread and butter done up in a piece of paper and carried with me for luncheon—this was my daily menu for the weeks that followed, varied on two occasions by the purchase of a half-pint of New Orleans molasses.

The advertisements for cigar and cigarette workers were very numerous; and as that sounded like humble work, I thought I might stand a better chance in that line than any other. Accordingly I applied to the foreman of a factory in Avenue A, who wanted " bunch-makers." He heard my petition in a drafty hallway through which a small army of boys and girls were pouring, each one stopping to insert a key in a time-register. They were just coming to work, for I was very early. The foreman, a young German, cut me off unceremoniously by asking to see my working-card; and when

THE LONG DAY

I looked at him blankly, for I had n't a ghost of an idea what he meant, he strode away in disgust, leaving me to conjecture as to his meaning.

Nothing daunted, however, for I meant to be very energetic and brave that morning, I went to the next factory. Here they wanted " labelers," and as this sounded easy, I approached the foreman with something like confidence. He asked what experience I 'd had, and I gave him a truthful reply.

" Sorry, but we 're not running any kindergarten here," he replied curtly and turned away.

I was still determined that I 'd join the rank of cigar-makers. Somehow, they impressed me as a very prosperous lot of people, and there was something pungent and wholesome in the smell of the big, bright workrooms.

The third foreman I besought was an elderly German with a paternal manner. He listened to me kindly, said I looked quick, and offered to put me on as an apprentice, explaining with much pomposity that cigar-making was a very difficult trade, at which I must serve a three years' apprenticeship before I could become a member of the union and entitled to draw union wages. I left him feeling very humble, and likewise disillusioned of my cigar-making ambitions.

" Girls wanted to learn binding and folding—
paid while learning." The address took me to
Brooklyn Bridge and down a strange, dark thoroughfare running toward the East River. Above was the
great bridge, unreal, fairy-like in the morning mist.
I was looking for Rose Street, which proved to be a
zigzag alley that wriggled through one of the great
bridge arches into a world of book-binderies. Rose
Street was choked with moving carts loaded with yellow-back literature done up in bales. The superintendent proved to be a civil young man. He did not
need me before Monday, but he told me to come back
that day at half-past seven and to bring a bone
paper-cutter with me. He paid only three dollars
a week, and I accepted, but with the hope that as this
was only Thursday, and not yet nine o'clock, I might
find something better in the meantime.

A Brooklyn merchant was in need of two " sales-
ladies—experience not necessary." A trolley-car
swirled me across the river, now glistering in the
spring sunshine. We were hurtled down interminable vistas of small shops, always under the grim
iron trestle of the elevated railroad. At the end of
an hour I entered the " Majestic," a small store
stocked with trash. After much dickering, Mr.
Lindbloom and his wife decided I 'd do at three and

a half dollars per week, working from seven in the morning till nine in the evening, Saturdays till midnight. I departed with the vow that if I must work and starve, I should not do both in Lindbloom's.

Five cents got me back to Cortlandt Street in Manhattan, where I called upon a candy-manufacturer who wanted bonbon-makers. The French foreman, in snowy cap and apron, received me in a great room dazzling with white-tile walls and floor, and filled with bright-eyed girls, also in caps and aprons, and working before marble tables. The Frenchman was polite and apologetic, but they never hired any but experienced workers.

It was half-past three, and I had two more names on my list. Rose-making sounded attractive, and I walked all the way up to Bond Street. Shabby and prosaic, this street, strangely enough, has been selected as the forcing-ground or nursery of artificial flowers. Its signs on both sides, even unto the top floor, proclaim some specialization of fashionable millinery—flowers, feathers, aigrets, wire hat-frames. On the third floor, rear, of a once fashionable mansion, now fallen into decay, I stumbled into a room, radiantly scarlet with roses. The jangling bell attached to the door aroused no curiosity whatever in the white-faced girls bending over these gay garlands. It was a signal, though, for a thick-set beetle-browed young fellow to bounce in from the next room and curtly demand my business.

"We only pay a dollar and a half to learners," he said, smiling unpleasantly over large yellow teeth. I fled in dismay. Down Broadway, along Bleecker, and up squalid Thompson Street I hurried to a paper-box factory.

The office of E. Springer & Company was in pleasant contrast to the flower sweat-shop, for all its bright colors. So, too, was there a grateful comparison between the Jew of the ugly smile and the portly young man who sat behind a glass partition and acknowledged my entrance by glancing up from his ledger. The remark he made was evidently witty and not intended for my ears, for it made the assistant bookkeeper—a woman—and the two women typewriters laugh and crane their necks in my direction. The bookkeeper climbed down from his high stool and opened the glass door. He was as kind now as he was formerly merry. Possibly he had seen my chin quiver the least bit, and knew I was almost ready to cry. He did not ask many questions; but presently he sent one typewriter flying up-stairs for the superintendent, and the other was sent to ask of the forewoman if all the jobs were filled. The superintendent proved to be a woman, shrewd, keen-faced, and bespectacled. The forewoman sent down word that No. 105 had not rung up that morning, and that I could have her key. The pay was three dollars a week to learners, but Miss Price, the superintendent, thought I could learn in a week's time, which opinion the portly gentleman heartily indorsed, and so I allowed him to enroll my name. He gave me a key, showed me how to " ring up " in the register at the foot of the stairs, and told me that henceforth I should be known as " 105."

I thanked him in as steady a voice as I could command, and reached the street door on the stroke of six, just in time to hear my shopmates of the morrow laughing and scrambling down-stairs in their mad effort to get away from that which I had been trying to obtain for so many weeks.

The street I stepped into had been transformed. Behind my blurred vision, as I hurried along, I saw no squalor, no wretchedness now. Through tears of thankfulness the houses, the streets, and the hurrying people were all glorified, all transfigured. Everything was right—the whole world and everybody in it.

Thus I sped homeward on that eventful evening,

eager to tell my good news to Mrs. Pringle, who, I knew, would be glad to hear it. As I drew near the block where I lived, I became half conscious of something strange and unusual in the atmosphere; I felt the strange sensation of being lost, of being in the wrong place. Men and women stood about in silent knots, and through the deep twilight I felt rather than heard the deep throbbing of fire-engines. Pressing through the little knots of men and women, I stood before the red mass of embers and watched the firemen pour their quenching streams upon the ashes of my lodging-house.

Dazed, stupefied, I asked questions of the bystanders. But nobody knew anything definite. One man said he guessed a good many lives had been lost; the woman next to him said she 'd heard the number was five.

The houses on both sides were still standing, the windows smashed in, and the tenants fled. There seemed to be not even a neighbor who might know of the fate of my lodging-house acquaintance or of my good friend Mrs. Pringle. I spoke to a policeman. He listened gently, and then conducted me to a house in Fifteenth Street, where they had offered shelter for the night to any refugees who might desire it.

THE LONG DAY

The basement of this house had been turned into a dormitory, one section for the men and the other for the women, who were in greater number and came straggling in one by one. A man-servant in livery passed hot coffee and sandwiches, which we swallowed mechanically, regarding one another and our surroundings with stupid bewilderment. I had never met any of these people before, though they had all been my fellow-lodgers.

The girl sitting on the cot next to mine passed her cup up for more coffee, and as she did so turned a quizzical gaze upon me. She was stupid and ugly. Her quizzical look deepened into curiosity, and by and by she asked:

" Youse did n't live there too, did youse? "

Our common misfortune inspired me to a cordial reply, and we fell into a discussion of the catastrophe. Her English was so sadly perverted and her voice so guttural that I could make out her meaning only with the greatest exercise of the imagination. But it was to the effect that the fire had started in a room on the top floor, whither poor old Mrs. Pringle had gone about three o'clock in the afternoon with a bucket of coal for the fire. Just what happened nobody knew. Every one on the top floor at the time had perished, including Mrs. Pringle.

" Did n't youse get nothin' out, neither? " asked my companion. And then it dawned upon me for the first time that I had nothing in all the world now but the clothes on my back and the promise of work on the morrow.

" Yes, I have lost everything," I answered.

" Youse got anything in the bank? " she pursued.

The question seemed to me ironical and not worthy of notice.

" I have. I 've got 'most five hundred dollars saved up," she went on.

" Five hundred dollars! "

The girl nodded. " Huh, that 's what! I could live tony if I wanted, but I like to save my money. I makes good money, too,—twelve dollars a week,— and I don't spend it, neither."

" What do you do? " I asked, regarding the large, rough hands with something like admiration for their earning abilities.

" I 'm a lady-buffer," she answered, with a touch of pride.

" A lady-buffer! What 's that? " I cried, looking at the slovenly, dirt-streaked wrapper and the shabby golf-cape that had slipped from her shoulders to the cot. She regarded me with pity for my ignorance, and then delivered herself of an axiom.

THE LONG DAY

"A lady-buffer is a lady what buffs." And, to render the definition still more explicit, she rolled up the sleeve of her wrapper, showed me mighty biceps, and then with her arm performed several rapid revolutions in midair.

"What do you buff?" I next ventured.

"Brass!"

This laconic reply squelched me completely, and I subsided without further conversation.

Despite my weariness, there was little sleep for me that night. Affairs had come to a crisis; my condition was about as bad as it could possibly be. Whatever was going to become of me? Why, in the name of all common sense, had I ever come to New York? Why was I not content to remain a country school-ma'am, in a place where a country school-ma'am was looked up to as something of a personage? That night, if I had had enough money to buy a ticket back to the town I had come from, my fate would have been settled definitely then and there.

Not the least distressing part of my condition was the fact that there was really no help for me save what I should be able to give myself. To be sure, I had certain distant relatives and friends who had warned me against my flight to the city, and to whom I might have written begging for money sufficient to carry me back to my native place, and the money, with many " I-told-you-so's," would have been forthcoming. To return discredited was more than my pride could bear. I had to earn my livelihood anyway, and so, on this night of grim adversity, owing my very bed and supper to charity, I set my teeth, and closed my tired lids over the tears I could not hide, and swore I 'd fight it out alone, so long as I had strength to stand and heart to hope; and then there was the prospect of a job at Springer's on the morrow, though the wage would hardly keep body and soul together.

The next morning, while her servants were giving us our breakfast, a stately middle-aged woman came down to the basement and passed among us, making inquiries regarding our various conditions, and offering words of well-meant, if patronizing, advice and suggestion wherever she thought them needed, but which somehow did not seem to be relished as her more material kindness had been. When it came my turn to be interviewed I answered her many questions frankly and promptly, and, encouraged by the evident interest which she displayed in my case, I was prompted to ask her if she might know of any place where I could get work. She looked at me a moment out of fine, clear eyes.

"You would not go into service, I suppose?" she asked slowly.

I had never thought of such an alternative before, but I met it without a moment's hesitation. "No, I would not care to go into service," I replied, and as I did so the lady's face showed mingled disappointment and disgust.

"That is too bad," she answered, "for in that case I 'm afraid I can do nothing for you." And with that she went out of the room, leaving me, I must confess, not sorry for having thus bluntly declared against wearing the definite badge of servitude.

V

THE " lady-buffer " and I were the last to
leave the house. We went out together
and parted company at Third Avenue, she
going south to her work, and I continuing along the
street westward. The catastrophe of the preceding
day seemed to have entirely evaporated from her
memory; she seemed also to have forgotten the incident of our meeting and conversation of the night
before, for she made no comment, nor even gave me
a parting greeting.

I was inclined to reproach such heartlessness as I
hurried along, when suddenly it was borne in upon
my consciousness that it was I, not she, who was open
to that charge. Here I was, speeding along to my
work with hope in my heart, sometimes almost forgetting that the woman who had been so kind to me
was probably lying in the morgue, awaiting burial
in the Potter's Field, unless saved from that ignoble

58

end by some friend. And yet I was powerless. I could not even spare time to go to the morgue or to make inquiries. I knew not a soul who could have helped me, and I had only one dollar and a half in all the world, no place to sleep that night, no change of garments, nothing except the promise of work that morning at Springer's. I stopped at the corner, strongly tempted by my innate sense of decency to the memory of the dead. But only for a moment: the law of life—self-preservation—again asserted itself, and for the time being I put the past behind me and hurried on toward Thompson Street.

It lacked but a few minutes of eight o'clock when, at last, I turned into the squalid street at the end of which stands Springer's. In the sunshine of the mild March morning the façade of the tall buff building looked for all the world like a gaunt, ugly, unkempt hag, frowning between bleared old eyes that seemed to coax—nay, rather to coerce me into entering her awful house.

The instant impression was one of repulsion, and the impulse was to run away. But there was fascination, too, in the hag-like visage of those grim brick walls, checkered with innumerable dirty windows and trussed up, like a paralytic old crone, with rusty fire-escapes. It was the fascination of the mysterious and of the evil; and, repulsive and forbidding as was its general aspect, nothing could now have induced me to turn back. Instinct told me that I was about to enter into no commonplace experience. And so, unresisting, I was borne along in the swift current of humanity that was swept down the street, like the water in a mill-race, to turn the wheels of workshop and factory. Before Springer's a great arm of this human mill-stream eddied inward, to be lost in another moment in the vortex of the wide black doors, whence issued muffled sounds of the pandemonium within. At the last moment I hesitated, obsessed once more with the indefinable horror of it all. Again there was the strong impulse to run away—far, far away from Springer's and from Thompson Street, when suddenly the old monody began to ring in my ears, " work or starve, work or starve! " Another moment, and I too had passed within the wide black doors.

The entrance passage was lighted by a sickly gas-jet, and in its flicker a horde of loud-mouthed girls were making frantic efforts to insert their keys in the time-register. I was jostled and tumbled over unceremoniously. I was pushed and punched unmercifully by the crowding elbows, until I found myself squeezed tight against the wall. From the scrambling and confusion it was evident everybody was late, and tones and language attested to racked nerves and querulous tempers. Suddenly there was a scuffle and the sharp scraping of feet on the floor.

" Get out, yez dirty Irish! " rang out in the stifling air.

" I wuz here fust! " snarled another voice.

" Call me dirty Irish ag'in and I 'll dirty Irish you! "

The black-haired girl had accepted the challenge, and the maligned daughter of Erin, cheeks aflame and eyes blazing, rushed at her detractor with clenched fist.

" Go for her, Rosie! She 's nothin' but a dirty black Ginney, nohow! "

" Pitch into her, Celie! Punch her! " yelled a chorus from the stairs who came swooping down from above, attracted by the scrimmage, and just in time to see the combatants rush at each other in a hand-to-hand struggle, punctuated with loud oaths.

The noise suddenly subsided at the screeching of a raucous nasal voice.

" Well, young ladies! What does this mean? " demanded the superintendent, and Rosie and Celie both began to talk at once.

" Never mind about the rest of it," snapped Miss

Price, cutting the tale short. "I'll dock you both half a day's pay; and the next time it happens you'll both be fired on the spot."

Then Miss Price turned to me, while the now silent wranglers meekly turned their keys in the register and marched up-stairs, whither their respective factions had since disappeared.

"I do hope to goodness you ain't high-tempered like some is," she remarked, with an effort toward affability, as we stepped before the time-register, where I inserted my key for the first time. "All I got to say is, don't get into no fights with the girls. When they say things to you, don't talk back. It's them that just takes things as they come, and lets bygones be bygones, that get the good checks at the end of the week. Some of them fight more 'n they work, but I guess you won't be that kind," she concluded, with an unctuous smile, displaying two rows of false teeth. Then, with a quick, nervous, jerky gait, she hopped up the flight of rough plank stairs, threw open a door, and ushered me into the bedlam noises of the "loft," where, amid the roar of machinery and the hum of innumerable voices, I was to meet my prospective forewoman.

"Miss Kinzer! Here's a lady wants to learn," shrilled the high nasal voice. "Miss Kinzer!

THE LONG DAY

Where 's Miss Kinzer? Oh, here you are!" as a young woman emerged from behind a pile of pasteboard boxes. " I 've a learner for you, Miss Kinzer. She 's a green girl, but she looks likely, and I want you to give her a good chance. Better put her on table-work to begin with." And with that injunction the little old maid hopped away, leaving me to the scrutiny and cross-questioning of a rather pretty woman of twenty-eight or thirty.

" Ever worked in a factory before?" she began, with lofty indifference, as if it did n't matter whether I had or had not.

" No."

" Where did you work?"

" I never worked any place before."

" Oh-h!" There was a world of meaning, as I afterward discovered, in Miss Kinzer's long-drawn-out " Oh-h!" In this instance she looked up quickly, with an obvious display of interest, as if she had just unearthed a remarkable specimen in one who had never worked at anything before.

" You 're not used to work, then?" she remarked insinuatingly, straightening up from the rude desk where she sat like the judge of a police-court. She was now all attention.

" Well, not exactly that," I replied, nettled by her

manner and, above all, by her way of putting things. " I have worked before, but never at factory-work."

" Then why did n't you say so? "

She now opened her book and inscribed my name therein.

" Where do you live? "

" Over in East Fourteenth Street," I replied mechanically, forgetting for the moment the catastrophe that had rendered me more homeless than ever.

" Home? "

" No, I room." Then, reading only too quickly an unpleasant interpretation in the uplifted eyebrows, a disagreeable curiosity mirrored in the brown eyes beneath, I added hastily, " I have no home. My folks are all dead."

What impression this bit of information made I was unable to determine as I followed her slender, slightly bowed figure across the busy, roaring workroom.

" Be careful you don't get hurt," she cried, as we threaded a narrow passage in and out among the stamping, throbbing machinery, where, by the light that filtered through the grimy windows, I got vague, confused glimpses of girl-faces shining like stars out of this dark, fearful chaos of revolving belts and wheels, and above the bedlam noises came girlish laughter and song.

"Good morning, Carrie!" one quick-witted toiler sang out as she spied the new girl in tow of the fore-woman, and suddenly the whole room had taken up the burden of the song.

"Don't mind them," my conductor remarked. "They don't mean nothing by it—watch out there for your head!"

Safe through the outlying ramparts of machinery, we entered the domain of the table-workers, and I was turned over to Phœbe, a tall girl in tortoise ear-rings and curl-papers. Phœbe was assigned to "learn" me in the trade of "finishing." Somewhat to my surprise, she assumed the task joyfully, and helped me off with my coat and hat. From the loud-mouthed tirades as to "Annie Kinzer's nerve," it became evident that the assignment of the job of "learner" is one to cause heartburning jealousies, and that Phœbe, either because of some special adaptability or through favoritism, got the lion's share of novices.

"That's right, Phœbe; hog every new girl that comes along!" amiably bawled a bright-faced, tidy young woman who answered to the name of Mrs. Smith. Mrs. Smith worked briskly as she talked, and the burden of her conversation appeared to be the heaping of this sort of good-natured invective upon the head of her chum—or, as she termed it, her " lady-friend," Phœbe. The amiability with which Mrs. Smith dealt out her epithets was only equaled by the perfect good nature of her victim, who replied to each and all of them with a musically intoned, " Hot air ! "

" Hot A—i—r ! " The clear tones of Phœbe's soprano set the echoes ringing all over the great workroom. In and out among the aisles and labyrinthine passages that wind through towering piles of boxes, from the thundering machinery far over on the other side of the " loft " to the dusky recess of the uttermost table, the musical cry reverberated.

" Hot a—i—r ! " Every few minutes, all through the long, weary day, Phœbe found occasion for sounding that magic call.

" The rest of the ladies get up their backs something awful," Phœbe explained as she dragged a big green pasteboard box from beneath the work-table. " They say she gives me more 'n my share of learners because I 'm easy to get on with, I guess, and don't play no tricks on them. . . . You have a right to put your things in here along with my lunch. Them girls is like to do 'most anything to a new girl's duds

66

if you wuz to hang them in the coat-room. Them Ginneys 'll do 'most anything. Wuz you down-stairs when Celie Polatta got into the fight with Rosie? "

" I just missed it," she sighed in reply to my affirmative. " I was born unlucky."

" Hello, Phœbe! So you 've hogged another! " a new voice called across the table, and I put a question.

" Why do they all want to teach the new girl? I should think they 'd be glad to be rid of the trouble."

" You mean *learn* her? Why, because the girl that learns the green hand gets all her work checked on to her own card while she 's learning how. Never worked in a box-factory before? " I shook my head.

" I guessed as much. Well, box-making 's a good trade. Have you an apron? "

As I had not, I was then ordered to " turn my skirt," in order that I might receive the inevitable coat of glue and paste on its inner rather than on its outer surface. I gently demurred against this very slovenly expedient.

" All right; call it hot air if you want to. I s'pose you know it all," tossing her curl-papers with scorn. " You know better 'n me, of course. Most learners do think they knows it all. Now looky here, I 've been here six years, and I 've learned lots of green girls, and I never had one as did n't think she had n't ought to turn her skirt. The ladies I 'm used to working with likes to walk home looking decent and respectable, no difference what they 're like other times."

With the respectability of my ladyhood thus impeached, and lest I infringe upon the cast-iron code of box-factory etiquette, there was nothing to do but yield. I unhooked my skirt, dropped it to the floor, and stepped out of it in a trice, anxious to do anything to win back the good will of Phœbe. Instantly she brightened, and good humor once more flashed over her grimy features.

" H-m! that 's the stuff! There 's one thing you had n't ought to forget, and mind, I 'm speaking as one lady-friend to another when I tell you these things—and that is, that you have a right to do as the other girls in the factory or you 'll never get 'long with them. If you don't they 'll get down on you, sure 's pussy 's a cat; and then they 'll make it hot for you with complaining to the forelady. And then she 'll get down on you after while too, and won't give you no good orders to work on; and— well, it 's just this way: a girl must n't be odd."

Continuing her philosophy of success, Phœbe proceeded to initiate me into the first process of my job,

which consisted in pasting slippery, sticky strips of
muslin over the corners of the rough brown boxes
that were piled high about us in frail, tottering tow-
ers reaching to the ceiling, which was trellised over
with a network of electric wires and steam-pipes.
Two hundred and fifty of these boxes remained to be
finished on the particular order upon which Phœbe
was working. Each must be given eight muslin
strips, four on the box and four on its cover; two
tapes, inserted with a hair-pin through awl-holes;
two tissue "flies," to tuck over the bonnet soon to
nestle underneath; four pieces of gay paper lace to
please madame's eye when the lid is lifted; and three
labels, one on the bottom, one on the top, and one
bearing the name of a Fifth Avenue modiste on an
escutcheon of gold and purple.

The job, as it progressed, entailed ceaseless shoving and shifting and lifting. In order that we
might not be walled in completely by our cumbersome
materials, every few minutes we bore tottering piles
across the floor to the "strippers."

These latter, who were small girls, covered the sides
with glazed paper on machines; and as fast as each
box was thus covered it was tossed to the "turner-
in," a still smaller girl, who turned in the overlap-
ping edge of the strip, after which the box was ready

to come back to the table for the next process at our hands.

By ten o'clock, with Mrs. Smith's gay violet-boxes and our own bonnet-boxes, we had built a snug bower all round our particular table. Through its pasteboard walls the din and the songs came but faintly. My mates' tongues flew as fast as their fingers. The talk was chiefly devoted to clothes, Phœbe's social activities, and the evident prosperity of Mrs. Smith's husband's folks, among whom it appeared she had only recently appeared as " Jeff's " bride. Having exhausted the Smiths, she again gave Phœbe the floor by asking:

" Are you going to-night? "

" Well, I should say! Don't I look it? "

To determine by Phœbe's appearance where she might be going were an impossibility to the uninitiated, for her dress was an odd combination of the extremes of wretchedness and luxury. A woefully torn and much-soiled shirt-waist; a gorgeous gold watch worn on her breast like a medal; a black taffeta skirt, which, under the glue-smeared apron, emitted an unmistakable frou-frou; three Nethersole bracelets on her wrist; and her feet incased in colossal shoes, broken and stringless. The latter she explained to Mrs. Smith.

THE LONG DAY

" I just swiped a pair of paw's and brought them along this morning, or I 'd be dished for getting into them high heels to-night. My corns and bunions 'most killed me yesterday—they always do break out bad about Easter. My pleasure club," she explained, turning to me—" my pleasure club, ' The Moonlight Maids,' give a ball to-night." Which fact likewise explained the curl-papers as well as the slattern shirt-waist, donned to save the evening bodice worn to the factory that morning and now tucked away in a big box under the table.

A whole side of our pretty violet-sprinkled bower caved in as a little " turner-in " lurched against it in passing with a top-heavy column of boxes. Through the opening daylight is visible once more, and from the region of the machines is heard a chorus of voices singing " The Fatal Wedding."

" Hot a—i—r ! " Phœbe intones derisively. " It 's a wonder Angelina would n't get a new song. Them strippers sing that ' Fatal Wedding ' week in and week out."

We worked steadily, and as the hours dragged on I began to grow dead tired. The awful noise and confusion, the terrific heat, the foul smell of the glue, and the agony of breaking ankles and blistered hands seemed almost unendurable.

WOMEN AT WORK

At last the hour-hand stood at twelve, and suddenly, out of the turmoil, a strange quiet fell over the great mill. The vibrations that had shaken the whole structure to its very foundations now gradually subsided; the wheels stayed their endless revolutions; the flying belts now hung from the ceiling like long black ribbons. Out of the stillness girl-voices and girl-laughter echoed weirdly, like a horn blown in a dream, while sweeter and clearer than ever rang Phœbe's soprano "Hot air!"

The girls lunched in groups of ten and twelve. Each clique had its leader. By an unwritten law I was included among those who rallied around Phœbe, most of whom she had "learned" at some time or other, as she was now "learning" me. The luncheons were divested of their newspaper wrappings and spread over the ends of tables, on discarded box-lids held across the knees—in fact, any place convenience or sociability dictated. Then followed a friendly exchange of pickles and cake. A dark, swarthy girl, whom they called "Goldy" Courtleigh, was generous in the distribution of the lukewarm contents of a broken-nosed tea-pot, which was constantly replenished by application to the hot-water faucet.

Although we had a half-hour, luncheon was swallowed quickly by most of the girls, eager to steal away to a sequestered bower among the boxes, there to lose themselves in paper-backed romance. A few of less literary taste were content to nibble ice-cream sandwiches and gossip. Dress, the inevitable masquerade ball, murders and fires, were favorite topics of discussion,—the last always with lowered voices and deep-drawn breathing. For fire is the box-maker's terror, the grim specter that always haunts her, and with good reason does she always start at the word.

"I 'm always afraid," declared Phœbe, "and I always run to the window and get ready to jump the minute I hear the alarm."

"I don't," mused Angelina; "I have n't sense enough to jump. I faint dead away. There 'd be no chance for me if a fire ever broke out here."

Once or twice there was mention of beaux and "steady fellows," but the flesh-and-blood man of every-day life did not receive as much attention in this lunch chat as did the heroes of the story-books.

While it was evident, of course, from scattered comments that box-makers are constantly marrying, it was likewise apparent that they have not sufficient imagination to invest their hard-working, sweat-grimed sweethearts with any halo of romance.

WOMEN AT WORK

Promptly at half-past twelve the awakening machinery called us back to the workaday world. Storybooks were tucked away, and their entranced readers dragged themselves back to the machines and steaming paste-pots, to dream and to talk as they worked, not of their own fellows of last night's masquerade, but of bankers and mill-owners who in fiction have wooed and won and honorably wedded just such poor toilers as they themselves.

VI

IN WHICH PHŒBE AND MRS. SMITH HOLD FORTH
UPON MUSIC AND LITERATURE

"DON'T you never read no story-books?" Mrs. Smith asked, stirring the paste-pot preparatory to the afternoon's work. She looked at me curiously out of her shrewd, snapping dark eyes as she awaited my answer. I was conscious that Mrs. Smith did n't like me for some reason or other, and I was anxious to propitiate her. I was pretty certain she thought me a boresome prig, and I determined I 'd prove I was n't. My confession of an omnivorous appetite for all sorts of story-books had the desired effect; and when I confessed further, that I liked best of all a real, tender, sentimental love-story, she asked amiably:

"How do you like ' Little Rosebud's Lovers '?"

"I 've never read that," I replied. "Is it good?"

"It 's fine," interposed Phœbe; "but I like ' Woven on Fate's Loom ' better—don't you?" The last addressed to Mrs. Smith.

" No, I can't say as that 's my impinion," returned
our vis-à-vis, with a judicious tipping of the head to
one side as she soused her dripping paste-brush over
the strips. "Not but what 'Woven on Fate's
Loom' is a good story in its way, either, for them
that likes that sort of story. But I think 'Little
Rosebud's Lovers' is more int'resting, besides being
better wrote."

" And that 's just what I don't like about it," retorted Phœbe, her fingers traveling like lightning up
and down the corners of the boxes. "You like this
hot-air talk, and I don't; and the way them fellows
and girls shoot hot-air at each other in that there
'Little Rosebud's Lovers' is enough to beat the
street-cars!"

" What is it about?" I asked with respectful interest, addressing the question to Mrs. Smith, who
gave promise of being a more serious reviewer than
the flippant Phœbe. Mrs. Smith took a bite of gingerbread and began:

" It 's about a fair, beautiful young girl by the
name of Rosebud Arden. Her pa was a judge, and
they lived in a grand mansion in South Car'lina.
Little Rosebud—that 's what everybody called her—
had a stepsister Maud. They was both beauties,
only Maud did n't have a lovely disposition like Lit-

tle Rosebud. A Harvard gradjate by the name of
Percy Fielding got stuck on Little Rosebud for the
wealth she was to get from her pa, and she was terrible stuck on him. She was stuck on him for fair,
though not knowing he was a villian of the deepest
dye. That 's what the book called him. He talked
her into marrying him clandestinely. Maud and her
mother put up a job to get rid of Little Rosebud, so
Maud could get all the moncy. So they told lies to
her pa, who loved her something awful; and one
night, when she came in after walking in the grand
garden with her husband, who nobody knew she was
married to, she found herself locked out. Then she
went to the hotel where he was staying, and told him
what had happened; but he turned her down flat
when he heard it, for he did n't want nothing to do
with her when she was n't to get her pa's money; and
then—"

She stopped her cornering to inspect my work,
which had not flagged an instant. Mrs. Smith took
another bite of gingerbread, and continued with increasing animation:

" And then Little Rosebud turned away into the
night with a low cry, just as if a dagger had been
punched into her heart and turned around slow. She
was only sixteen years old, and she had been brought

up in luxury and idolized by her father; and all of a sudden she found herself homeless, with nowheres to sleep and no money to get a room at the hotel, and scorned by the man that had sworn to protect her. Her pa had cursed her, too, something awful, so that he burst a blood-vessel a little while afterwards and died before morning. Only Little Rosebud never found this out, for she took the midnight express and came up here to New York, where her aunt lived, only she did n't know the street-number."

"Where did sh get the money to come to New York with?" interrupted the practical Phœbe. "That 's something I don't understand. If she did n't have no money to hire a room at a hotel down in South Carolina for overnight, I 'd like to know where she got money for a railroad ticket."

"Well, that 's just all you know about them swells," retorted Mrs. Smith. "I suppose a rich man's daughter like that can travel around all over the country on a pass. And saying she did n't have a pass, it 's only a story and not true anyway.

"She met a fellow on the train that night who was a villian for fair!" she went on. "His name was Mr. Paul Howard, and he was a corker. Little Rose-bud, who was just as innocent as they make 'em, fell right into his clutches. He was a terrible man; he would n't stop at nothing, but he was a very elegant-looking gentleman that you 'd take anywheres for a banker or 'Piscopalian preacher. He tipped his hat to Little Rosebud, and then she up and asked if he knew where her aunt, Mrs. Waldron, lived. This was nuts for him, and he said yes, that Mrs. Waldron was a particular lady-friend of his. When they got to New York he offered to take Little Rosebud to her aunt's house. And as Little Rosebud had n't no money, she said yes, and the villian called a cab and they started for Brooklyn, him laughing to himself all the time, thinking how easily she was going to tumble into the trap he was getting fixed for her."

" Hot air!" murmured Phœbe.

" But while they were rattling over the Brooklyn Bridge, another man was following them in another cab—a Wall-street broker with barrels of cash. He was Raymond Leslie, and a real good man. He 'd seen Rosebud get into the cab with Paul Howard, who he knew for a villian for fair. They had a terrible rumpus, but Raymond Leslie rescued her and took her to her aunt's house. It turned out that he was the gentleman-friend of Little Rosebud's cousin Ida, the very place they were going to. But, riding along in the cab, he fell in love with Little Rosebud,

and then he was in a terrible pickle because he was
promised to Ida. Little Rosebud's relations lived
real grand, and her aunt was real nice to her until she
saw she had hooked on to Ida's gentleman-friend;
then they put her to work in the kitchen and treated
her terrible. Oh, I tell you she had a time of it, for
fair. Her aunt was awful proud and wicked, and
after while, when she found that Raymond Leslie was
going to marry Little Rosebud even if they did make
a servant of her, she hired Paul Howard to drug her
and carry her off to an insane-asylum that he ran up
in Westchester County. It was in a lonesome place,
and was full of girls that he had loved only to grow
tired of and cast off, and this was the easiest way to
get rid of them and keep them from spoiling his
sport. Once a girl was in love with Paul Howard,
she loved him till death. He just fascinated women
like a snake does a bird, and he was hot stuff as long
as he lasted, but the minute he got tired of you he
was a demon of cruelty.

" He did everything he could, when he got Little
Rosebud here, to get her under his power. He tried
his dirty best to poison her food, but Little Rosebud
was foxy and would n't touch a bite of anything, but
just sat in her cell and watched the broiled chicken
and fried oysters, and all the other good things they

sent to tempt her, turn to a dark-purplish hue.   One
night she escaped disguised in the turnkey's daughter's dress.   Her name was Dora Gray, and Paul
Howard had blasted her life too, but she worshiped
him something awful, all the same-ee.   Dora Gray
gave Little Rosebud a lovely dark-red rose that was
soaked with deadly poison, so that if you touched it
to the lips of a person, the person would drop dead.
She told Little Rosebud to protect herself with it if
they chased her.   But she did n't get a chance to see
whether it would work or not, for when she heard
them coming back of her after while with the blood-
hounds barking, she dropped with terror down flat
on her stummick.   She had suffered so much she
could n't stand anything more.   The doctors said
she was dead when they picked her up, and they
buried her and stuck a little white slab on her grave,
with ' Rosebud, aged sixteen ' on it."

" Hot air ! " from the irrepressible Phœbe.

I felt that courtesy required I should agree upon
that point, and I did so, conservatively, venturing to
ask the name of the author.

Mrs. Smith mentioned the name of a well-known
writer of trashy fiction and added, " Did n't you
never read none of her books? "

My negative surprised her.   Then Phœbe asked:

"Did you ever read 'Daphne Vernon; or, A Coronet of Shame'?"

"No, I have n't read them, either," I replied.

"Oh, mama! Carry me out and let me die!" groaned Mrs. Smith, throwing down her paste-brush and falling forward in mock agony upon the smeared table.

"Water! Water!" gasped Phœbe, clutching wildly at her throat; "I 'm going to faint!"

"What 's the matter? What did I say that was n't right?" I cried, the nature of their antics showing only too plainly that I had " put my foot in it " in some unaccountable manner. But they paid no attention. Mortified and utterly at sea, I watched their convulsed shoulders and heard their smothered giggles. Then in a few minutes they straightened up and resumed work with the utmost gravity of countenance and without a word of explanation.

"What was it you was asting?" Phœbe inquired presently, with the most innocent air possible.

"I said I had n't read the books you mentioned," I replied, trying to hide the chagrin and mortification I felt at being so ignominiously laughed at.

"Eyether of them?" chirped Mrs. Smith, with a vicious wink.

82

"Eyether of them?" warbled Phœbe in her mocking-bird soprano.

It was my turn to drop the paste-brush now. Eye-ther! It must have slipped from my tongue unconsciously. I could not remember having ever pronounced the word like that before.

I did n't feel equal, then and there, to offering them any explanation or apologies for the offense. So I simply answered:

"No; are they very good? are they as good as 'Little Rosebud's Lovers'?"

"No, it ain't," said Mrs. Smith, decisively and a little contemptuously; "and it ain't two books, eye-ther; it 's all in one—'Daphne Vernon; or, A Coronet of Shame.'"

"Well, now I think it is," put in Phœbe. "Them stories with two-handled names is nearly always good. I 'll buy a book with a two-handled name every time before I 'll buy one that ain't. I was reading a good one last night that I borrowed from Gladys Carringford. It had three handles to its name, and they was all corkers."

"Why don't you spit 'em out?" suggested Mrs. Smith. "Tell us what it was."

"Well, it was 'Doris; or, The Pride of Pember-

ton Mills; or, Lost in a Fearful Fate's Abyss.'
What d' ye think of that?"

"It sounds very int'*rest*ing. Who wrote it?"

"Charles Garvice," replied Phœbe. Did n't you
ever read none of his, e—y—e—ther?"

"No, I must say I never did," I answered, ignor-
ing their mischievous raillery with as much grace as
I could summon, but taking care to choose my words
so as to avoid further pitfalls.

"And did you never read none of Charlotte M.
Braeme's?" drawled Mrs. Smith, with remorseless
cruelty—"none of Charlotte M. Braeme's, eye-
ther?"

"No."

"Nor none by Effie Adelaide Rowlands, e—y—e—
ther?" still persisted Mrs. Smith.

"No; none by her."

"E—y—e—ther!" Both my tormentors now
raised their singing-voices into a high, clear, full-
blown note of derisive music, held it for a brief moment at a dizzy altitude, and then in soft, long-
drawn-out cadences returned to earth and speaking-
voices again.

"What kind of story-books do you read, then?"
they demanded. To which I replied with the names
of a dozen or more of the simple, every-day classics

that the school-boy and -girl are supposed to have read. They had never heard of " David Copperfield " or of Dickens. Nor had they ever heard of " Gulliver's Travels," nor of " The Vicar of Wakefield." They had heard the name " Robinson Crusoe," but they did not know it was the name of an entrancing romance. " Little Women," " John Halifax, Gentleman," " The Cloister and the Hearth," " Les Misérables," were also unknown, unheard-of literary treasures. They were equally ignorant of the existence of the conventional Sunday-school romance. They stared at me in amazement when I rattled off a heterogeneous assortment from the fecund pens of Mrs. A. D. T. Whitney, " Pansy," Amanda M. Douglas, and similar good-goody writers for good-goody girls; their only remarks being that their titles did n't sound interesting. I spoke enthusiastically of " Little Women," telling them how I had read it four times, and that I meant to read it again some day. Their curiosity was aroused over the unheard-of thing of anybody ever wanting to read any book more than once, and they pressed me to reciprocate by repeating the story for them, which I did with great accuracy of statement, and with genuine pleasure to myself at being given an opportunity to introduce anybody to Meg and

Jo and all the rest of that delightful March family. When I had finished, Phœbe stopped her cornering and Mrs. Smith looked up from her label-pasting.

" Why, that 's no story at all," the latter declared.

" Why, no," echoed Phœbe; " that 's no story— that 's just everyday happenings. I don't see what 's the use putting things like that in books. I 'll bet any money that lady what wrote it knew all them boys and girls. They just sound like real, live people; and when you was telling about them I could just see them as plain as plain could be— could n't you, Gwendolyn? "

" Yep," yawned our vis-à-vis, undisguisedly bored.

" But I suppose farmer folks likes them kind of stories," Phœbe generously suggested. " They ain't used to the same styles of anything that us city folks are."

While we had been trying to forget our tired limbs in a discussion of literary tastes and standards, our workmates had been relieving the treadmill tedium of the long afternoon by various expedients. The quartet at the table immediately in front of us had been making inane doggerel rhymes upon the names of their workmates, telling riddles, and exchanging nasty stories with great gusto and frequent fits of wild laughter. At another table the forthcoming ball of the " Moonlight Maids " was under hot discussion, and at a very long table in front of the elevator they were talking in subdued voices about dreams and omens, making frequent reference to a greasy volume styled " The Lucky Dream Book."

Far over, under the windows, the stripper girls were tuning up their voices preparatory to the late-afternoon concert, soon to begin. They hummed a few bars of one melody, then of another; and at last, Angela's voice leading, there burst upon the room in full chorus, to the rhythmic whir of the wheels, the melodious music and maudlin stanzas of " The Fatal Wedding."

Phœbe lent her flute-like soprano to the next song, the rather pretty melody of which was not sufficient to redeem the banality of the words:

> "The scene is a banquet where beauty and wealth
>   Have gathered in splendid array;
>   But silent and sad is a fair woman there,
>   Whose young heart is pining away.

> " A card is brought to her—she reads there a name
>   Of one that she loved long ago;
>   Then sadly she whispers, 'Just say I 'm not here,
>   For my story he never must know.'

WOMEN AT WORK

"That night in the banquet at Misery Hall
  She reigned like a queen on a throne;
But often the tears filled her beautiful eyes
  As she dreamed of the love she had known.

"Her thoughts flowed along through the laughter
    and song
  To the days she could never recall,
And she longed to find rest on her dear mother's
   breast
  At the banquet in Misery Hall.

"The time passes quickly, and few in the throng
  Have noticed the one vacant chair—
Till out of the beautiful garden beyond
  A pistol-shot rings on the air.

"Now see, in the moonlight a handsome youth lays—
  Too quickly his life doth depart;
While kneeling beside him, the woman he 'd loved
  Finds her picture is close to his heart."

"What is the name of that song?" I asked when
the last cadence of Phœbe's voice, which was sustained long after every other in the room was hushed,
had died away.

"That! Why, it 's 'The Banquet in Misery
Hall,'" answered Mrs. Smith, somewhat impatient
of my unfolding ignorance. But I speedily forgot
the rebuke in a lively interest in the songs that fol-

lowed one another without interlude. Phœbe was counting her pile of boxes and ranging them into piles of twelve high; so she could n't sing, and I, consequently, could not catch all the words of each song. The theme in every case was a more or less ungrammatical, crude, and utterly banal rendition of the claptrap morality exploited in the cheap story-books. Reduced to the last analysis, they had to do with but one subject—the frailty of woman. On the one side was presented Virtue tempted, betrayed, repentant; on the other side, Virtue fighting at bay, persecuted, scourged, but emerging in the end unspotted and victorious, with all good things added unto it.

It was to me an entirely new way of looking at life; and though I could n't in the least explain it to myself, it seemed, to my unsophisticated way of looking at such matters, that the propensity to break the seventh commandment was much exaggerated, and that songs about other subjects would have been much more interesting and not nearly so trying to the feelings. For the sweet voices of the singers could not but make the tears come to my eyes, in spite of the fact that the burden of the song seemed so unworthy.

" You all sing so beautifully ! " I cried, in honest

admiration, at the close of one particularly melodious and extremely silly ditty. " Where did you learn? "

Phœbe was pleased at the compliment implied by the tears in my eyes, and even Mrs. Smith forgot to throw out her taunting " eye-ther " as she stood still and regarded my very frank and unconcealed emotion.

" I guess we sort of learn from the Ginney girls," explained Phœbe. " Them Ginneys is all nice singers, and everybody in the shop kind of gets into the way of singing good, too, from being with them. You ought to hear them sing Dago songs, ought n't she, Gwendolyn? "

" Yep," answered Gwendolyn; " I could just die hearing Angela and Celie Polatta singing that — what-d'ye-call-it, that always makes a body bu'st out crying? "

" You mean ' Punchinello.' Yep, that 's a corker; but, Lord! the one what makes me have all kinds of funny cold feelings run up my back is that ' Ave Maria.' Therese Nicora taught them — what she says she learned in the old country. I would n't want anything to eat if I could hear songs like that all the time."

The clock-hands over Annie Kinzer's desk had now crept close to the hour of six, and Angela had only begun the first stanza of —

THE LONG DAY

"Papa, tell me where is mama," cried a little girl one
    day;
"I 'm so lonesome here without her, tell me why she
    went away.
You don't know how much I 'm longing for her
    loving good-night kiss!"
Papa placed his arms around her as he softly whispered
    this:

"Down in the City of Sighs and Tears, under the
    white light's glare,
Down in the City of Wasted Years, you 'll find your
    mama there,
Wandering along where each smiling face hides its
    story of lost careers;
And perhaps she is dreaming of you to-night, in the
    City of Sighs and Tears."

The machinery gave a ponderous throb, the great
black belts sagged and fell inert, the wheels whirred
listlessly, clocks all over the great city began to toll
for one more long day ended and gone, while the
voices of the girl toilers rose superbly and filled the
gathering stillness with the soft crescendo refrain:

"Wandering along where each smiling face hides its
    story of lost careers;
And perhaps she is dreaming of you to-night, in the
    City of Sighs and Tears—
In the City of Sighs and Tears."

VII

IN WHICH I ACQUIRE A STORY-BOOK NAME AND
MAKE THE ACQUAINTANCE OF MISS
HENRIETTA MANNERS

BEFORE entering upon my second day's work at the box-factory, and before detailing any of the strange things which that day brought forth, I feel it incumbent upon me to give some word of explanation as to my whereabouts during the intervening night. It will be remembered that when I left the factory at the end of the first day, I had neither a lodging nor a trunk. I will not dwell upon the state of my feelings when I walked out of Thompson Street in the consciousness that if I had been friendless and homeless before, I was infinitely more so now. I will say nothing of the ache in my heart when my thoughts traveled toward the pile of ruins in Fourteenth Street, with the realization of my helplessness, my sheer inability even to attempt to do a one last humble little act of love and gratitude for the dead woman who had been truly my friend.

THE LONG DAY

Briefly stated, the facts are these: I had, all told, one dollar, and I walked from Thompson Street straight to the Jefferson Market police-station, which was not a great distance away. I stated my case to the matron, a kindly Irishwoman. I was afraid to start out so late in the evening to look for a lodging for the night. I would have thought nothing of such a thing a few weeks previous, but the knowledge of life which I had gained in my brief residence in Fourteenth Street and from the advice of Mrs. Pringle had showed me the danger that lurked in such a course. The police matron said my fears were well founded, and she gave me the address of a working-girls' home over on the East Side, which she said was not the pleasantest place in the world for a well-brought-up girl of refinement and intelligence, such as she took me to be, but was cheap, and in which I would be sure of the protection which any young, inexperienced woman without money needs so badly in this wicked city. She wrote down the address for me, and I had started to the door of her little office when her motherly eye noticed how fagged out and lame I was—and indeed I could scarcely stand—and with a wave of her plump arm she brought me back to her desk.

"Why don't you stay here with me to-night?"

she asked. " You need n't mind; and if I was you I would do it and save my pennies and my tired legs. You can have a bite of supper with me, and then bundle right off to bed. You look clean tuckered out."

So to my fast-growing list of startling experiences I added a night in the station-house; but a very quiet, uneventful night it was, because the matron tucked me away in her own little room. That is, it was quiet and uneventful so far as my surroundings were concerned, though I slept little on account of my aching bones. All night I tossed, pain-racked and discouraged; for, after all the long, hard day's work of the day before, Phœbe's card had only checked one dollar and five cents, which represented two persons' work. Such being the case, how could I expect to grow sufficiently skilful and expeditious to earn enough to keep body and soul together in the brief apprenticeship I had looked forward to? Unable to sleep, I was up an hour earlier than usual, and after I had breakfasted—again by the courtesy of the matron—I was off to work long before the working-day began.

I had thought to be the first arrival, but I was not. A girl was already bending over her paste-pot, and the revelers of the " Ladies' Moonlight Pleasure

Club " came straggling in by twos and threes. Some
of the weary dancers had dropped to sleep, still wearing their ball-gowns and slippers and bangles and
picture-hats, their faces showing ghastly white and
drawn in the mote-ridden sunbeams that fell through
the dirty windows. Others were busy doffing Cin-
derella garments, which rites were performed with
astounding frankness in the open spaces of the big
loft.

" Oh, Henrietta, you had ought to been there,"
Georgiana gushed, dropping her lace-trimmed petticoats about her feet and struggling to unhook her
corsets. " It was grand, but I 'm tired to death; and
oh, dear! I 've another blow-out to-night, and the
' Clover Leaf ' to-morrow night! " With a weary
yawn, the society queen departed with her finery.

" You did n't go to the ball? " I suggested to the
girl addressed as Henrietta, and whom I now recalled
as one who had worked frantically all the day before.

" Me? No. I don't believe in dancing," she replied, without looking up. " Our church 's down on
it. I came early to get ahead with my order. You
can do more work when there 's not so many round."

Such strict conformity to her religious scruples,
combined with such pathetic industry, seemed to
augur well for the superior worth of this tall, blonde,

blue-eyed girl. I was anxious to make a friend of her, and accordingly proffered my services until Phœbe should come to claim me. She accepted gladly, and for the first time looked up and rewarded me with a smile. I caught a glimpse of an unprepossessing countenance—despite rather good features and fine hair—the most striking characteristics of which were a missing front tooth and lips that hung loose and colorless.

As we worked, the conversation became cordial. She inquired my name, and I repeated the plain, homely Scotch-Irish cognomen that had been handed down to me by my forefathers.

" Why don't you get a pretty name? " she asked, in a matter-of-fact tone. " All the girls do it when they come to the factory to work. It don't cost no more to have a high-sounding name."

Much interested, I protested, half in fun, that I did n't know any name to take, and begged her to suggest one. She was silent for a moment.

" Well, last night," she went on—" last night I was reading a story about two girls that was both mashed on the same feller. He was rich and they was poor and worked, and one of them was called ' Rose Fortune.' "

" That 's a very pretty name," I remarked.

" Is n't it, though? Rose Fortune—ever so much prettier than your own. Say, why don't you take it, and I 'll begin calling you by it right away."

" And what 's your name? " I ventured.

" Mine? Oh, mine 's Henrietta Manners; only," she added hastily—" only that 's my real name. I was born with it. Now most of the girls got theirs out of story-books. Georgiana Trevelyan and Goldy Courtleigh and Gladys Carringford and Angelina Lancaster and Phœbe Arlington—them girls all got theirs out of stories. But mine 's my own. You see," and she drew near that no other ear might hear the secret of her proud birth—" you see, Manners was my mother's name, and she ran away and married my papa against her rich father's wishes. He was a banker. I mean mama's papa was a banker, but my papa was only a poor young gentleman. So grandfather cut her off without a cent in his will, but left everything to me if I would take the name of Manners."

The heroine of this strange romance stopped for breath, and if I had cherished any doubts of the truth of her story in the beginning, at least I was sure now that she believed it all herself; one glance into her steady blue eyes, in which a telltale moisture was already gathering, was proof of that.

" No, indeed," continued Miss Manners; " I
have n't always been a working-girl. I used to go
to boarding-school. I thought I 'd be a governess
or something, and once I tried to learn bookkeeping,
but my eyes give out, and the figures mixed up my
brain so, and then I got sick and had to come to this
box-factory. But I 'm the first Manners that ever
worked."

I was now thoroughly ashamed of my first unjust
suspicions that Henrietta might not be strictly
truthful, and I inquired with sincere interest as to
the fate of her ill-starred family.

" All dead and sleeping in our family vault," she
replied wistfully. " But don't let us talk anything
more about it. I get so worked up and mad when I
talk about the Mannerses and the way they treated
me and my poor parents ! "

The threatened spell with Henrietta's nerves was
averted by a sudden turning on of the power, and
the day's work began. Phœbe did not appear to
claim me, and I worked away as fast as I could to
help swell Henrietta's dividends.

" I guess you can stay with her the rest of the
day," Annie Kinzer said, stopping at the table. The
' Moonlight Maids ' must have been too much for
Phœbe. Guess she won't show up to-day."

THE LONG DAY

Henrietta was naturally delighted with the arrangement, which would add a few pennies to her earnings. " I only made sixty cents yesterday, and I worked like a dog," she remarked. " It was a bad day for everybody. We ought to make more than a dollar to-day. Phœbe says you 're a hustler."

Our job was that of finishing five hundred ruching-boxes. Henrietta urged me frequently to hurry, as we were away behind with the order. I soon discovered that for all her Manners blood and alleged gentle breeding, she was a harder taskmaster than the good-natured but plebeian Phœbe. Her obvious greed for every moment of my time, for every possible effort of my strength and energy, I gladly excused, however, when she revealed the fact that all her surplus earnings went toward the support of a certain mission Sunday-school in which she was a teacher. The conversation drifted from church matters to my own personal affairs.

" Is n't it awful lonesome living alone in a room? "

" How did you know I lived in a room? " I inquired in surprise, with the uncomfortable feeling that I had been the subject of ill-natured gossip.

" Oh, Annie Kinzer told me. Say, I would n't tell her anything about my affairs. She 's an awful clack."

99

We were silent for a moment, while I wondered if Henrietta, if Annie Kinzer, if any girl in all the world could ever guess how lonely I had been every moment since I had come to this great city to work and to live. Then came the unexpected.

" Would n't you like to come and room with me? "

" With you? " I was half pleased, half doubtful.

" Yes. I 've got plenty of room."

" Perhaps I could n't afford it."

" Yes, you can. I don't put on style. It won't cost us more than a dollar and a half a week for each—rent, eating, and everything else. I was thinking, as you 're a learner, it will be a long time before you can make much, and you 'd be glad to go halvers with somebody. Two can always live cheaper than one."

A dollar and a half a week! That was indeed cheaper than I had been living. I had something less than two dollars in my purse, and pay-day, for me, was still a week off.

And so I accepted the proposition, and by lunch-time the news was all over the factory that the new girl was to be Henrietta's room-mate. Annie Kinzer—everybody, in fact—approved, except, possibly, Emma. Emma was a homely, plainly dressed girl who had worked ten years here at Springer's. She bore the reputation of being a prudey and a kill-joy. Thus far she had never deigned to look at me, but now she took occasion to pass the time of day when we met at the water-faucet, and asked, in a doubtful tone, how long I had known Henrietta Manners.

Meanwhile we "cornered" and "tissued" and "laced" and "labeled." Higher and higher grew our pasteboard castle, which we built as children pile up brightly colored blocks. At eleven Henrietta sent me below for trimmings.

"How do you like your job?" asked the young fellow who filled my order. This was strictly conventional, and I responded in kind. While Charlie cut tapes and counted labels, he made the most of his opportunity to chat. Dismissing, with brief comment, the weather and the peculiar advantages and disadvantages of box-making as a trade, he diplomatically steered the talk along personal and social lines by suggesting, with a suppressed sigh, the probability that I should not always be a box-maker. I replied heartily that I hoped not, which precipitated another question: "Is the day set yet?" My amused negative to the query, and intimation that I had no "steady," were gratefully received, and warranted the suggestion that, as a matter of course, I liked to go to balls.

"My pleasure club has a blow-out next Sunday night," he remarked significantly, as I gathered up my trimmings and departed.

During my five minutes' absence the most exciting event of the day had occurred. Adrienne, one of the strippers, had just been carried away, unconscious, with two bleeding finger-stumps. In an unguarded moment the fingers had been cut off in her machine. Although their work does not allow them to stop a moment, her companions were all loud in sympathy for this misfortune, which is not rare. Little Jennie, the unfortunate girl's turner-in and fellow-worker for two years, wept bitterly as she wiped away the blood from the long, shining knife and prepared to take the place of her old superior, with its increased wage of five dollars and a half a week. The little girl had been making only three dollars and a quarter, and so, as Henrietta remarked, "It's a pretty bad accident that don't bring good to somebody."

"Did they take her away in a carriage?" Henrietta asked of Goldy Courtleigh, who had stopped a moment to rest at our table.

"Well, I should say! What's the use of getting your fingers whacked off if you can't get a carriage-ride out of it?"

"Yes, and that's about the only way you'd ever

squeeze a carriage-ride out of this company," commented Henrietta. " Now I 've two lady-friends who work in mills where a sick headache and a fainting-spell touch the boss for a carriage-ride every time!"

The order on which we worked was, like most of the others on the floor that day, for late-afternoon delivery. Our ruching-boxes had to be finished that day, even though it took every moment till six or even seven o'clock. Saturday being what is termed a " short-day," one had to work with might and main in order to leave at half-past four. This Henrietta was very anxious to do, partly because she had her Easter shopping to do, and partly because this was the night I was to be installed in my new quarters. Lunch-time found us still far behind. Therefore we did not stop to eat, but snatched bites of cake and sandwich as hunger dictated, and convenience permitted, all the while pasting and labeling and taping our boxes. Nor were we the only toilers obliged to forgo the hard-earned half-hour of rest.

The awakening thunder of the machinery burst gratefully on our ears. It meant that the last half of the weary day had begun. How my blistered hands ached now! How my swollen feet and ankles throbbed with pain! Every girl limped now as she crossed the floor with her towering burden, and the procession back and forth between machines and tables began all over again. Lifting and carrying and shoving; cornering and taping and lacing—it seemed as though the afternoon would never wear to an end.

The whole great mill was now charged with an unaccustomed excitement—an excitement which had in it something of solemnity. There was no sign of the usual mirth and hilarity which constitute the mill's sole attraction. There was no singing—not even Angelina's "Fatal Wedding." No exchange of stories, no sallies. Each girl bent to her task with a fierce energy that was almost maddening in its intensity.

Blind and dizzy with fatigue, I peered down the long, dusty aisles of boxes toward the clock above Annie Kinzer's desk. It was only two. Every effort, human and mechanical, all over the great factory, was now strained almost to the breaking-point. How long can this agony last? How long can the roar and the rush and the throbbing pain continue until that nameless and unknown something snaps like an overstrained fiddle-string and brings relief? The remorseless clock informed us that there were two hours more of this torture before the signal to " clean up "—a signal, however, which is not given until the last girl has finished her allotted task. At half-past two it appeared hopeless even to dream of getting out before the regular six o'clock.

The head foreman rushed through the aisles and bawled to us to " hustle for all we were worth," as customers were all demanding their goods.

" My God! ain't we hustling? " angrily shouted Rosie Sweeny, a pretty girl at the next table, who supplied most of the profanity for our end of the room. " God Almighty! how I hate Easter and Christmas-time! Oh, my legs is 'most breaking," and with that the overwrought girl burst into a passionate tirade against everybody, the foreman included, and all the while she never ceased to work.

There were not many girls in the factory like Rosie. Hers were the quickest fingers, the sharpest tongue, the prettiest face. She was scornful, impatient, and passionate—qualities not highly developed in her companions, and which in her case foreboded ill if one believed Annie Kinzer's prophecy: " That Rosie Sweeny 'll go to the bad yet, you mark my words."

Three o'clock, a quarter after, half-past! The terrific tension had all but reached the breaking-point. Then there rose a trembling, palpitating sigh that seemed to come from a hundred throats, and blended in a universal expression of relief. In her clear, high treble Angelina began the everlasting "Fatal Wedding." That piece of false sentiment had now a new significance. It became a song of deliverance, and as the workers swelled the chorus, one by one, it meant that the end of the day's toil was in sight.

By four o'clock the last box was done. Machines became mute, wheels were stilled, and the long black belts sagged into limp folds. Every girl seized a broom or a scrub-pail, and hilarity reigned supreme while we swept and scrubbed for the next half-hour, Angelina and her chorus singing all the while endless stanzas of the "Fatal Wedding."

Henrietta sent me for a fresh pail of water, which I got from the faucet in the toilet-room; and as I filled my bucket I made a mental inventory of my fellow-toilers' wardrobes. Hanging from rows of nails on all sides were their street garments—a collection of covert-cloth jackets, light tan automobile coats, black silk box-coats trimmed in white lace, raglans, and every other style of fashionable wrap that might be cheaply imitated. Sandwiched among the street garments were the trained skirts and evening bodices of the "Moonlight Maids" of the night before, and which were to be again disported at some other pleasure-club festivity that Easter evening, now drawing near. Along the walls were ranged the high-heeled shoes and slippers, a bewildering display of gilt buckles and velvet bows; each pair waiting patiently for the swollen, tired feet of their owner to carry them away to the ball. The hats on the shelf above were in strict accord with the gowns and the cloaks and the foot-gear—a gorgeous assortment of Easter millinery, wherein the beflowered and beplumed picture-hat predominated.

I hurried back with my bucket of water, hoping in my heart that the pleasure their wearers got out of this finery might be as great as the day's work which earned it was long and hard. And so indeed it must have been, if Henrietta was any authority on such questions.

"I love nice clothes, even if I do have to work hard to get them," she remarked, as we turned into Bleecker Street a few minutes later, four one-dollar bills safely tucked away in her stocking. "But say, you ought to see my new hat. It 's elegant," and drawing my arm through hers, my new room-mate hurried me through the Saturday-evening crowd of homeward-bound humanity.

VIII

WHEREIN I WALK THROUGH DARK AND DEVIOUS
WAYS WITH HENRIETTA MANNERS

IT had been an ideal day for March—a day touched with pale-yellow sunshine in which one felt the thrill and the promise of the spring-time, despite the chill east wind.

Into the murky, evil-smelling squalor of Thompson Street this shy primrose sunshine had poured in the earlier part of the afternoon; but, being a north-and-south thoroughfare, it had all filtered out by half-past four, only to empty itself with increased warmth and glory into the east-and-west cross-streets, leaving Thompson dim and cold by comparison when Henrietta Manners and I emerged from Springer's.

Henrietta wore a dusty picture-hat of black velvet with a straight ostrich feather and streamers of soiled white tulle, and a shabby golf-cape of blue and white check which was not quite long enough to conceal the big brass safety-pins with which her trained skirt was tucked up, and which she had forgotten to remove until we had gone some yards down the street. While we stopped long enough for her to perform this most important sartorial detail, my eye traversed the street before us, which with a gentle descent drops downward and stretches away toward the south—a long, dim, narrow vista, broken at regular intervals by brilliant shafts of gold streaming from the sunlit cross-streets, and giving to the otherwise squalid brick-walled cañon the appearance of a gay checkered ribbon. But if the March sunshine had deserted Thompson Street, the March winds still claimed it as their own. Up and down they had swept all day, until the morning mud on the cobblestones had been long dried up and turned to dust, which now swirled along, caught up in innumerable little whirlwinds that went eddying down the street.

Grabbing up her demi-train in her bare hand, Henrietta and I also eddied down the street and were lost to view for a few moments in the whirlwind which struck us at the crowded corner of Bleecker Street.

This whirlwind was the result partly of physical and partly of human forces. For it was Saturday night, and life was running at flood-tide all over the great city. Always tempestuous, always disturbed with the passion and pain and strife of its struggle to maintain the ground it had gained, never for one brief moment calm, even at its lowest ebb—now, on this last night of the long, weary week, all the currents and counter-currents of the worker's world were suddenly released. At the stroke of bell, at the clang of deep-mouthed gong, at the scream of siren whistle, the sluice-gates were lifted from the great human reservoirs of factory and shop and office, and their myriad toilers burst forth with the cumulative violence of six days' restraint.

It was a shabby carnival of nations that jostled one another at this windy corner—Italian, Spanish, German, Slav, Jew, Greek, with a preponderance of Irish and " free-born " Americans. The general air was one of unwonted happiness and freedom. The atmosphere of holiday liberty was vibrant with the expectation of Saturday-night abandon to fun and frolic or wild carousal.

For " the ghost had walked " through the workaday world that day, and everybody had his " envelop " in his pocket. It is a pleasant sensation to feel the stiff-cornered envelop tucked safely away in your vest pocket, or in the depths of your stocking, where Henrietta had hidden hers safe out of the reach of the wily pickpocket, who, she told me, was lurking at every corner and sneaking through every crowd on that Saturday evening, which was also Easter Eve.

Easter Eve! I had almost forgotten the fact which accounted for this more than usual activity on the part of the hurrying crowds, and for the unmistakable holiday air which Bleecker Street displayed. As far as we could see, lined up on both sides of the curb were the pushcart peddlers, and at every step a sidewalk fakir, all crying their Easter wares.

Henrietta lingered first about one pushcart, then about another, opening her gaudy side-bag, then shutting it resolutely and marching on, determined not to succumb to the temptation to squander her hard-earned pennies. She succeeded admirably until we came upon a picturesque Italian and his wife who were doing a flourishing business from a pushcart piled high with sacred images. Henrietta showed a lively interest in the cut prices at which they were going: ten cents for St. Peter in a scarlet robe and golden sandals; fifteen cents for St. John in purple; and only twenty-five for the Blessed Virgin in flowing blue clasping the Holy Babe.

They were " dirt-cheap," Henrietta declared, as we watched the plaster casts pass over the heads of the crowd, out of which by and by emerged our shopmate, little Angela, clasping a Madonna under her arm and counting her change.

The three of us resumed our homeward walk together, without any comment until Angela had satisfied herself about the correctness of her change.

" What a slop you are! " remarked Henrietta, as her critical eye swept over the undeveloped little figure in the long, greasy black-taffeta coat, which, flapping open in front, disclosed the pasty surface of a drabbled blue skirt. " Why don't you never turn your skirt, Angela? "

" Oh, what 's the dif? " replied Angela. " There ain't no fellows going to look at me any more now."

This reply, commonplace enough, might have passed unnoticed had there not been a note of tragedy in her deep contralto voice.

" Why, what 's the matter? " I asked.

" Don't you know? " she demanded, scowling at Henrietta's silly, vacant " tee-hee."

" Know? Know what? " I asked.

" That I 'm a grass-widow."

" A grass-widow! " I echoed in astonishment, and looked upon the childish creature in sheer unbelief — for child I had always considered her. " Why, how old are you, anyway, Angela? "

" Fifteen—I mean I 'm 'most fifteen."

THE LONG DAY

" And you 're really married ! " I exclaimed again, quite aghast and altogether innocent of the construction which Angela immediately put upon the qualifying adverb.

" Well, if you don't believe me look at that ! " she cried, and stuck out a tiny, dirty hand, with finger-nails worn to the quick, and decorated with a gold band broad enough and heavy enough to have held a woman ten times Angela's weight and size in the bands of indissoluble matrimony ; " I was married for fair, and I was married lawful. A priest did it."

" Oh, I did n't mean to question that," I hastened to apologize with some confusion. " Only you seemed so very young, I thought you were just joking me."

" Well, it 's no joke to be married and have a baby, specially when you 've got to s'port it," returned the girl, her lips still pouting.

" And you 've a baby, too—you ! "

The bedraggled little prima donna nodded ; the pout on the lips blossomed into a smile, and a look of infinite tenderness transformed the tired, dark little face. " It 's up to the crèche—that 's where I 'm going now. The ladies keeps it awful good for me."

" And it 's such a lovely baby, too ! " declared Henrietta, softly. " I seen it once."

" She 's cute ; there 's no lie 'bout that," assented

the little mother. " Look what I bought her—here, you hold this Peter a minute—Henrietta, just hang on to the Holy Virgin," and thrusting them into our hands, she opened the box under her arm and drew forth a gaily painted hen that clucked and laid a painted egg, to the uproarious delight of Henrietta.

Henrietta meanwhile had begun counting the change in her side-bag.

" I don't never like to break a bill unless I 've got to," she remarked, returning the Holy Virgin to Angela's arms; "but I 'm going to have one of them chickens too," and away she went after the fakir. A moment later she emerged from the crowd with a little brown box under her arm, and we three continued our walk westward along Bleecker, dropping little Angela at the corner of the street which was to lead her to the day-nursery where she would pick up her baby and carry it home.

" That was a ' fatal wedding ' for fair, was n't it? " I remarked, as my eyes followed the little figure.

But my companion paid no attention to my attempt to be facetious, if indeed she heard the remark at all. She seemed to be deep in a brown study, and several times I caught her watching me narrowly from the corner of her eye. I was already begin-

ning to have some misgivings as to the temperamental
fitness of my strange "learner" and new-found
friend as a steady, day-in-and-day-out person with
whom to live and eat and sleep. And this feeling
increased with every block we covered, for by and by
I found myself studying Henrietta in the same furtive manner as she was evidently studying me.

At last, when we had exchanged the holiday gaiety
and the sunshine of Bleecker Street for a dark,
noisome side-street, she broke out explosively:

"Hope to God you ain't going to turn out the
way my last room-mate did!"

"Why? What did she do?"

"Went crazy," came the laconic reply, and she
shivered and drew the old golf-cape more closely
about her shoulders; for the damp of the dark, silent
tenements on either side seemed to strike to the mar-
row. Something in her manner seemed to say, "Ask
no more questions," but nevertheless I pursued the
subject.

"Went crazy! How?"

"I d' know; she just went sudden crazy. She
come to Springer's one day just like you, and she
said how she was wanting to find a place to board
cheap; and she was kind of down in the mouth, and
she come home with me; and all of a sudden in the

night I woke up with her screamin' and going on
something fearful, and I run down and got the Dago
lady in the basement to come up, and her man run
for the police. They took her away to the lock-up
in the hurry-up wagon, and the next day they said
she was crazy,—clean crazy,—and she 's in the
crazy-house over on the Island now."

"What island?" I asked, not with any desire to
know this minor detail, but because I was too disturbed for the moment to make any other comment.
It seemed to Henrietta, however, a most senseless
question, for she remarked rather testily:

"Why, just the Island, where they send all the
crazy folks, and the drunks, and the thieves and
murderers, and them that has smallpox."

"Mercy! what an awful place it must be!" I
cried. "And that 's where the poor girl went?"

"That 's where she went—say, tell me honest now,
did n't you run away?"

"Run away! Where from?"

"Run away from home—now did n't you?"

"Mercy, no! What put such an idea as that in
your head?" I asked, laughing.

"Fanny Harley did."

"Who 's Fanny Harley?"

"She 's the girl they took to the crazy-house."

THE LONG DAY

" But," I argued, " is that any reason for you to suppose that I ran away from home too? "

" Yep, it is.   You 're ever so much like Fanny Harley.   You talk just alike, and you 've got just the same notions she had, from what I can make; and she did run away from home.   She told me so. She lived up-state somewhere, and was off a farm just like you; and—"

" But I 'm not a farmer, and never was," I put in.

" Why, you told me yourself you was born in the country, did n't you? " and I saw there was no use trying to point out to Henrietta the difference between farmers and those born in the country, both of which were terms of contempt in her vocabulary. We were still threading the maze of strange, squalid streets which was to lead us eventually to the former brief abiding-place of Fanny Harley; and, filled with curiosity regarding my own resemblance to my unfortunate predecessor, I revived the subject by asking carelessly:

" How is it I talk and act that makes me like Fanny Harley? "

" Well, you 've got a kind of high-toned way of talking," she explained.   " I don't mind the way you talk, though,—using big words and all that. That ain't none of our business, I tell the girls;

but you do walk so funny and stand so funny, that it is all I can do to keep from bu'stin' out laughing to see you. And the other girls says it 's the same with them, but I told them it was because you was just from the country, and that farmers all walk the same way. But really, Rose,—you 're getting used to that name, ain't you?—you ought to get yourself over it as quick as you can; you ain't going to have no lady-friends in the factory if you 're going to be queer like that."

" But I walk as I always did. How else should I walk? How do I walk that makes me so funny? " I asked, mortified at the thought of my having been the butt of secret ridicule. Henrietta was cordial in her reply.

" You walk too light," she explained; " you don't seem to touch the ground at all when you go along, and you stand so straight it makes my back ache to watch you."

Then my mentor proceeded to correct my use and choice of diction.

" And what makes you say ' lid ' when you mean a cover? Why, it just about kills us girls to hear you say ' lid.' "

" But," I remonstrated, aggravated by her silly " tee-hee " into defense of my English, " why

118

should n't I say ' lid ' if I want to? It means just the same as cover."

" Well, if it means the same, why don't you say ' cover '? " my " learner " retorted, with ill-disguised anger that I should question her authority; and I dropped the subject, and the remainder of the walk was continued in silence.

It was growing more and more apparent that I had not made a wise selection in my room-mate, but it seemed too late to back out now—at least until I had given her a trial of several days.

I felt as though I had obtained, as if by magic, a wonderfully illuminating insight into her nature and character during this short walk from the factory. I had thought her at the work-table a kind-hearted, honest toiler, a bit too visionary, perhaps, to accord with perfect veracity, and woefully ignorant, but with an ignorance for which I could feel nothing but sorrow and sympathy, as the inevitable result of the hard conditions of her life and environment. But now I recognized with considerable foreboding, not only all this, but much more besides. Henrietta Manners, that humble, under-fed, miserable box-maker, was the very incarnation of bigotry and intolerance, one by whom any idea, or any act, word, or occurrence out of the ordinary rut set by box-factory canons of taste and judgment, must be condemned with despotic severity. And yet, in the face of all these unpleasant reflections upon poor Henrietta's unbeautiful mental characteristics, I felt a certain shamefaced gratitude toward the kind heart which I knew still beat under that shabby golf-cape.

Meanwhile, Henrietta had again lapsed into a silent, sullen mood, as she pitched along in the nervous, jerky, heavy-footed gait which she had urged me to emulate, and which I thought so hideous. I did not know then, but I do know now, that such gait is invariably a characteristic of the constitution in which there is not the proper coördination of muscular effort. In the light of knowledge gained in later years, I can now see in that long, slouching, shuffling figure, in that tallow-colored face with the bloodless, loose lips and the wandering, mystic eyes of periwinkle blue—I can see in that girl-face framed by a trashy picture-hat, and in that girl-form wrapped in the old golf-cape, one of the earth's unfortunates; a congenital failure; a female creature doomed from her mother's womb—physically, mentally, and morally doomed.

I was, however, on this memorable Easter Eve most happily innocent of my Lombroso and my Mantagazza, else I had not been walking home with

THE LONG DAY

Henrietta Manners, in all the confidence of an unsophisticated country-girl. So much confidence did
I have in my shop-mate that I did not yet know the
name of the street on the West Side where my
future home was, nor did I know any of the strange,
dark, devious paths by which she led me through a
locality that, though for the most part eminently
respectable, is dotted here and there, near the river-
front, with some of the worst plague-spots of moral
and physical foulness to be found in New York.

In later and more prosperous years I have several
times walked into Thompson Street, and from that
as a starting-point tried to retrace our walk of that
night, bordering along old Greenwich Village, but
as well have tried to unravel the mazes of the Cretan
Labyrinth.

The last westward street we traversed, dipping
under the trellis of an elevated railroad, led straight
into a lake of sunset fire out of which the smoking
funnels of a giant steamship lying at her dock rose
dark and majestic upon the horizon.

A little cry of admiration escaped me at sight of
the splendid picture, and I hoped secretly that our
way might continue to the water's edge; but instead,
reaching the line of the elevated, we turned in and
followed the cold, black street above which the noisy

121

trains ran. The street itself presented the appearance of a long line of darkened warehouses, broken occasionally by a dismal-looking dwelling, through the uncurtained windows of which we could see slattern housewives busy getting supper.

It was the most miserable and squalid of all the miserable and squalid streets I had thus far seen, and it had the additional disadvantage of being practically deserted of everything save the noise and smoke overhead. There were no foot-passengers, no human sounds. It was all so hideous and fearsome that after five minutes' walk I was not surprised to see Henrietta select the most wretched of all the wretched houses as the one we should enter. As we climbed the high stoop, I could see, through the interstices of rusted ironwork that had once been handsome balusters, the form of an Italian woman sitting in the basement window beneath, nursing a baby at her breast.

"That 's the lady what come up to help hold Fanny Harley," my room-mate remarked as we passed inside.

IX

INTRODUCING HENRIETTA'S "SPECIAL GENTLEMAN-FRIEND"

"SAY! ain't you got no special gentleman-friend?"

Henrietta's voice, breaking a pregnant silence, startled me so that I nearly jumped off the empty soap-box where for some minutes I had sat watching her bend over a smoking skillet of frying fat.

An answer was not to be given unadvisedly, such was the moral effect of the question. It had n't been asked in a casual way, but showed, by its explosive form of utterance, that it was the result not so much of a pent-up curiosity as of a careful speculation as to the manner in which I would receive it. So I tried to look unconscious, and at this critical juncture the thunder of an elevated train came adventitiously to my rescue and gave me a few moments in which to consider what I should reply. And as I considered unconsciously my eye took in an inventory of the room. The heavily carved woodwork hinted of the fact that it had once been a lady's bedchamber in the bygone days when this was a fashionable quarter of New York, and its spaciousness and former elegance now served rather to increase the squalor as well as to accentuate the barrenness of its furnishings. The latter consisted of two wooden boxes, one of which I sat upon; an empty sugar-barrel, with a board laid across the top; a broken-down bed in an uncurtained alcove; a very large, substantial-looking trunk, iron-bound and brass-riveted; and last, but not least, a rusty stove, now red-hot, which might well have been the twin sister of my own " Little Lottie " at the ill-fated Fourteenth-street house. This stove, connected with the flue by a small pipe, fitted into what had once been a beautiful open fireplace, but which was now walled up with broken bricks, and surmounted by a mantel of Italian marble sculptured with the story of Prometheus's boon to mankind, and supported on either end by caryatides in the shape of vestal virgins bearing flaming brands in their hands. Overhead the ceiling showed great patches of bare lath, where the plaster had fallen away, and the uncarpeted floor was strewn with bread-crumbs and marked by a trail of coal-siftings from the stove to a closet-door from which the fire was replenished. The door to the closet was gone, and in its recess a pair of trousers hung limply, while Henrietta's scant wardrobe was ranged along the black-painted wall outside. The long, cobweb-hung windows, bare of blind or curtain, showed a black-mirrored surface against the batten shutters.

All these details I could descry but dimly by the light of the smoking oil-lamp that sat on the mantel-shelf above the stove, and which cast a ghastly light upon a row of empty bottles—the sole burden of the once spotless, but now sadly soiled, vestal virgins.

Henrietta was bending over the smoking skillet, with the lamp-light falling across her pale face. As she boiled the coffee and fried the eggs I studied her profile sketched against the blue, smoky background, and tried in vain to grasp the secret of its fleeting, evanescent beauty. For beautiful Henrietta was—beautiful with a beauty quite her own and all the more potent because of its very indefinableness. I watched her as one horribly fascinated,—that high, wide white forehead, that weak chin, those soft, tremulous lips, on which a faint smile would so often play, and those great, wide eyes of blue that now looked purple in the lamp-light. And then, gradually, I saw, as I watched, an expression I had never seen there before; the wavering suggestion of the smile left the lips and they fell apart, loose and bloodless, with a glimpse of the missing front tooth. It was an expression that lasted but the fraction of a second, but it stamped her whole countenance with something sinister.

Then Henrietta lifted the eggs, carried the coffee-pot across to the table, which was none other than the board-capped barrel, and went back for the lamp. All these things she insisted upon doing herself, just as she had stubbornly refused to allow me to help with the cooking of the supper.

Setting the lamp down upon the improvised table, she threw open one of the shutters to let in a breath of fresh air, and as she did so the room was filled with the roar and dust of the elevated train which passed so close to our windows, and after it came a cold draft of air caused by the suction of the cars. Henrietta closed the window and returned to the table.

Then I answered her question: "Well, that depends upon what you mean by gentleman-friend," I said.

"I mean just what I said," replied Henrietta, sliding an egg upon her plate and passing the remaining one to me. " I mean a *special* gentleman-friend."

" Well, no ; I guess I have n't. I used to know lots of boys in the country where I lived, but there is n't one of them I could call my special gentleman-friend, and I don't know any men here." I uttered this speech carefully, so as not to imply any criticism of Henrietta's use of the expression " gentleman-friend," nor to call down upon my own head her criticism for using any other than the box-factory vernacular in discussing these delicate amatory affairs.

" Oh, go and tell that to your grandmother ! " she retorted, with a sly little laugh. " Don't none of the girls there have gentlemen-friends, or is farmers so different that they never stand gentlemen-friends to them ? "

" Oh, dear me, yes ! " I answered hastily, trying to avoid the unpleasant *double entendre*, and choosing to accept it in its strictly explicit phase. " Why, certainly, the girls get married there every day. There are hardly any old maids in my part of the country. They get engaged almost as soon as they are out of short dresses, and the first thing you know, they are married and raising families." Then I

added, " but have you got a gentleman-friend yourself? "

" Yep," she answered, nodding and pouring out
the coffee; " I have a very particular gentleman-
friend what 's been keeping company with me for
nearly a year, off and on."

" Oh! " I cried, eager to turn the conversation
toward Henrietta's personal affairs instead of my
own, which I felt she completely misconstrued. " Do
tell me about him; what is his name—and are you
engaged to him yet? "

" My! ain't you fresh, though? " she said; but
there was cordiality in the rebuff. " I met him at
the mission where I teach Sundays," she went on.
" He 's brother Mason, and he 's the Sunday-school
superintendent. He give me all that perfume on
the mantel," and she pointed a dripping knife
toward the row of empty bottles.

" Why, is he in the perfumery business? " I asked
innocently, my eyes ranging over the heterogeneous
collection on the mantel. Henrietta took the remark
as exceedingly funny, for she immediately fell into
a paroxysm of tittering, choking over a mouthful of
food before she could attain gravity enough to
answer.

" Lord! no; you do ask the funniest questions! "

THE LONG DAY

Thus checked, I did not press for further information as to brother Mason's vocation, but proceeded to satisfy my hunger, which was not diminished by the unappetizing appearance of the food on the barrel.

It was a matter of great surprise to me to see how little Henrietta ate, and I was likewise ashamed of my own voracious appetite. Henrietta noticed this and frowned ominously.

"God! but you do eat!" she commented frankly, poising her knife in air.

"I 'm hungry. I 've worked hard to-day," I replied with dignity.

"Maybe you won't eat so much, though, after a while," she said hopefully.

"Maybe not," I agreed. "But you, Henrietta—you are not eating anything!"

"Me? Oh, I 'm all right. I 'm eating as much as I ever do. The works takes away my hunger. If it did n't, I don't know how I 'd get along. If I eat as much as you, I 'd be likely to starve to death. I could n't make enough to feed me. When I first begun to work in the factory I 'd eat three or four pieces of bread across the loaf, and potatoes and meat, and be hungry for things besides; but after a while you get used to being

129

hungry for so long, you could n't eat if you had it to eat."

"How long have you been working?" I ventured.

Henrietta put her cup on the table and shot a suspicious glance at me before she answered:

"Oh, off and on, and for five or six years, ever since my uncle died. He was my guardian—that 's his house up there."

I looked in the direction of Henrietta's pointed finger to a cheap chromolithograph that was tacked on the wall between the windows and immediately over the barrel where we were eating. I recognized it at once as a reproduction of a familiar scene showing a castle on the Rhine. I had seen the same picture many times, once as a supplement with a Sunday newspaper. That this stately pile of green and yellow variegated stones should be the residence of Henrietta's uncle and guardian seemed obviously but a bit of girlish fun, of a piece with her earlier talk regarding her aristocratic ancestry; for by this time I had construed that strange story into a hoax that was never meant to be taken seriously.

But one glance now at Henrietta's face showed me my mistake. It was plainly to be seen that she had come to believe every word of what she had told me.

My eye had traveled to the row of garments on the

pegs behind the door and had rested with curiosity upon a "lassie" bonnet and cloak. Henrietta did not wait for the question on my lips.

"Them 's my adjutant's uniform," she said, with a touch of pride. "You did n't know I used to be an adjutant in the Salvation Army, did you?"

I shook my head.

"Well, I was, all right. Adjutant Faith Manners, that 's what I was," and rising, she limped across the floor, and burrowing in the depths of the trunk, returned in a moment with an envelop which she handed me with the command to read its contents. The envelop, postmarked "Pittsburg, Pa.," was addressed to Adjutant Faith Manners.

"But how does it come you have two names?" I inquired.

"Well," the girl replied slowly, "I thought as how it sounded better for a professing Christian to have some name like that, than Henrietta. Henrietta is kind of fancy-sounding, specially when you was an adjutant officer and was supposed to have give yourself to Jesus."

I read the letter; it was a curious epistle, written in a beautiful, flowing hand, well worded, and complimenting Adjutant Manners upon her "persist-

ence in the good work for Jesus," and winding up
with the offer of a small post, at a salary to be determined later on, in the Pittsburg barracks of the
Salvation Army. The name of the writer, which for
obvious reasons it is best not to divulge, was that of
an officer who, I have since discovered, is well and
favorably known in Pittsburg. The whole thing
was a bewildering paradox. There was no doubt of
its being a bona-fide letter, nor of Adjutant Faith
Manners and my room-mate being one and the same
person. And yet, how explain the ludicrous incon-
sistency of such an experience in the life of such a
girl?

I had opened my mouth to ask some question to
this end, when we started as a heavy step resounded
in the hallway outside. Then the latch rattled, the
door swung open, and a thick-set, burly, bearded
man stood upon the threshold. I screamed before I
noticed that Henrietta regarded the new-comer quite
as a matter of course.

The man stood in the doorway, evidently surprised
for the moment at seeing me there; then, closing the
door behind him, he advanced awkwardly, tiptoeing
across the floor, and sat down upon the edge of the
bed without so much as a word.

" Will you have a cup of coffee, brother Mason? "

asked Henrietta, shaking the pot to determine whether its contents would warrant the invitation.

"I don't care if I do, sister Manners," returned brother Mason, removing his hat as if it were an afterthought, and drawing forth a large red handkerchief with which he mopped his forehead and thick red neck.

"This is my lady-friend, Rose Fortune," said Henrietta as she drained the coffee-pot, and nodding first to the visitor, then to myself; "my gentleman-friend, brother Mason."

Brother Mason had risen and tiptoed forward, his hands thrust into the bulging pockets of his overcoat, whence he proceeded gravely to draw forth and deposit upon the barrel-top a heterogeneous love-offering, as follows: two oranges; a box of mustard; a small sack of nutmegs; a box of ground pepper; a package of allspice; a box containing three dozen bouillon capsules; a bottle of the exact size and label as the innumerable empty vessels on the mantel; a package of tea done up in fancy red-and-gold paper; and, last, a large paper sack of pulverized coffee.

Henrietta now handed a cup to the donor of these gifts, which he accepted meekly and carried on tiptoe back to his place on the edge of the bed.

WOMEN AT WORK

Brother Mason drank his coffee with a great deal of unnecessary noise, while Henrietta gathered up the dishes, after again rebuffing me almost rudely for presuming to offer my services. Thus there was nothing left for me to do, apparently, but to sit on the soap-box and look at brother Mason, who regarded me in rather sheepish fashion over the top of his cup.

I judged him to be a good-natured man on the near side of fifty. His close-cropped hair was an iron-gray, and his stubby beard and mustache a fierce red, the ferocity of which was tempered by the mildness of deep-set, small blue eyes. His general appearance would, I thought, have been more in accord with the driver of a beer-truck than anything so comparatively genteel as driving a grocer's wagon —his occupation, I discovered, which explained the source of his offerings to Henrietta. Despite the burliness of brother Mason, there was that about him which rather encouraged confidence than aroused suspicion, although it was difficult to reconcile him with the superintendence of a mission Sunday-school. The latter incongruity had just popped into my mind when he broke the silence by asking in a deep guttural, and with a vigorous nod in my direction as he put down his empty cup:

THE LONG DAY

" Ha! Cat'lic? "

" Oh, no," I answered, eager to break the embarrassing silence—" oh, no; I 'm a Protestant."

" Ha! But you be Irish, be n't you? "

I laughed. " No; American! "

" Ha! Father and mother Irish, mebbe? "

" No, they were American, too; but my great-great-grandfather and -grandmother were Irish."

" Aye, that 's it! I knowed you was Irish the minute I seen them red cheeks, eh! sister Manners? " chuckled brother Mason in a rich brogue, rubbing his hands and looking across at my room-mate, who had been apparently oblivious to our conversation, as she washed and wiped the dishes out of a tin basin which I recognized as that from which we had washed our hands and faces after we got home from work. She now fixed the visitor with her periwinkle eyes, and replied severely:

" I ain't got nothing to say against my lady-friend's looks, as you certainly know, brother Mason."

Something in this answer—no doubt, a hint of smothered jealousy—made brother Mason throw his hand to his mouth and duck his head as he darted a sly look toward me. But I met the look with a serious face, and indeed I felt serious enough without getting myself into any imbroglio with this strange pair of lovers.

"You 're Irish, I suppose, Mr. Mason?" I asked when he had recovered his gravity after this mirth-provoking incident.

"Me? I 'm from County Wicklow, but I ain't no Cat'lic Irish. I 'm a Methody. Cat'lic in the old country, Methody here. Got converted twenty years ago at one of them Moody and Sankey meetings—you 've heard tell of Moody and Sankey, mebbe? Eh? Ha!"

These latter ejaculations the Catholic apostate repeated alternately and with rhythmic precision as he proceeded to press tobacco into a clay pipe with numerous deft movements of his large red thumb, regarding me fixedly all the while.

"Yes, yes," I repeated many times, but not until he had lighted the pipe and drawn a deep whiff of it did brother Mason choose to regard his question as answered.

"Well, it was them that brought me to the mourners' bench, for fair. It was Moody and Sankey that did the damage; and I 've got to say this much for them gentlemen, I 've never seen the day I was sorry they did it. I 'm the supe of a mission Sunday-school now, meself; and I 've done me dirty best to push the gospel news along." Here he turned to Henrietta. "Be your lady-friend coming over to-morrow afternoon, sister Manners?"

"I don't hinder her, nor nobody's, doing what they like!" answered Henrietta, again with that air of severity, not to say iciness, in her manner; and I shifted myself uncomfortably on the box as I met her glance of patient scorn. She had now finished her dish-washing, and seated herself upon the edge of the box, which brother Mason had already appropriated with his large, clumsy bulk.

"Come now, you do care, ye know you care!" he said gruffly, as he threw an arm carelessly across the girl's shoulder and patted her kindly; the scowl immediately left her face and her head dropped upon his brawny, red-shirted breast and snugly settled itself there, much to my embarrassment. Then, between long-drawn whiffs of the rank-smelling pipe, brother Mason descanted upon himself and his achievements, religious, social, financial, and political, with no interruption save frequent fits of choking on the part of poor Henrietta, whom even the clouds of rank smoke could not drive from her position of vantage.

Brother Mason, so he informed me, was not only an Irishman and a Methodist, but a member of

Tammany Hall and a not unimportant personage in
the warehouses of the wholesale grocers for whom he
drove the delivery wagon, and from whom, I now
have n't a doubt in the world, he had stolen for the
benefit of his lady-love many such an offering of
sweet perfume and savory spice as he had carried her
that Easter Eve. I found his talk eminently enter-
taining, with the charm that often goes with the talk
of an unlettered person who knows much of life and
of men. He was densely ignorant from the school-
master's point of view, and openly confessed to an
inability to write his name; but his ignorance was
refreshing, as the ignorance of man is always refreshing when compared with the ignorance of woman; which fact, it has often appeared to me, is the
strongest argument in favor of the general superior-
ity of the male sex. For hidden somewhere within
brother Mason's thick, bullet head there seemed to
be that primary germ of intelligence which was apparently lacking in the fair head snuggled on his
breast. It was therefore with a mingled feeling of
relief and regret that, after a couple of hours of conversation, I saw him gently push Henrietta away and
announce his departure,—relief from the embarrassment which this open love-making had caused me,
and regret that I was once more to be left alone with

THE LONG DAY

Henrietta in that dark, cavernous house. It was then after midnight, and Henrietta suggested, as brother Mason drew on his overcoat, that she accompany him as far as the corner saloon, where she wanted to buy a quarter-pint of gin; and they went off together, leaving me alone.

When their resounding footsteps had died away down the stairs, I picked up the lamp and walked about, examining the shadowy corners of the room, peering into the black abyss of the alcove where the unwholesome bed stood, and not neglecting, like the true woman I was, to look underneath and even to poke under it with the handle of a broom. I raised the windows and threw open the batten-shutters, and through the darkness tried to measure the distance to the street below. Not only that, but I also speculated upon being able to climb out upon the railroad tracks, should the worst come to the worst.

What worst? What did I fear? I don't know. I did not exactly know then, and I scarcely know now. It may have been the promptings of what is popularly termed "woman's intuition." No more do I know why I then and there resolved that I should sleep with my shoes and stockings on; and further, if possible, I determined to keep awake through the long night before me.

I closed the windows and returned to a further inspection of the room, stopping before the open trunk to examine some of the many books it contained. One by one I opened and examined the volumes; a few of them were romances of the Laura Jean Libbey school of fiction, but the majority were hymnals inscribed severally on the fly-leaf with the names " Faith Manners," " Hope Manners," " Patience Manners." Across the room the bottles on the mantel shone vaguely in the shadow. I carried the lamp over, and placing it in the little cleared-out space among them, began to examine the bottles with idle curiosity. " Wild Crab Apple," " Jockey Club," " Parma Violet," " Heliotrope," I read on the dainty labels, lifting out the ground-glass corks and smelling the lingering fragrance which yet attached to each empty vial. Of these there must have been two dozen or more.

And there were other bottles, also empty, but not perfume-bottles. Of these others there were more than a dozen. At first I did not quite comprehend the purport of the printing on their labels, and it was not until I had studied some half a dozen of them that the sickening horror of their meaning dawned upon me fully. There was no mistaking them; the language was too unblushingly plain. They were

THE LONG DAY

the infamous nostrums of the malpractitioner; and in the light of this loathsome revelation there was but one thing for me to do: I had to get out of that room, and before Henrietta should return; and so, grabbing up my hat and jacket, I rushed in a panic out of the awful place into the midnight blackness of the empty street.

X

IN WHICH I FIND MYSELF A HOMELESS WANDERER
IN THE NIGHT

IN making my escape I had not counted upon my chances of meeting Henrietta returning from the saloon. I had thought of nothing but to get as far away as possible from the horror of it all. Dashing headlong down the street, I was going I knew not where, when suddenly Henrietta's vacuous " tee-hee " rang out in the darkness and echoed among the iron girders of the elevated trestle; and, looking ahead of me, I saw her in the light of the corner gas-jet coming toward me, a man on either side of her, and all three evidently in the best of spirits. I sank back into the darkness of a doorway that stood open, motionless until they had passed and their voices had died away.

In the few minutes of waiting, I had collected my wits sufficiently to determine upon a plan of action. I would find my way back to the Jefferson Market, and stay there until daylight, and then go to the Working Girls' Home recommended by the police matron.

But no sooner had I determined on this plan, which was really the only thing I could have done, than I heard women's voices close at hand; and before I could creep out of the doorway, two figures, groping up to it through the darkness, dropped down upon the threshold. They muttered and mumbled to each other for a little while, then their deep breathing told me they had fallen into a doze.

Again and again I had crept out of my hiding-place, looked at the two bowed, crouching figures, which I could see only in vague outline, and then withdrew again into the comparative safety of the black hallway. I hesitated to waken them, and I could not creep over them asleep—not until I heard the low, guttural voice of a drunken man in the darkness above, and the uncertain shuffle of feet feeling their way to the head of the staircase. Then, my heart in my mouth, quite as much for the fear of what was before me as for what was fumbling about in the darkness behind, I came boldly out and stood over the huddled figures. Now I saw that they were old women, very old, and both fast asleep, with their arms locked about each other for protection against the cold. Both were bare-headed and scantily dressed, and each wore a little wisp of gray hair drawn into a button at the back of her head, just as Mrs. Pringle had worn hers. I touched the nearest bundle on the shoulder. She awoke with a start, and peered around at me with a pitiful whimper. I explained that I only wanted to pass, and that she would oblige me very much to allow me to do so.

"You want to git out, do ye, dearie? Well, you jist shall git out," came the rejoinder in a high, quavering voice, and slowly the old woman lifted herself, with many groans and "ouches" for her stiffened joints.

"Dearie! dearie! I thought ye wuz the cop," the old crone went on, as she grasped my arm in a hand whose thinness I could feel through my thin jacket. "A nice arm it is ye have got, and yit ye don't speak as if ye be one of we uns, be you?" The withered hand held me as though in a vise, while I could feel the gin-laden breath of the unfortunate creature as she peered close into my face.

"Please—please let me go!" I whispered, for I could hear the stumbling footsteps within near the bottom of the stairs. "Please let me go! I must go to the drug-store to find a doctor; some one is sick."

"Sure, dearie, sure!" and the thin fingers relaxed

their hold. " Do ye know where the drug-store is? and might n't I make bold enough to ask to go with ye? It 's late for a lady to be out, with the streets full of drunks and lazy longshoremen; and I know you *be* a lady."

I was in a quandary. Naturally I did not want to accept this drunken woman's offer to pilot me, and yet I really had not the heart to offend the old creature, for there was genuine sympathy betrayed in her voice at the mention of sickness. She seemed to take my silence for acceptance, however; and placing her arm on mine, conducted me down the dark street. At the corner we passed under a gas-lamp, when we saw each other distinctly for the first time. She was dark and swarthy, with deep-set black eyes, and her thin, coarse, bristling gray hair, I noticed, was full of wisps of excelsior and grass box-packing. She was about sixty-two or -three, and had a spare, brawny frame with heavy, stooped shoulders. Evidently she had taken just as careful an inventory of my appearance, for we had not gone far before she was giving me all manner of good advice about taking care of myself in a big, wicked city, with repeated asseverations that she always knew a lady when she saw one, and that if I was n't one of that enviable species, then her name was n't Mrs. Bridget

Reynolds; and the latter being " a proper married
woman and the mother of a family all dead now, God
rest their souls! " who should know a lady better
than she? And why was Mrs. Bridget Reynolds, a
proper married and equally proper widowed woman
of her reverend years, sitting upon a doorstep at
three o'clock of a cold March morning? Och! God
bless ye, just a little trouble with the landlord, no
work for several weeks, and a recent eviction; a
small matter that had often happened before, and
was like as not to happen ag'in, God willing! And
who was Mrs. Bridget Reynolds's sleeping mate left
behind on the doorstep? Divil a bit did Mrs. Bridget Reynolds know about her, only that she had
found her that night in the empty warehouse, where
she had gone like herself to sleep, among the pack-
ing-cases, under the straw and excelsior, which made
a bed fit for a queen, and where they might still have
been taking their ease had not a heartless cop chased
them out, bad luck to him!

Such was the gist of Mrs. Reynolds's discourse.
I have not the courage to attempt to transcribe her
rich brogue and picturesque phraseology; and even
were I able to do so, it could give the reader no ade-
quate idea of the wealth of optimism and cheerfulness that throbbed in her quavering voice. Hers

could be a violent tongue, too, as the several men who
accosted us on our dark way discovered at their first
approach to familiarity; and on one occasion, when
a drunken sailor leered up to my side, Mrs. Bridget
spat at him like an angry tabby-cat. Somehow, I
no longer felt afraid under her protection and guidance.

At last, after a very long walk, we came in sight
of the brightly lighted windows of a drug-store, and
Mrs. Reynolds said we were on Bleecker Street. I
had now to explain that my asking the way to a
drug-store had been merely a bit of subterfuge,
which I did in fear and trembling as to how Mrs.
Reynolds would accept such deception on my part.
But she was all good humor.

" Sure, dearie, it 's all right! I 'm glad to do a
good turn for yez, being as you 're a poor body like
mesilf, even if ye air a lady! "

We were now standing in the glare of the big
colored-glass carboys in the drug-store window at
the corner of Bleecker Street and some one of its in-
tersecting alleys. It was now four in the morning,
and the streets were almost deserted. My companion smiled at me with the maudlin tenderness which
gin inspires in the breast of an old Irishwoman, and
as we stood irresolute on the corner I noticed how

thinly clad she was. The sharp wind wrapped her calico skirt about her stiffened limbs, and her only wrap was a little black knitted fascinator which did not meet over the torn calico blouse.

"A wee nip of gin would go right to the spot now, would n't it, dearie?" the old soul asked wistfully, which reminded me of something I had forgotten: that I still had my precious dollar and a half snugly stowed away in my petticoat pocket. So I suggested that we go to a lunch-room and have a good meal and a cup of hot coffee, and sit there till daylight, which now was not far off.

The prospect of something to eat and something hot to drink infused great cheerfulness into my strange chaperon; she grasped my arm with the gaiety of a school-girl, and we walked eastward until we came to a dairy lunch-room upon the great plate-glass windows of which was enameled in white letters a generous bill of fare at startlingly low prices. The place was of the sort where everybody acts as his own waiter, buying checks for whatever he wants from the cashier and presenting them at a long counter piled up with eatables. Mrs. Reynolds was modesty itself in accepting of my bounty.

When we had finished it was daylight, and I parted from my duenna at the door, she with in-

numerable terms of maudlin endearment, and an
invocation to all the saints in the calendar that they
should keep a kindly eye upon me. As to my own
feelings, I felt heartless to be obliged to leave the
poor creature with nothing more than a twenty-five-
cent piece, and with no proffer of future help—if,
indeed, she was not beyond help. But I was powerless; for I was as poor as she was. I had suggested her applying to the authorities for aid, but
she had received it scornfully, even indignantly,
declaring that Mrs. Bridget Reynolds would die
and rot before she 'd be beholden to anybody for
charity. Anything in the shape of organized
authority was her constitutional enemy, and the
policeman was her hereditary foe. Hospitals were
nefarious places where the doctors poisoned you and
the nurses neglected you in order that you should
die and furnish one more cadaver to the dissecting-
rooms; almshouses were the last resort of the broken
in heart and spirit, institutions where unspeakable
crimes were perpetrated upon the old and helpless.
Therefore, was it any wonder this independent old
dame of Erin preferred deserted warehouses and
dark doorways as shelter?

And so, early in this Easter morning, I left Mrs.
Bridget Reynolds at the door of the Bleecker Street

lunch-room, she to go her way and I to go mine. I looked back when I had got half a block away, and she was still standing there, apparently undetermined which way to turn. I watched a moment, and presently she ambled across the street and rattled the door of the " ladies' " entrance to the saloon on the corner. Then I turned my face toward the reddening east, against which the shabby housetops and the chimneys and the distant spires and smokestacks stretched out in a broken, black sky-line. I was going to find the home for working girls which the good matron at Jefferson Market had recommended, and the address of which I still had in the bottom of my purse.

XI

I BECOME AN "INMATE" OF A HOME FOR WORKING GIRLS

THE spirit of the early Easter Day had breathed everywhere its own ineffable Sabbath peace, and when at last I emerged into Broadway, it was to find that familiar thoroughfare strangely transformed. On the six days preceding choked with traffic and humming with ten thousand noises, it was now silent and deserted as a country lane—silent but for the echo of my own footsteps upon the polished stone flagging, and deserted but for the myriad reflections of my own disheveled self which the great plate-glass windows on either side of the street flashed back at me.

My way lay northward, with the spire of Grace Church as a finger-post. Grace Church had become a familiar landmark in the preceding weeks, so often had I walked past it in my hopeless quest, and now I approached it as one does a friend seen

suddenly in a crowd of strangers. The fact that
I was approaching an acquaintance, albeit a dumb
and unseeing one, now made me for the first time
conscious of my personal appearance so persistently
reflected by the shop windows. Before one of them
I stopped and surveyed myself. Truly I was a
sorry-looking object. I had not been well washed
or combed since the last morning at Mrs. Pringle's
house; for two days I had combed my long and
rather heavy hair with one of the small side-combs I
wore, and on neither morning had I enjoyed the
luxury of soap. And two successive mornings without soap and the services of a stout comb are likely
to work all sorts of demoralizing transformations in
the appearance of even a lady of leisure, to say
nothing of a girl who had worked hard all day in a
dirty factory.

Fortunately the street was deserted. I stepped
into the entrance of a big, red-sandstone building,
and standing between the show-windows, took off my
hat, laid it on the pavement, and proceeded to unroll
my hair and slick it up once more with the aid of the
side-comb, of which I had now only one left, having
lost the other somewhere in my flight from Henrietta's. That I should have thought to put on my
hat in preparing for that flight I do not understand,

for I forgot my gloves, a brand-new pair too; my handkerchief; and, most needful of all else, my ribbon stock-collar, without which my neck rose horribly long and thin above my dusty jacket-collar. Looking at it ruefully, I began to feel for the first time what was for me at least the very quintessence of poverty—the absolute impossibility of personal cleanliness and of decent raiment. I had known hunger and loneliness since I had come to New York, but never before had I experienced this new, this infinitely greater terror—lack of self-respect. That I had done nothing to lower my self-respect had nothing whatever to do with it, since self-respect is often more a matter of material things than of moral values. It is possible for a hungry woman to walk with pride, and it is possible for the immoral and utterly degraded woman to hold her own with the best of her sisters, when it comes to visible manifestation of self-respect, if only she is able to maintain her usual degree of cleanliness and good grooming. But unacquainted with soap for two days! and without a collar! How could I ever summon courage to present myself to anybody in such a condition? Had I been an old woman, I might n't have cared. But I was a girl; and, being a girl, I suffered all of a girl's heartache and melancholy wretchedness when I remembered that it was Sunday and that there was no hope of buying either collar or comb for twenty-four hours—if, indeed, I dared to spend any of my few remaining dimes and nickels for these necessities, which had suddenly soared to the heights of unattainable luxuries.

In the full consciousness of my disreputable appearance, I hung in the doorway, reluctant to fare forth in the cruel light of the thoroughfare. Hitherto I had had the street all to myself, so it had not mattered so much how I looked. But now an empty car hurtled by, its gong breaking for the first time the silence of the long vista stretching away and dipping southward to the Battery. Then another car came speeding along from the opposite direction, whirled past Grace Church, and northward around the curve at Fourteenth Street; and following in the wake of the car, a hansom-cab with a jaded man and woman locked in each other's arms and fast asleep. As the latter passed close to the curb, I drew into the embrasure of the door as far as possible so as to avoid being seen by the cabman —as if it made the least difference whether he saw me or not; but such is the all-absorbing self-consciousness and vanity of girlhood. It was then that I noticed for the first time the glaring sign that had been staring at me during all these ineffectual attempts to " primp."

" Wanted—Girls to learn flower-making. Paid while learning. Apply Monday morning at nine o'clock."

I repeated the street-number over and over, so as to make sure of remembering it; and then, screwing up my courage, walked hurriedly up the street, trying to ignore the glances which were cast at me by occasional pedestrians. I happened to think of a large dairy lunch-room on Fourteenth Street where I had several times gone for coffee and rolls, and where the cashier and waitresses knew me by sight, and where I thought, by investing in a cup of coffee, I might tidy up a bit in the toilet-room. If only the place should be open on Sunday morning!

And it was. The cashier had just stepped into her cage-like desk, and the waitresses were lined up in their immaculate white aprons and lace head-dresses. I was their first customer, apparently. The cashier, a pretty, amiable girl, suppressed any surprise she may have felt at my appearance, and greeted me with the same dazzling smile with which she greeted every familiar face. I explained to her what I wanted to do, apologizing for my slovenliness. She was all sympathetic attention, her eyes

snapped with good-humored interest, and she told
me to go back and take all the time I wanted to
wash up. In a few minutes she sent me, by one of
the waitresses, a fresh piece of soap, a comb, a bit of
pumice-stone, a whisk-broom, a nail-file, a pair of
curved nail-scissors, a tiny paper parcel containing
some face-powder, and, wonder of wonders, a beautifully clean, fresh, shining collar!

Before the big, shimmering mirrors I washed and
splashed to my heart's content and to the infinite
advantage of my visage. How delicious it was to
see and hear and feel the clear, hot water as it rushed
from the silver faucet into the white porcelain bowl!
I washed and I washed, I combed and I combed, until
there was absolutely no more excuse for doing
either; then I powdered my face, just enough to
take the shine off, filed my finger-nails, brushed my
clothing, put on my borrowed collar, and stepped
out into the eating-room, feeling, if not looking,
like the " perfect lady " which the generous-hearted
cashier declared I resembled " as large as life."

" Never mind about the collar; you can just keep
it," she said when I returned her toilet articles.
" It 's not worth but a few cents, anyway, and I 've
got plenty more of them. . . . Don't mention it at
all; you 're perfectly welcome. I did n't do any-

thing more for you than I 'd expect you to do for me if I was in such a pickle. If we working girls don't stand up and help one another, I 'd like to know who 's going to do it for us. . . . So long!"

" So long!" It was not the first time that I had heard a working girl deliver herself of that laconic form of adieu, and heretofore I had always execrated it as hopelessly vulgar and silly, which no doubt it was and is. But from the lips of that kind-hearted woman it fell upon my ears with a sort of lingering sweetness. It was redolent of hope and good cheer.

The home for working girls I found, not very far away from this lunch-room, in one of the streets south of Fourteenth Street and well over on the East Side. It was a shabby, respectable, unfriendly-looking building of red brick, with a narrow, black-painted arched door. On the cross-section of the center panel was screwed a silver plate, with the name of the institution inscribed in black letters, which gave to the door the gruesome suggestion of a coffin set on end.

A polite pull at the rusty handle of the bell-cord brought no response, and I rang again, a little louder. A chain was rattled and a bolt drawn back. The lid of the black coffin flew open, disclosing, with the suddenness of a jack-in-the-box, a withered old beldam with a large brass key clutched in a hand that trembled violently with palsy.

She grumbled inarticulately, and with a jerk of her head motioned me into a small room opening off the hall, while she closed and locked the door with the great brass key.

The little reception-room, or office, was no more cheerful than the front door, and, like it, partook somewhat of an ecclesiastical aspect. Arranged in a sort of frieze about the room were a series of framed scriptural texts, all of which served to remind one in no ambiguous terms of the wrath of God toward the froward-hearted and of the eternal punishment that awaits unrepentant sinners. And then, at intervals, the vindictive utterances were broken by pictures—these, too, of a religious or pseudo-religious nature.

One of these pictures particularly attracted my attention. It was entitled "Hope leaning upon Faith," and showed an exceedingly sentimental young girl leaning heavily upon an anchor, her eyes lifted heavenward, where the sun was just breaking through black clouds, and all against a perspective of angry sea. I was trying to apply its symbolism to my own case, when a sharp, metallic voice inquired abruptly:

THE LONG DAY

" What did you wish? "

I turned about quickly. A tall, hard-faced woman of forty or thereabouts stood in the door, and looked at me coldly through spectacles that hooked behind ears the natural prominence of which was enhanced by her grayish hair being drawn up tightly and rolled into a " bun " on the very top of the head. She was the personification of neatness, if such be the word to characterize the prim stiffness of a flat-figured, elderly spinster. She wore large, square-toed, common-sense shoes, with low heels capped with rubber cushions, which, as I was shortly to discover, had earned for the lady the sobriquet of " Old Gum Heels." What her real name was I never found out. Nobody knew. She was the most hated of all our tormentors; and in all of the weeks I was to remain in the house over which she was one of the supervisors, I never heard her referred to by any other than the very disrespectful cognomen already quoted. But I am anticipating.

" I would like to get board here," I replied timidly, for the very manner of the woman had in it an acid-like quality which bit and burned the sensibilities like vitriol does the flesh.

" Have you any money? "

" Not very much."

" How much? " she demanded.

" About one dollar."

" What baggage have you? "

" None," I replied, and related as well as my embarrassment would allow me the story of the fire and of my flight from Henrietta, not forgetting the generosity of the cashier in the dairy lunch-room. She listened in silence, and when I had finished I thought I saw the repression of a smile, which may or may not have been of the sardonic order. Then she motioned me to follow her through the long, gloomy hall to the rear of the house, where, turning an angle, we came to a staircase down which a flood of sunlight streamed from the big window on the landing. The sunlight showed walls of shimmering whitewashed purity and unpainted oaken stairs scoured white as a bone. " Old Gum Heels " stopped here, and was beginning to give me directions for finding the matron's room on the floor above, when a door at the back opened and a very little girl appeared with a very large pitcher of hot water, which she held tight in her arms as though it were a doll, jiggling at every step a little of the contents upon the floor.

" Julia, take this girl along with you to Mrs. Pitbladder's room, and tell her that she wishes to make arrangements about board and lodging."

And then to me: "Mrs. Pitbladder is the matron.
You will pay your money to her, and she will tell
you the rules and regulations for inmates.—And
then, Julia, hurry back to the kitchen; I 'll need
you right away."

"Yes, ma'am," replied the child, timidly, with a
shy glance at me as she proceeded laboriously up the
stairs. At the landing she stopped to draw breath,
putting the pitcher upon the floor and relaxing her
thin little arms. She was such a mite of a child,
hardly more than eight or nine, if judged from the
size of the spindly, undeveloped figure. This was
swaddled in the ugly apron of blue-checked gingham, fastened down the back with large bone buttons, and so long in the sleeves that the little hands
were all but lost, and so long in the skirt that only
the ends of the small copper-toed shoes showed beneath. Judged, however, by the close-cropped
head and the little sallow face that surmounted the
aproned figure, she might have been a woman of
twenty-five, so maturely developed was the one, so
shrewd and knowing the other. The child leaned
her shoulders upon the whitewashed wall and stared
at me in bold, though not unfriendly curiosity,
which, undoubtedly, I reciprocated. She was evidently sizing me up. I smiled, and she screwed her

full, sensitive mouth into a judicial expression, puckering her forehead; then, in a deep, contralto voice, she spoke. What she said I did n't hear, or rather did n't grasp, in my wonder at the quality and timbre of that great voice, which, issuing from the folds of the checked apron, seemed fairly to fill the big hall below and the stair-well above with a deep, beautiful sound. I apologized and asked her to repeat what she had said.

"Your skirt—it 's so stylish," she said, and the little hand stole out and began stroking the snugly-fitting serge of that very unpretentious garment.

"I 'm very glad you like it," I laughed, "for it 's the only skirt I have"; and I picked up the heavy pitcher and carried it up the rest of the way, the child following me, holding up her apron skirts with both hands to keep from stumbling, and making a ringing, metallic noise as the copper toes struck the wood at every rise. She took the pitcher at the head of the stairs without comment, but with a look full of diffident gratitude. Stopping before one of the doors, the child rapped timidly—so timidly, in fact, that it could scarcely be heard. No answer coming, she rapped again, this time a little louder, and a woman's shrill voice screamed, "Come in!"

THE LONG DAY

"Mis' Pitbladder, the lady down-stairs says as this is a young girl what wants to have a talk with youse about coming here," my little guide announced all in one breath, and almost before the door had entirely swung open upon the group within, consisting of an old lady and two little girls. The old lady was in a comfortable state of dishabille; the little girls each wore big checked gingham aprons like Julia's, and buttoned down the back with the same big, white bone buttons. One of them was waving Mrs. Pitbladder's hair with a crimping-iron which she heated in a gas-jet before the bureau; the other child was laboriously working at one of the pudgy hands with a pair of nail-scissors.

"Come in, come in, and don't stand there with the door open," mumbled the bowed figure in the arm-chair, who held a twisted bit of uncrimped forelock between her teeth to keep it from getting mixed with what was already waved, and which fell over her face so that I could not see her features.

"So you want to come here to board with us, my dear?" began the masked one, which was the signal for an exchange of grave winks between the hairdresser, the manicure, and the little slavey, Julia, who was pouring the hot water into the pitcher on the washstand.

" If I could arrange it," I replied quickly, taking courage from the woman's kindly manner of putting the question, which was in such startling contrast to that of the dragon down-stairs.

" You are a working girl, are you, my dear? "

" I want to be. I 'm looking for work now, and I hope to get a job in a few days. I understand your rates are very low, and that I can live here cheaper than almost anywhere else."

" And who sent you here, my dear? "

In answer to this I told her my story almost in totality, leaving out only such details as could not possibly have concerned her. Perfect candor, I was fast learning, was the only way in which one in my desperate situation could hope for any degree of sympathetic treatment, as the time for all silly pride was passed.

Then Mrs. Pitbladder explained the system upon which the house was run. I could have a room all to myself for a dollar and a half a week, or I could sleep in the dormitory for ten cents a night, or fifty cents a week; all terms payable in advance. The latter fact she was particular to impress upon me. As to food, she named a price which fairly took away my breath. Six cents each for meals—six cents each for breakfast, dinner, and supper! I said at once I would become a boarder, and that I would take a cot in the dormitory, for which I would pay from night to night.

At this juncture the girl who answered to the name of May finished undulating the last strand of gray hair, and as she lifted it off her mistress's face that lady raised her head and we looked at each other for the first time. She was somewhere between sixty-five and seventy, and very fat. Mrs. Pitbladder's face was a surprise to me, for all it was a round, red face—the very sort of face in which one would have expected good nature to repose. Its predominating features were a huge, beaked nose and high cheek-bones which encroached to an alarming degree upon the eye-sockets, wherein little dark, furtive eyes regarded me fixedly. It was a face which even the most unsophisticated observer could scarcely fail to characterize as that of a woman hardened in every sort of petty tyranny, a woman who, having the power to make others uncomfortable, found infinite pleasure in doing so, quite apart from any motive of selfish interest. To be sure, I did not read all this in Mrs. Pitbladder's face by the end of our first meeting. The supreme question to be settled, the only one which had for me a vital interest then, was how long I might still put off utter destitution in the event of my not finding work within the ensuing week.

The terms were always in advance, Mrs. Pitbladder again repeated, as she entered my name and age in a long book which May brought from the dark mahogany desk that matched the rest of the well-made furniture in the spacious room. I would now pay her, she said, ten cents for the bed I was to sleep in that night, and my board money would be paid meal by meal to the woman in charge of the dining-room. I gave her a twenty-five-cent piece. I had remaining three other silver quarters. I watched my twenty-five-cent piece drop into Mrs. Pitbladder's purse, and heard the greedy mouth of that receptacle snap shut.

" Mintie," Mrs. Pitbladder spoke briskly, " show this girl to the sitting-room, and then go and find Mrs. Lumley and tell her to come to me at once."

Mintie, who had now finished lacing the matron's shoes, rose eagerly and, with a shy glance toward me, made for the door. I hesitated, and looked at Mrs. Pitbladder.

" You may go now," she said, with a wave of the pudgy hand.

" Excuse me," I replied, considerably abashed, quite as much by the curious looks of the little girls

as by the annoyance of having to remind the matron about the fifteen cents change still due me—
" excuse me, but I gave you twenty-five cents."

" And I gave you your change, my dear," the matron returned suavely but decisively.

" I beg your pardon for contradicting you," I replied firmly, and without taking my eyes from hers, which blinked unpleasantly. "You did *not* give me any change."

" Look in your purse and see," said Mrs. Pitbladder.

" It is quite unnecessary," I replied; "but I will do so to satisfy you "; and I opened the purse again and showed my three remaining silver pieces, which to further satisfy her I took out upon my palm and then turned the purse's lining inside out.

But Mrs. Pitbladder did not seem impressed. I for my part resolved to be equally insistent, inspired as I was with the determination that comes to desperate people. There were fifteen cents due me, and nobody should cheat me out of a single one of those precious pennies if I could possibly prevent it. There was a short silence in which we took each other's measure, the children looking on in evident enjoyment of the situation. Finally the old lady opened the purse again and gave me the change due, though she grumblingly maintained that it was I, not she, who was in error.

When the door closed at last upon us, my small companion clutched my hand and gave it a jubilant squeeze. " Golly! that did me good," she whispered as we were going down-stairs. " She always lets on to make mistakes about the girls' change, only most of 'em is so scairt of her they just let her beat them out of it."

While the child went to find Mrs. Lumley I waited in the sitting-room. It was an empty, ugly place, with bare floors and whitewashed walls, the latter decorated, like those of the office, with framed scriptural texts. Its furniture consisted of several long, slat-bottomed settees and a single large rocking-chair which, crowded with children, was swinging noisily over the bare boards. At our entrance the chair stopped rocking, and one of the children climbed out.

It was Julia. She came promptly over to my side, while a half-dozen of the other children jumped off the benches and ran to the rocking-chair to squabble over the question of who should take the vacant place.

" Did yez have a row? " she asked eagerly. " Say, did yez? "

THE LONG DAY

I evaded the question, thinking it neither advisable nor proper to satisfy the curiosity of the little mite. To divert her attention, I began questioning her about herself and her little companions—who were they, what were they, and how did they come to be here?

"Why, don't you know?" the little one asked, looking at me in amazement. "We 're waifs!"

"Waifs! What sort of waifs?"

"Why, just waifs."

"But I did n't know this was an orphan-asylum," I said, looking about at the children sitting in rows of two and three upon the scattered settees.

"Oh, no, ma'am. We 're not orfants," the child hastened to correct me; "we 're just waifs."

"And where are your fathers and mothers, then?" I cried.

"We ain't got none," Julia replied promptly, the little hand again stealing through the long sleeve and stroking my much-admired skirt. She had now snuggled down beside me upon the settee, and instinctively, rather than from any desire to show friendliness, I drew my arm about the small shoulders, which overture was interpreted as an invitation for the cropped head to nestle closer.

"But if you have n't father or mothers, then you

169

must be orphans," I reasoned,—an argument which made Julia straighten up suddenly and look at me in puzzled wonderment.

" No, we ain't orfants, neither, exceptin' just a few that did onct have fathers and mothers, mebbe; but me and May Wistaria and Mintie Delancy— they was the girls you seen up-stairs in HER room— we never did have no fathers and mothers, we 're just waifs, and so 's them kids waifs too that 's playing in the rocking-chair. They was all foundling-asylum kids."

At this moment a thick-set woman in a black dress appeared in the doorway, which was a signal for all the little girls to make an onslaught upon her. They twined their arms about her large waist, they hung three and four upon each of her generous, kindly arms, and the smaller girls held on to her skirts.

Thus encumbered, the good Mrs. Lumley introduced herself in an asthmatic voice which was scarcely more than a whisper, and in a manner as kindly as it was humble. Then she shoved the children back to their benches, and led me up-stairs to the dormitory; showing me the cot where I was to sleep, the lavatory where I would make my toilet in the mornings, and the bath-room where I had the privilege of taking a bath once a week. She also told me the rules of the house: first bell at six o'clock, when everybody in the dormitory must rise and dress; second bell at half-past six, when everybody must leave the dormitory, not to return until bedtime. As to that hour, it came at various times: for the waifs it was seven o'clock; for the regular lodgers, ten o'clock; and for the transients, from seven till twelve o'clock, at which hour the house was closed for the night.

All this Mrs. Lumley repeated in a dreary monotone which seemed strangely out of keeping with the half-concealed kindliness which was revealed in her homely countenance. She was a working matron, a sort of upper servant, and had been three years in the place, which, I gradually gleaned from her, had been started as a home for destitute children and had eventually assumed the character and discharged the functions of a girls' lodging-house. Under what auspices the house was conducted she did n't know any more than did I, any more than I know to this day. There was a board of managers, —ladies who sometimes came to look at the dormitories and the bath-rooms and then went away again in their carriages; there was the matron, Mrs. Pitbladder, who had been there four or five years, she

171

thought, but was n't certain; there were several under-matrons, who acted as teachers to the children. What did the children study? Reading and writing and arithmetic and the Bible; and then, as soon as they were old enough, they were turned into the sewing-room, where they were taught dress-making, or into the laundry, where they learned to do fine laundry-work.

All this sounded just and good, and I began to alter my opinion of the place. I even began to think that perhaps Mrs. Pitbladder was merely absent-minded and a little crotchety; that she had not meant to forget my fifteen cents change. I did not know until several days later that the house did a large dressmaking and laundry business, and that their advertisement appeared, and does to this day appear, in all the daily newspapers. It was from the older girls in the dormitory, in whispered talks we had at night after we were in bed, that I learned this and innumerable other things, which my own observation during the weeks that followed served to confirm.

To this home for working girls the waifs, the foundlings, came at all sorts of tender years, came from God only knows where—I could never find out exactly—some of them, perhaps, from city asylums, some from the families upon which they had been left as an encumbrance. They came as little children, and they went away as grown women. For them the home was practically a prison. Locked in here from morning till night, week in, week out, year after year, they were prisoners at all save certain stated times when they were taken abroad for a walk under charge of the matrons. In return for a scant education in the rudimentary branches, and a very generous tuition in the drudgery of the kitchen, the laundry, and the sewing-room, they received in all these years only their board and clothes and a certain nominal protection against the vices and corruptions of the street and the gutter from which they had been snatched.

" You won't eat here? " Mrs. Lumley inquired as we were going down-stairs again. To which I replied with a " Yes, why not? I have arranged with Mrs. Pitbladder to do so."

We were on the landing where the stairs turned into the ground-floor. She glanced apprehensively at Mrs. Pitbladder's door, into which a small blue-aproned figure at this moment was passing with a tray laden with Mrs. Pitbladder's breakfast. When it had closed again, she looked at me hesitatingly, as if fearful of taking me too far into her confidence. Then, perhaps reading a certain unconscious reassurance there, she replied with a brief—

" I would n't, if I was you. You can't stand it."

" But I 'll have to stand it," I returned; " I 'm as poor as anybody here."

She shook her head. " But you could n't work on it—you 're not used to it. I can see that. Besides, it is n't so cheap as you think it 'll be. You 'd better go out. I would n't even eat here to-day. I would n't begin it. There 's a little lunch-room over on Third Avenue where you can get enough to eat, and just as cheap as here."

The woman's manner was so mysterious, and withal so very earnest, not to say urgent, that I felt instinctively that there was something more in all she said than the mere depreciation of the quality of the victuals she warned me against. So I was not surprised when she said slowly and insinuatingly, as though feeling every step of the way:

" You know the misunderstanding you had this morning—about the change? "

" Yes," I answered, more mystified than ever. Then, as she looked me full in the eyes, light dawned upon me, and I saw the old woman up-stairs in a character as startling as it was infamous.

174

THE LONG DAY

"Well," Mrs. Lumley said, when she saw that I understood; and with that she again dropped into her habitual expression of bovine stolidness. We parted at the foot of the stairs, she to disappear into the back of the house, and I to join the waifs in the unfriendly sitting-room.

The afternoon I spent sitting in Union Square, whence I went at half-past five for a bite of supper in the dairy lunch-room where I had made my toilet in the morning. I had had no luncheon, feeling that I could not afford more than two meals a day now. I sat a long time over my cup of coffee and three hard rolls. I did not want to return to that dreary house until the lamps should be lighted and it was time to go to bed. The very thought of returning to sit with those forlorn waifs, in that cheerless whitewashed sitting-room, was appalling.

I returned a few minutes before seven, just in time to hear the children singing the last stanza of "Beulah Land" as I passed up-stairs to the dormitory on the third floor. An old woman sat outside the door, crocheting a shawl in such light as she could get from a blue-shaded night-lamp that hung in the middle of the great whitewashed room within. She looked up from her work long enough to challenge me with a shrewd, impertinent look of inquiry, demanded to know if I had any lead-pencils about my person, and, receiving a polite negative, allowed me to pass.

I was not the first arrival. In the dim light I could make out, here and there, a bulging surface in the row of gray-blanketed cots, while in the quiet I could hear the deep breathing of the sleepers. For they all seemed to be asleep, save one who tossed from one side to the other and sighed wearily. The latter was not far away from my own cot, and before I had finished undressing she was sitting up looking at me.

"I 'd give anything for a drink of water," she said softly.

"Why, is there no water?" I whispered.

The words were not out of my mouth before there was a thumping upon the floor outside, and the voice of the beldame spoke sharply:

"No talking, girls!"

The thirsty girl dropped back to her pillow, and I crept under the blanket. Later on I learned that each must have her drink of water before entering the dormitory, because, once there, it was an iron-clad rule that we should not leave until after the rising-bell had rung at six the next morning. I also learned, later on, that had there not been also an

iron-clad rule against carrying lead-pencils into the
dormitory, the snowy-white walls were like as not to
be scrawled with obscenities during the night hours.

All sorts of girls seeking a night's refuge drifted
into this working-girls' home. Most of them were
" ne'er-do-weels "; some of them were girls of lax
morality, though very few were essentially " bad."
When, however, they did happen to be " bad," they
were very bad indeed. And these lead-pencil in-
scriptions they left behind them were the frightful
testimony of their innate depravity.

Fortunately for me, I was quite ignorant on this
first night of what the character of the girls under
the gray blankets might in all possibility have been,
and I settled myself to go to sleep with the thought
that a working-girls' home was not half bad, after
all.

A little while later there was a fresh burst of
childish voices and the clatter of shoes on the stairs.
It was the orphans marching up to bed singing
" Happy Day! " The music stopped when they
reached the dormitory door, which they entered silently, two by two. Their undressing was but the
matter of a few moments, so methodical and precise
was every movement. The small aprons and petticoats were folded across the foot of each cot, and,

on top, the long black stockings laid neatly.   Each pair of copper-toed shoes was placed in exactly the same spot under the foot of each cot, and each little body, after wriggling itself into a gray flannellet nightgown, dropped to its knees and bowed its head upon the blanket in silent prayer.

After they had tucked themselves in bed a voice very near me, and which I recognized as Julia's, whispered:

" May, are yez asleep? "

" No," muttered May.

" Say, is to-morrow bean day or molasses day? "

" Bean," replied May; and then all was silent in the dormitory, and so remained save for the interruption caused by the tiptoe entrance of some newly arrived " transient," some homeless wanderer driven here to seek a night refuge.

In the morning we washed and combed in a large common toilet-room.   There were only a dozen facebowls, and these we had to watch our chance to pounce upon.   I waited until the rush was over, and after the orphans had scurried down to their breakfast I performed a more leisurely toilet.   Two other girls were there, doing the same thing.   I recognized them as transient lodgers, like myself, wanderers that had drifted in.

THE LONG DAY

Both were very young, and one, whom I had heard sigh, and who groaned continuously in her sleep, very, very pretty. The latter entered into conversation as we combed before the long, narrow glass. " Do you stay here all the time? " I asked. No, she had been living with her " lady-friend "; and that lady-friend having departed to the country for lack of employment until times would pick up, she was looking about for a boarding-house. The subject of work gave me my opportunity, and I asked her if she knew of a job. She shook her head. She was a skirt-hand; she had worked in a Broadway sweat-shop, and did n't know anything about any other sort of work. As we talked she finished her toilet, putting on as the finishing touch a great picture-hat and a scanty black Eton. Ready for the street, you would have little dreamed that she had slept in a ten-cent lodging-house. After going through a sort of inspection by the old woman at the entrance, during which it was ascertained we had not pilfered anything, we were allowed to depart.

XII

IN WHICH I SPEND A HAPPY FOUR WEEKS MAKING ARTIFICIAL FLOWERS

BRIGHT and early, after a four-cent breakfast, I was on my way to find the place where I had read the sign, " Flower-makers Wanted.—Paid while learning."

It was not difficult to find, even had I not had the number so securely tucked away in my memory.

" Flowers & Feathers," in giant gilded letters, I read a block away, as I dodged electric cars and motor vehicles, and threaded the maze of delivery wagons and vans. I had a hasty interview with the superintendent, a large and effusively polite man, whose plump white hands sparkled with gems. He put me on the freight-elevator and told the boy to show me to Miss Higgins. At the third floor the iron doors were thrown open, and I stepped into what seemed to be a great, luxuriant garden. The room was long and wide, and golden with April sunshine, and in the April breeze that blew through the half-open windows a million flowers fluttered and danced in the ecstacy of spring. Flowers, flowers, flowers everywhere; piled high on the tables, tossed in mad confusion on the floor, and strung in long garlands to the far end of the big room.

" The lady with the black hair, sitting down there by them American Beauties," said the elevator-boy, waving his hand toward the rear.

I passed down a narrow path between two rows of tables that looked like blossoming hedges. Through the green of branches and leaves flashed the white of shirt-waists, and among the scarlet and purple and yellow and blue of myriad flowers bobbed the smiling faces of girls as they looked up from their task long enough to inspect the passing stranger. Here were no harsh sounds, no rasping voices, no shrill laughter, no pounding of engines. Everything just as one would expect to find it in a flower-garden—soft voices humming like bees, and gentle merriment that flowed musically as a brook over stones.

" The lady with the black hair " sat before a cleared space on a table banked on either side with big red roses. In front of her were three or four glasses, each containing one salmon-colored rose, fresh and fragrant from the hothouse.

WOMEN AT WORK

Leaning forward, with her elbows on the table and her chin in her palm, she was staring intently at these four splendid blooms. Then she picked up a half-finished muslin rose and compared them. All this I saw while I waited timidly for her to look up. But she did not see me. She was absorbed in the study of the living rose. At last I summoned courage to inquire if she was Miss Higgins. She started, looked up quickly, and nodded her head, with a smile that displayed a row of pretty teeth. Her manner was cordial.

"Have you ever worked at flowers before?" she asked.

"No."

"Ever worked at feathers?"

"No."

"Well, the best I can do is to put you at blossom-making to-day, and see how you take to it. It's too bad, though, you don't know anything about feathers; for the flower season ends in a month, anyway, and then I have to lay off all my girls till September, unless they can make feathers too. Then they get jobs on the next floor. There'll be lots of work here, though, for a month, and we might take you back in September."

The tone was so kindly, the interest so genuine,

that I was prompted to explain my situation, assuring her I should be glad to get work even for four weeks. As a result, I was put on Rosenfeld's payroll for three and a half dollars per week, with half a day's extra pay for night work: the latter had been a necessity three or four nights every week for six months, and was likely to continue for two, maybe three, weeks longer. Besides the assurance of extra pay from this source, Miss Higgins also intimated, as she conducted me to one of the tables, that if I was " able to make good " she would raise me to four dollars at the end of the week.

Soon I was " slipping up " poppies under the instruction of Bessie, a dreamy-eyed young Jewess. The process was simple enough, to watch the skilled fingers of the other girls, but it was very tedious to my untried hand. In awkward, self-conscious fashion I began to open out the crimped wads of scarlet muslin which came to us hot from the crimping-machine.

" You must n't smooth the creases out too much," Bessie protested; and with a deft touch, the right pull here, the proper flattening there, the muslin scrap blossomed into a fluttering corolla.

" Don't get discouraged. We 've all got to

learn," one of the girls at the far end of the table called out cheerily.

"Yes, and don't be afraid of making a mistake," put in my vis-à-vis, a pretty Italian. "We all make mistakes while we 're learning; but you 'll find this a nice place to work, and Miss Higgins is so lovely — she 's awful nice, too, to the new girls."

"Yes, indeed," added Bessie. "It is n't many years since she worked at the table herself. I 've often heard her tell about the first day she went to work down at Golderberg's."

"That 's the worst in town," piped another; "I stayed there just two days. That was enough for me. Whenever the girls disagree down there, they step out into the hall and lick each other. First day I was there, one girl got two ribs broken. Her rival just walked all over her."

"What did they do with the girls?"

"Oh, nothing. They made it all up, and were as sweet as two turtle-doves, walking around the work-room with their arms around each other."

"Well, that 's what it is to work in those cheap shops," commented Annie Welshons, of the big blue eyes and yellow hair. "If they ever do get respect-able girls, they won't stay long."

As we worked the conversation ran easily. The

talk was in good, up-to-date English. There was
rarely a mispronounced word, or a slip in grammar;
and there was just enough well-selected slang to
make the dialogue bright and to stamp the chatter-
ers as conversant with the live questions of the day.
The topics at all times bespoke clean minds and an
intelligent point of view.

"Are you American born?" Bessie inquired by
and by.

The question sounded unusual, almost unnecessary, until I discovered that out of the eight girls
in our immediate circle, only half were native Americans. My vis-à-vis, Therese, was a Neapolitan;
Mamie, a Genoese; Amelia was born in Bohemia;
the girl with the yellow hair was North German;
and Nellie declared she was from County Killarney
and mighty glad of it.

"Well, I 'm an American," said Bessie, tossing
her head in mock scorn, as she cleared away a quan-
tity of the flowers that had been meanwhile accumu-
lating on the wire lines.

Therese laughed. "But only by the skin of your
teeth—an eleventh-hour arrival." Then she turned
to me and whispered that Bessie was born only two
weeks after her mother came to this country.

"Better late than never," laughed Bessie, casting

a backward and withering glance at the aliens as she moved away with her trayful of scarlet blossoms to the branchers' table, where another relay of workers twisted green leaves among the scarlet and tied them in wreaths and bunches.

By eleven o'clock I had made two dozen poppies, which Amelia told me was " just grand for a beginner." I began to feel confident that I should hold the job, and my fingers flew. Into the glue-pot at my right hand I dipped my little finger, picking up at the same moment with my other hand a bit of paper-covered wire. On the end of the wire was a bunch of short yellow threads, which were touched lightly with my glue-smeared finger, the wire being held between the thumb and forefinger. With the free left hand, I caught up a fluttering corolla, touching its perforated center with glue; then I " slipped up " the wire about an inch, took up another corolla in the same way, and then drew the two to the " pipped " or heart end of the wire, where they now became a big red flower with a golden eye. A bit of dark-green rubber tubing drawn over the wire completed the process, the end was bent into a hook, and the full-blown poppy hung on the line.

At a quarter past eleven a little girl wearing an

immense flower-hat and carrying a large market-basket came and asked us for our lunch orders. She carried a long piece of pasteboard and wrote as the girls dictated. One could buy anything one wanted, Bessie explained; bread and butter, eggs, chops, steak, potatoes, canned goods, for which there was ample provision for cooking on the gas-stoves used by the rose-makers to heat their pincers. When the little girl was gone I learned that she was one of the errand-runners, and that this was her daily task.

" How far does she go to market? "

" Over to First Avenue."

" Is n't that pretty far for a small girl to carry such a heavy load? "

" Oh, she does n't mind it. All the errand-girls are tickled to death to get the job. The grocers pay them ten per cent. commission on all they buy."

It lacked but a few minutes of twelve when the child returned, panting under her burden.

" How much did you clear to-day? " somebody asked.

" Twenty-one cents," the child answered, blushing as red as the poppies.

When Miss Higgins slipped her tall, light figure into her stylish jacket and began to pin on her hat it was always a sign that the lunch-hour had come.

WOMEN AT WORK

One hundred and twenty girls popped up from their hiding-places behind the hedges, which had grown to great height since morning. In a trice spaces were cleared on the tables. Cups and saucers and knives and forks appeared as if by magic. In that portion of the room where the crimping-machines stood preparations for cooking commenced. The pincers and tongs of the rose-makers, and the pressing-molds of the leaf-workers, were taken off the fires, and in their place appeared stew-pans and spiders, and pots and kettles. Bacon and chops sputtered, steak sizzled; potatoes, beans, and corn stewed merrily. What had been but lately a flower-garden, by magic had become a mammoth kitchen filled with appetizing sounds and delicious odors. White-aproned cooks scurried madly. It was like a school-girls' picnic. As they moved about I noticed how well dressed and neat were my shop-mates in their white shirt-waists and dark skirts. Indeed, in the country village I had come from any one of them would have appeared as the very embodiment of fashion.

Cooked and served at last, we ate our luncheon at leisure, and with the luxury of snowy-white table-cloths and napkins of tissue-paper, which needs of the workroom were supplied in prodigal quantities.

During this hour I heard a great deal about the

girls and their work. They told me, as they told all new-comers, of the wonderful rise of Miss Higgins, who began as a table-worker at three and a half dollars a week, and was now making fifty dollars. They told me of her rise from the best rose-maker in New York to designer and forewoman. They dwelt on her kindness to everybody, discussed her pretty clothes, and wondered which of her beaux she was going to marry.

All afternoon I " slipped up " poppies. At five Miss Higgins came to tell me I was " doing fine," and that I should have four dollars instead of three and a half. This made the work easier than ever, and my fingers flew happily till six o'clock. Then we cooked dinner as we did our luncheon, but we took only half an hour for our evening meal, so as to get off at half-past nine instead of ten. At night the work was harder, as the room became terribly hot from the gas-jets and from the stoves where the rose-makers heated their tools. The faces grew tired and pale, and the girls sang to keep themselves awake. " The Rabbi's Daughter," " The City of Sighs and Tears," and " The Banquet in Misery Hall " were the favorite songs. A rising breeze swept up Broadway, now almost deserted, and rushed through the windows, setting all our blossoms fluttering. Outside a soft, warm spring rain began to fall on the tired, sleepy city.

One week, two weeks, passed in these pleasant surroundings. I was still "slipping up" poppies all day long, and every evening till half-past nine. Then I went home to the little cot in the dormitory of the "home." It would seem that all the world's wife and daughters were to wear nothing but poppies that season. But ours was only a small portion of Rosenfeld's output. Violets, geraniums, forget-me-nots, lilies-of-the-valley, apple-blossoms, daisies, and roses of a score of varieties were coming to life in this big garden in greater multitudes even than our common poppies. Forty girls worked on roses alone. The rose-makers are the swells of the trade. They are the best paid, the most independent, and always in competitive demand during the flower season. Any one can learn with patience how to make other kinds of flowers; but the rose-maker is born, and the thoroughly experienced rose-maker is an artist. Her work has a distinction, a touch, a "feel," as she calls it, which none but the artist can give.

The star rose-maker of the shop, next to the fore-woman (who was reputed the finest in America), was about twenty-five. Her hair was fluffy and brown, and her eyes big and dark blue. She was of Irish birth, and had been in America about fourteen years. One day I stopped at her chair and asked how long it took her to learn.

" I 'm still learning," she replied, without looking up from the tea-rose in her fingers. " It was seven years before I considered myself first-class; and though I 'm at it now thirteen, I don't consider I know it all yet." She worked rapidly, flecking the delicate salmon-colored petals with her glue-finger, and pasting them daintily around the fast-growing rose. I watched her pinch and press and crease each frail petal with her hot iron instruments, and when she had put on a thick rubber stem and hung the finished flower on the line she looked up and smiled.

" Want to see a rose-maker's hand? " she remarked, turning her palm up for my inspection. She laughed aloud at my exclamation of horror. Calloused and hard as a piece of tortoise-shell, ridged with innumerable corrugations, and hopelessly discolored, with the thumb and forefinger flattened like miniature spades, her right hand had long ago lost nearly all semblance to the other.

" It is the hot irons do that," she said, drawing

her pincers from the fire and twirling them in the air until they grew cool enough to proceed with the work. "We use them every minute. We crease the petals with them, and crinkle and vein and curl the outer edges. And we always have to keep them just hot enough not to scorch the thin muslin."

"How many can you make a day?"

"That depends on the rose. This sort—" picking up a small, cheap June rose—"this sort a fair worker can make a gross of a day. But I have made roses where five single flowers were considered a fine day's job. Each of those roses had one hundred and seventy-five pieces, however; and there were eighteen different shapes and sizes of petals; and besides that, every one of those pieces had to be put in its own place. If one piece had been wrongly applied, the whole rose would have been spoiled. But they don't make many of such complicated roses in this country. They have to import them. They have n't enough skilled workers to fill big orders, and it does n't pay the manufacturers to bother with small orders."

The girl did all the fine work of the place, and had always more waiting to be done than she could have accomplished with four hands instead of two. She had no rival to whom this surplus work could be turned over. The dull season had no terrors for her, nor would it have had for her comrades had they been equally skilled. She made from twenty-two to twenty-five dollars a week, all the year round, and was too busy ever to take a vacation. The other girls averaged nine dollars, and if they got eight months' work a year they considered themselves fortunate. They were clever and industrious, but they had not learned to make the finer grade of roses.

The third week came and went all too quickly, and we were now entering on the fourth. Plainly the season was drawing to its close. The orders that had come pouring in from milliners and modistes all over the land for six months were now dwindling daily. The superintendent and the " boss " walked through the department every day, and we heard them talk about overproduction. Friday the atmosphere was tense with anxiety. The girls' faces were grave. Almost without exception, there were people at home upon whom this annual " lay-off " fell with tragic force. I have not talked with one of them who did not have to work, and they have always some one at home to care for. A few were widows with small children at home or in the day nursery. One can tell little, by their appearance, about these secret burdens. Each girl wears a mask.

The neat costume, made with her own hands in midnight hours snatched from hard-earned rest, is no evidence of extravagance, or even of comfortable circumstances. It is only that manifestation of proper pride and self-respect which the best type of wage-earning woman is never without. If they sometimes talk happily about theaters and parties and beaux, if occasionally there is a brief spell of innocent hilarity in the workroom, it is only the inevitable and legitimate outcropping of healthy and wholesome animal spirits, of a vigorous hope which not even the hard conditions of life can crush.

On Saturday morning many of the girls sat idle. "Don't work too fast, or you 'll work yourself out of a job," one cried in jest; but the meaning was one of dead earnest. And as the day passed the prophecy came true to one after another. In the afternoon we made a feint of work by papering wires and opening petals for those who were still busy. The hours passed drearily. Miss Higgins was going over her pay-roll, checking off the names of the girls who could make feathers as well as flowers. All others were to be laid off indefinitely that night. We watched anxiously for the moment, which was not far off.

"I hope Miss Higgins won't cry—she did last

year. It breaks her up terribly to let us off," somebody remarked.

" It 's a long time to be idle—till September," I suggested to the girl across the work-table. She looked up in surprise.

" Idle!" she exclaimed. " But we are never idle. We dare n't. We get other jobs."

" What? "

" Oh, everything: waitress in a summer boarding-house, novelty goods, binderies, shirt-waists, stores, anything we can get."

" She 's coming," some one whispered. Everybody tried to look unconcerned. Those who had no work to claim attention looked carefully at their finger-nails, or found sudden necessity to adjust collars and belts. Miss Higgins passed along the tables, bending over the heads and speaking to each in a low voice. The tears were running down her cheeks. Those retained concealed their happiness as best they could, and spoke words of sympathy and encouragement to their less fortunate companions. The warrants were received with a stoicism that was more pathetic than tears. From the far end of the room I heard an unaccustomed sound, and turning, I saw the forewoman, who had dropped into a chair at the forget-me-not table, her face buried in her arms, and sobbing like a child. It was the signal that her cruel duty was done, that the last " lay-off " sentence had been pronounced, that the work for the day and for the " season " was over, that it had come time to say good-by.

" Good-by! " The voices echoed as we trooped down-stairs to the street door. " Good-by! Good-by! " The lingering farewells rose faintly above the noises of Broadway, as we scattered at the corner. Good-by to Rosenfeld's—now no longer a reality, but rather a memory of idyllic beauty—the workroom bright with sunshine and flashing with color, with the faces of the workers bent over the fashioning of rose and poppy, and best of all, the kind hearts and the quick sympathy that blossomed there as luxuriantly as the flowers themselves.

Good-by to my four happiest weeks in the workaday world.

XIII

THREE " LADY-FRIENDS," AND THE ADVENTURES THAT BEFALL THEM

INTO every human experience there must come sooner or later the bitter consciousness that Nature is remorselessly cruel; that she laughs loudest when we are most miserable; that she is never so bright, never so beautiful as in the darkest hour of our need; that she ever makes mock of our agony and ever smiles serenely at our despair.

Such, at least, were my feelings in those long, beautiful June days that followed close on the " lay-off " at Rosenfeld's.

Dear little Bessie! poor unhappy Eunice! This chapter of my experiences is so dominated by their personalities that I shall devote a few words to recounting the circumstances which brought us together and sent us faring forth on a summer's day to seek new fortunes, three " lady-friends," arm in arm. I make no apology for saying " lady-friends."

WOMEN AT WORK

I know all the prejudices of polite society, which smiles at what is esteemed to be a piece of vulgar vanity characteristic of the working-girl world. And yet I use the term here in all seriousness, in all good faith; not critically, not playfully, but tenderly. Because in the humble world in which our comradeship was formed there is none other to designate the highest type of friendship, no other phrase to define that affection between girl and girl which is as the love of sisters. In the great workaday world where we toiled and hoped and prayed and suffered together for a brief period we were called " the three lady-friends " by our shop-mates, and such we were to each other always, and such we shall be throughout the chapter; and I know, if Bessie and Eunice were here to-night, looking over my shoulder as I write the account of that sordid little tragedy and the part they played in it,—I know they would clasp their rough little hands in mine and nod approval.

Bessie had been my " learner " at Rosenfeld's. I still remember her exactly as I saw her that first time, a slender little figure bending over the worktable. Her shirt-waist was snowy-white, and fastened down—oh, so securely!—under the narrow leather belt; she had a wealth of straight blonde hair of that clear, transparent quality which, when heaped high on her head, looked like a mass of spun glass; her cheeks, which were naturally very pale, burned a deep crimson as they reflected the light on the poppies beneath; and after a while, when she raised her head, I saw that her eyes were blue, and that her profile, sharp and clear cut, was that of a young Jewess. I had thought her to be about twenty-two,—for, pretty and fresh as she was, she looked every day of it,—but I found out later that she was not then eighteen.

We had not been long getting acquainted—that is, as well acquainted as was possible in a busy shop like Rosenfeld's. Indeed, it would be a strange, sad world—stranger and sadder than it really is—if Bessie and I had not sooner or later established a certain bond of intimacy. Sitting opposite at the same work-table, we made poppies together and exchanged our little stories. She had been working, since she was fifteen, at all sorts of odd jobs: cash-girl in a department store; running errands for a fashionable modiste; cashier in a dairy lunch-room; making picture-frames. This was her second season at flower-making, and she liked it better than anything she had ever tried, if only there was work all the year round; for she could n't afford to sit

idle through the long summer months—well, I
should say not!—with eight small brothers and sisters at home, and a rather incompetent father, and
sixteen dollars a month rent! The experiences of a
score of shops, and the motley crew of people she
had worked with in these busy years, Bessie in her
careless, simple narrative had the power to invest
with lifelike reality.

Scarcely less interesting than all this to me was
my own story to Bessie, which found ready sympathy in her tender heart, especially that part of it
that had to do with the home for working girls
where I was now living. For to Bessie, with her in-
born racial love of family, nothing was so much to
be pitied as the unfortunates who found shelter
there. She seemed to take a certain sort of consola-
tion for her own hard life in hearing the sordid details of the wretched waifs and strays that came
wandering into the " home " at all hours of the day
and night. I told her about the dormitory where
we slept side by side in gray-blanketed cots, each
girl's clothes folded neatly across the footboard; of
the cross old dragon who sat outside in the brightly
lighted passageway, and snored all night long, when
she should have been attending to her duties,—which
duties were to keep an eye on us lest we rob one

another of the few pennies we might have under our pillows, or that we might not scrawl obscene verses on the whitewashed walls, in case we had succeeded in smuggling in a forbidden lead-pencil. For such offenses, and they happened only too often, we were all held equally guilty in the eyes of the sour, autocratic matron. As each night brought a fresh relay of girls to the dormitory, it was productive of a new series of episodes, which I related faithfully to Bessie.

That is how she became interested in Eunice. The latter had come tiptoeing into the dormitory one night long after the other girls were fast asleep, and without undressing threw herself on the vacant cot next to mine. In the lamplight that shone from the passageway full on her face, I saw, as I peeped above the rough blanket, that the new-comer was no common type of waif and stray. There was an elusive charm in the glimpse of profile and in the delicate aquiline features, a certain suggestion of beauty, were it not for the white, drawn look that enveloped them like a death-mask. As I was gazing furtively at her she turned on her side, moaning as only a girl can moan when peace of mind is gone forever. Such sounds were not uncommon in the dormitory. Several times, waking in the night, I had listened pityingly to the same half-smothered lament. On this night I had fallen asleep as usual, when suddenly a shriek rang out, and I wakened to hear the angry accents of the beldam protesting against "hysterics," and the indistinct muttering of the girlish sleepers whose rest the stranger had so inconsiderately disturbed. In a few moments everything was quiet again, our old woman had renewed her snoring, and then the new-comer, repressing her anguish as best she could, slid kneeling to the floor.

It was then, all sleep gone for that night, I reached out my hand and touched the sleeve of her black dress.

From that moment we became friends. The information which she vouchsafed about herself was meager and not of a character to throw much light upon her former condition and environment. It was obvious that there had been a tragedy in her life, and I instinctively guessed what that tragedy was, although I respected the reserve she threw around her and asked no indiscreet questions. She was fairly well educated, had been brought up in a small New Jersey village, and had been a stenographer until she went to a telephone office to tend a switchboard. Between that job and her advent in the " home " was an obvious hiatus, which at times she vaguely referred to as a period wherein she " lost her grip on everything." She had no money, and her clothes were even shabbier than my own, and she was too discouraged even to look for work. Her cot and three meager meals a day, consisting of bread and tea for breakfast and supper, and bread and coffee and soup for dinner, she received, as did all the transient boarders, in return for a ten-hour-day's work in the " home " kitchen. After a few nights she ceased moaning, and settled gradually into a hopeless apathy, while over her deep gray eyes there grew a film of silent misery.

Stirred by my fragmentary accounts of Eunice's wretchedness, the generous-hearted Bessie one day suggested that we take her with us to look for a job as soon as the anticipated " lay-off " notice came into effect at Rosenfeld's. And so, on the Monday morning following that dreaded event, Bessie met Eunice and me at the lower right-hand corner of Broadway and Grand Street, and together we applied for work at the R—— Underwear Company, which had advertised that morning for twenty operators.

" Ever run a power Singer? " queried the foreman.

" No, but we can learn. We 're all quick," an-

swered Bessie, who had volunteered to act as spokes-
man.

"Yes, I guess you can learn all right, but you
won't make very much at first. All come together?
. . . So! Well, then, I guess you 'll want to work
in the same room," and with that he ushered us into
a very inferno of sound, a great, yawning chaos of
terrific noise. The girls, who sat in long rows up
and down the length of the great room, did not raise
their eyes to the new-comers, as is the rule in less
strenuous workrooms. Every pair of eyes seemed
to be held in fascination upon the flying and endless
strip of white that raced through a pair of hands to
feed itself into the insatiable maw of the electric
sewing-machine. Every face, tense and stony, bespoke a superb effort to concentrate mind and body,
and soul itself, literally upon the point of a needle.
Every form was crouched in the effort to guide the
seam through the presser-foot. And piled between
the opposing phalanxes of set faces were billows
upon billows of foamy white muslin and lace—the
finished garments wrought by the so-many dozen per
hour, for the so-many cents per day,—and wrought,
too, in this terrific, nerve-racking noise.

The foreman led us into the middle of the room,
which was lighted by gas-jets that hung directly

over the girls' heads, although the ends of the shop had bright sunshine from the windows. He seemed a good-natured, respectable sort of man, of about forty, and was a Jew. Bessie and me he placed at machines side by side, and Eunice a little farther down the line. Then my first lesson began. He showed me how to thread bobbin and needle, how to operate ruffler and tucker, and also how to turn off and on the electric current which operated the machinery. My first attempt to do the latter was productive of a shock to the nerves that could not have been greater if, instead of pressing the harmless little lever under the machine with my knee, I had accidently exploded a bomb. The foreman laughed good-naturedly at my fright.

"You 'll get used to it by and by," he shouted above the noise; "but like as not for a while you won't sleep very good nights—kind of nervous; but you 'll get over that in a week or so," and he ducked his head under the machine to adjust the belt. Suddenly, above all the frenzied crashing of the machines came a sound, half scream, half cackle:

"Yi! yi! my pretty one, you 'll get used to it by and by; you 'll get used to anything in this world." It was an old woman's voice, and looking across the table, I saw a merry-eyed, toothless old crone, who was grinning and nodding at me.

"Hello! hello there, Miriam! what 's eating you now?" shouted the foreman, emerging and scrambling to his feet as he turned to get Bessie started. But the strange old creature only grinned wider and screeched, "Yi! yi!" louder than ever.

But I had not time, either, to look at or listen to her now, as I leaned over the machine and practised at running a straight seam. Ah, the skill of these women and girls, and of the strange creature opposite, who can make a living at this torturing labor! How very different, how infinitely harder it is, as compared with running an ordinary sewing-machine. The goods that my nervous fingers tried to guide ran every wrong way. I had no control whatever over the fearful velocity with which the needle danced along the seam. In utter discouragement, I stopped trying for a moment, and watched the girl at my right. She was a swarthy, thick-lipped Jewess, of the type most common in such places, but I looked at her with awe and admiration. In Rachel Goldberg's case the making of muslin, lace-trimmed corset-covers was an art rather than a craft. She was a remarkable operator even among scores of experts at the R——. Under her stubby,

ill-kept hands ruffles and tucks and insertion bands
and lace frills were wrought with a beauty and soft-
ness of finish, and a speed and precision of workman-
ship, that made her the wonder and envy of the shop.
And with what ease she seemed to do it all, despite
the riveted eyes and tense-drawn muscles of her ex-
pressionless face! Suddenly her machine stopped,
she looked up with a loud yawn, and stretched her
arms above her head. She acknowledged the flattery of my look with a patronizing smile and
a "How-do-you-think-you're-going-to-like-your-
job?" I answered the conventional question in the
usual way, and remarked that she sewed as if she had
done it for ever and ever, and as if it were no work
at all.

She shook her head. "Yes, I 've worked a long
time at it, but my shoulder aches as bad this morning
as it did when I was a learner like you," and she
pressed the power-lever and again bent over the
tucking.

At my left Bessie was also practising on running
seams, and a little farther down we saw poor Eunice
struggling at the same hopeless lesson. The foreman, whose name proved to be Isaacs,—" Abe "
Isaacs,—brought us our first " lot " of work. Mine
consisted of six dozen coarse muslin corset-covers,

which were already seamed together, and which I
was shown how to " finish " with an embroidery yoke
and ruffled edging about the arm's-eye. There is
no basting, no pinning together of pieces; all the
work is free-hand, and must be done with infinite
exactness. I must hold the embroidery and the finishing strips of beading on the edge of the muslin
with an exact nicety that will insure the edges of all
three being caught in one seam; a process difficult
enough on any sewing-machine, under any circumstances, but doubly so when the lightest touch sends
the three-ply fabric under the needle with an incalculable velocity. Result of my first hour's work: I
had spoiled a dozen garments. Try as I would, I
invariably lost all control of my materials, and the
needle plunged right and left—everywhere, in fact,
except along the straight and narrow way laid out
for it. And, to make matters still worse, I was painfully conscious that my old woman vis-à-vis was
laughing at my distress with her irritating " Yi,
yi! "

As I spoiled each garment I thrust it into the
bottom of a green pasteboard box under the table,
which held my allotment of work, and from the top
of the box grabbed up a fresh piece. I glanced over
my shoulder and saw that Bessie was doing the same

thing, although what we were going to do with them,
or how account for such wholesale devastation of
goods, we were too perturbed to consider. At last,
however, after repeated trials, and by guiding the
seam with laborious care, I succeeded in completing
one garment without disaster; and I had just
started another, when—crash!—flying shuttles and
spinning bobbins and swirling wheels came to a
standstill. My sewing-machine was silent, as were
all the others in the great workroom. Something
had happened to the dynamo.

There was a howl of disappointment.

" Yi, yi! " screamed the old woman, throwing up
her hands in a gesture of unutterable disgust; and
then, catching my eye, her wrinkled old lips parted
in a smile of friendly interest.

" How many did ye bungle? " she chuckled, leaning over and looking furtively up and down the
room, as if afraid of being caught talking to me. I
blushed in confusion that was half fright, and she
raised a forefinger menacingly:

" Yi! yi! ye thought I did n't see ye sneaking the
spoiled truck into the green box; but old Miriam 's
got sharp eyes, she has, and she likes to watch you
young uns when you comes in first. You 're not the
only one. They all spoil lots before they learn to

make a living out of it. There 's lots like ye!" and stooping over, she drew a handful of my botched work out of the box and began to rip the stitching.

"That 's all right; I 'm glad to help ye!" she protested. "And sure, if we don't help each other, who 's a-going to help us poor devils, I 'd like to know?"

I, too, busied myself with the task of ripping, which I saw Bessie and Eunice were also doing; in fact, all the new-comers of the morning could be thus singled out. The practised hands availed themselves of the enforced rest by yawning and stretching their arms, and by comparing the earnings of the morning; for we all worked on piece-work. Rachel Goldberg had finished four dozen of extra-fine garments, which meant seventy-five cents, and it was not yet eleven o'clock. She would make at least one dollar and sixty cents before the day was over, provided we did not have any serious breakdowns. She watched the clock impatiently,—every minute she was idle meant a certain fraction of a penny lost,—and crouched sullenly over her machine for the signal.

"What are you thinking about, Miriam?" a frowsy-headed girl asked, giving the wink to the crowd.

THE LONG DAY

The generous-hearted old lady looked up from the task she was helping me to do, and raising her hand to shield her eyes from the glare of the gaslight, peered down the long line of girls until she placed the speaker.

"Yi, yi! Ye want to know what I 'm thinking about? Well, mebbe, Beckie Frankenstein, I 'm thinking what a beautiful world this is, and what a fine time you and me has," and the strange creature broke into a laugh that was more terrible than a sob.

"Ah, there you go again, Miriam! What 's eatin' you to-day?" cried the foreman, as he came along to inspect the work; and seeing Miriam undoing my blunders, asked, "Who did that?"

Before I could put in a half-frightened acknowledgment, my intercessor had spoken up:

"And whose 'u'd them be but mine, Abe Isaacs?" —scowling at me to keep silence when I opened my mouth to contradict her.

The foreman looked incredulous. "You, Miriam! Do you mean to tell me it was you spoiled all that work? What 's the matter with you to-day, anyway? If you don't do better, I 'll have to fire you."

There was a good-natured tone, a kindly compassion, in Abe Isaacs's voice which was not in accord with the words; and when he turned and asked me what I had done, there was no fear in my heart. I answered by looking significantly at old Miriam.

"I thought as much," he muttered under his breath, and passed on to Bessie.

"Poor old Miriam, she 's teched up here," one of the girls explained, tapping her forehead. "They say it was the old sweat-shops put her out of her mind, and I guess it 's so, all right. My mother knows two ladies that was made crazy sewing pants up to Sternberg's. But that was long ago, when they used to treat the girls so bad. Things is ever so much better now, only Miriam can't get used to the improvements. She 's a hundred years behind the times."

I was still lost in admiring wonder of Rachel Goldberg's skill. I asked her how long it would take me to learn to do it as well. She did not have a chance to answer before a harsh laugh was heard and a new voice asserted itself.

"Oh-ho! you 'll never learn to work like her, and you 'd better find it out now. I seen you running your machine, and I says to myself, 'That girl 'll never make her salt making underclothes.' Pants 'd be more in your line. To make money on muslin you 've got to be born to 't."

" That 's no lie, either," muttered another.

" You bet it ain't!" declared the expert Rachel. " My mother was working on shirts for a straight ten months before I was born."

In half an hour we had resumed work, and at half-past twelve we stopped for another half-hour and ate luncheon—Bessie, Eunice, and I in a corner by ourselves.

We held a conference, and compared notes of the morning's progress, which had been even more discouraging to poor Eunice than to us; for to her it had brought the added misfortune of a row of stitches in her right forefinger. We counted up our profits for the morning, and the aggregate earnings of the three of us did not amount to ten cents. Of course we would learn to do better, but it would take a long, long time, Bessie was firmly convinced, before we could even make enough to buy our lunches. It was decided that one of us should resign the job that night, and the other two keep at it until the delegate found something better for us all and had tested the new job to her satisfaction. Bessie was of course appointed, and the next morning Eunice and I went alone, with plausible excuses for the absent Bessie, for we had a certain delicacy about telling the real facts to so kind a foreman as " Abe."

WOMEN AT WORK

The second day we had no better luck, and the pain between the shoulder-blades was unceasing. All night long I had tossed on my narrow cot, with aching back and nerves wrought up to such a tension that the moment I began to doze off I was wakened by a spasmodic jerk of the right arm as it reached forward to grasp a visionary strip of lace. That evening, as we filed out at six o'clock, Bessie was waiting for us, her gentle face full of radiance and good news. Even the miserable Eunice was affected by her hopefulness.

" Oh, girls, I 've got something that 's really good—three dollars a week while you 're learning, and an awful nice shop; and just think, girls!—the hours—I never had anything like it before, and I 've knocked around at eighteen different jobs—half-past eight to five, and—" she paused for breath to announce the glorious fact—" Girls, just think of it!—*Saturday afternoons off*, all the year round."

XIV

IN WHICH A TRAGIC FATE OVERTAKES MY "LADY-FRIENDS"

THE next morning we met on the corner, as usual, and Bessie led us to our new job—led us through a world that was strange and new to both Eunice and me, though poor Eunice had little heart for the newness and the strangeness of it all. In and out, and criss-cross, we threaded our way through little narrow streets bordered with stately "sky-scrapers," and at last turned into Maiden Lane. We walked arm in arm till we came to an alley which Bessie said was Gold Street. It is more of a zigzag even than Maiden Lane, and is flanked by dark iron-shuttered warehouses and factories. Wolff's, our destination, was at the head of the street, and in a few minutes we were sitting side by side at the work-table, while our new forewoman, a cross-eyed Irish girl, was showing us what to do and how to do it.

215

WOMEN AT WORK

Making jewel- and silverware-cases was now our work. In the long, whitewashed workroom there were thirty other girls performing the same task, and on each of the five floors beneath there were as many more girls, pasting and pressing and trimming cases that were to hold rings, watches and bracelets, and spoons, knives, and forks—enough to supply all Christendom, it seemed to me. As beginners we were given each a dozen spoon-boxes to cover with white leather and line with satin. It is light, pleasant work, and was such an improvement on the sweat-shop drudgery that even Eunice smiled a little after a while.

"Is youse lady-friends?" the forewoman asked when, in the course of ten minutes, she came to inspect our progress; on receiving an affirmative reply, she scowled.

"Fiddlesticks! If I 'd knowed youse was lady-friends, I 'd jist told Izzy he could get some other girls," and she walked off, still scowling. The girls about us giggled.

"Why does n't Miss Gibbs like us to be lady-friends?" asked Bessie.

A young Italian answered, "Because they always git to scrappin'."

We all laughed—even Eunice—at such an ending to our friendship.

" We had a fearful row here yesterday," spoke up another; " and they wuz lady-friends—thicker than sardines, they wuz—till they got on the outs about a feller down on Pearl Street; a diamond-cutter he wuz, and they wuz both mashed on him—a Dutch-man, too, he wuz, that wore ear-rings. I could n't get mashed on a Dutchman, ear-rings or no ear-rings, could you? "

" What did they do? " asked Bessie.

" Do! They snapped at each other all morning over the work-table, and then one of them called the other a name that wuz something awful, and she up and spit in her face for it."

" Well, I don't blame that girl for spitting in her face," interrupted a voice. " I don't blame her; lady-like or not lady-like, I 'd have done the same thing. I 'd spit in the President's face if I was in the White House and he was to call me such a name! "

" And then what happened? " asked Bessie.

" Oh, they just up and at each other like two cats, tumbling over a stack of them there white velvet necklace-cases, and bloodying up each other's faces something fierce; and then Miss Gibbs she called Izzy; and Izzy he fired them on the spot."

Despite these tales of strenuous conflicts, we were happy in our work at Wolff's. Our shop-mates were quiet, decent-looking girls, and their conversation was conspicuously clean—not always a characteristic of their class. Miss Gibbs, despite her justifiable prejudice against lady-friends, proved not unkind, and we congratulated ourselves as we bent over our work and listened to the cheerful hum of voices.

After each case was finished,—after the satin linings and interlinings and the tuftings had been fitted and glued into their proper places, and the bit of leather drawn across the padded cover,—we could raise our eyes for a moment and look out upon a strange, fascinating world. The open windows on one side of the shop looked into the polishing-room of a neighboring goldsmith, and on the other side into a sunshiny workroom filled with swirling black wheels and flying belts among which the workmen kept up a dialogue in a foreign tongue. The latter place was near enough for a good-looking young man to attempt a flirtation with Bessie, in such moments as he was not carefully watching what seemed to be a clumsy mass of wax on the end of a wooden handle. All the long forenoon he kept up his manœuvers, watching his ugly bludgeon as if it were the very apple of his eye; carrying it to the window one moment and examining it under the microscope; then carrying it back to his wheel and beginning all

THE LONG DAY

over again. Late in the afternoon he came to the window for the hundredth time, and brandishing the bludgeon so that the sunshine fell directly upon it, held it aloft for us to admire the great glittering gem that now sparkled deep-bedded in the ugly wax.

"I gif you dat if you marry me!" cried the diamond-cutter, striking a dramatic attitude for Bessie's benefit.

Thus one, two days passed swiftly, and we had learned to make jewel-cases with tolerable rapidity. We had a half-hour for luncheon, during which Bessie, Eunice, and I went off by ourselves to the rear of the shop, where we ate our sandwiches in silence and gazed out upon the forest of masts that filled the East River lying below.

On the fourth day Eunice and I ate luncheon alone. Bessie did not come that morning, nor send any excuse. Her absence gave me an opportunity, in this half-hour's respite from work, to get better acquainted with my silent and mysterious fellow-boarder; anything more than a most meager acquaintance was impossible at the place where we lived. Like the majority of semi-charitable institutions, the "home" was conducted on the theory that the only safety to morals, as well as to pocket-books, was espionage and isolation.

"It 's awful up there, is n't it?" she remarked suddenly after we had discussed every possible cause for Bessie's absence.

"Yes, is n't it?" I replied, somewhat surprised, for this was the first time the girl had ever expressed any opinion about anything, so fearful did she seem of betraying herself.

"I suppose you often wonder what brought me there that night?" she went on. "You 've told me your story, and you don't know anything at all about mine. You must often wonder, though you are too considerate to ask. But I 'm going to tell you now without asking. It was to keep me from going there," pointing through the window down to the river.

"I 'd had a lot of trouble,—oh, a terrible lot of trouble,—and it seemed as if there was n't any place for me; and I walked down to the edge of the river up there at the end of East Fourteenth Street, and something stopped me just when I was ready to jump in. Why I did n't, I don't know," and the girl turned a stony face to the window.

"Why, it was hope and renewed courage, of course!" I replied quickly. "Everybody gets blue spells—when one is down on one's luck."

Eunice shook her head. "No, it was n't hope.

It was because I was afraid—it was because I 'm a coward. I 'm too much of a coward to live, and I 'm too much of a coward to die. You never felt as I do. You could n't. I 've lost my grip on everything. Everything 's gone against me, and it 's too late now for things to change. You don't know —*you don't know*, you and Bessie. If you did, you 'd see how useless all your kindness is, in trying to get me to brace up. I 've tried—my God! I have tried to feel that there 's a life before me, but I can't—I can't. Sometimes, maybe for a minute, I 'll forget what 's gone by, and then the next minute the memory of it all comes back with a fearful stab. There is something that won't let me forget."

" Hush! Eunice; don't talk so loud," I whispered as her passionate voice rose above the hum of the other girls in a far portion of the room.

" I tell you it 's no use—it 's no use. I 've lost my grip on things, and I can never catch hold again. I thought, maybe, when I started out with you and Bessie, and got to working again, there 'd be a change. But there is n't any difference now from— from the night I went into that dormitory first. Now with you it would be different. What 's happened to me might, maybe, happen to you; but you could fight it down. There 's something inside of you that 's stronger than anything that can hurt you from the outside. Most girls are that way. They get hurt —and hurt bad, and they cry a lot at the time and are miserable and unhappy; but after a while they succeed in picking themselves up, and are in the end as good, sometimes better, than ever. They forget in a little while all about it, and wind up by marrying some man who is really in love with them, and they are as happy as if nothing had ever happened."

I looked at the occupant of cot No. 11 with mingled feelings of pity and amazement—pity for the hopelessness of her case, now more apparent than ever; amazement at her keen and morbid generalizations.

" How old are you, Eunice? "

" Twenty-four," she replied—" oh, I know what you 're going to say: that I have my whole life before me, and all that. But I have n't. My life is all behind me."

> " ' I am the Captain of my Soul,
> I am the Master of my Fate,' "

I quoted.

" Yes, you are; but I am not," she replied simply, and turned and looked at me with her hopeless eyes.

Poor, unfortunate Eunice; That night, as we

walked home together, she revealed a little more about herself by telling me that she had recently been discharged from the hospital on " the Island." I did not need to inquire the nature of the illness that had left her face so white and drawn. Brief as my experience had been among the humble in- mates of the " home," I had learned the expediency of not being too solicitous regarding the precise facts of such cases.

The next day was Saturday, and still no Bessie. As we worked we speculated as to her absence, and decided to spend the afternoon looking her up. Meanwhile, although I had been managing to do my work a little better each day, Eunice had not been succeeding so well. Her apathy had been increas- ing daily, until she had lost any interest she might ever have had in trying to do her work well. On this morning the forewoman was obliged to give her repeated and sharp reproofs for soiling her materials and for dawdling over her work.

" You seem to like to work," Eunice said once, breaking a long silence.

" Not any better than you do, only I 've got to, and I try to make the best of it."

" Yes, you do. You like to work, and I don't, and that 's the difference between us. And it 's all the difference in the world, too.   If I liked work for its own sake, like you do, there 'd be some hope for me living things down."

" I wonder," she whispered, again breaking a long silence—" I wonder if Bessie had any man after her."

I looked up suddenly, perhaps indignantly, and my reply was not encouraging to any conjectures along this line, as Eunice saw quickly.

" I 'm sorry I offended you," she added hastily; " but I did n't think anything wrong of Bessie— you know I did n't.   Only I 've watched the boss following her around with his eyes ever since we came here to work.   You did n't see, for you don't know as much about their devilment as I do; but I tell you, if anything was ever to happen that poor little girl through any man, I 'd choke him to death with my own hands!"

The satin-tufted box she was working on dropped from her fingers and clattered on the floor, bringing the forewoman down upon her with many caustic remarks.   When the flurry was over I assured her that I thought Bessie fully capable of taking care of herself, although I had seen more of the manager's advances than Eunice gave me credit for observing.

THE LONG DAY

At last noon came, and with it our first half-holiday. With the first shriek of the whistle we jumped up and began folding our aprons, preparatory to rushing out to find Bessie.

" Where does she live? " asked Eunice.

I looked at her in blank amazement, for I did n't know. I had never even heard the name of the street. I knew it was somewhere on the East Side; that was all. In all our weeks of acquaintanceship no occasion had arisen whereby Bessie should mention where she lived. I thought of Rosenfeld's. Perhaps some one there might know, and we took a Broadway car up-town. But Miss Higgins was away on her vacation, and none of the girls who still remained in the flower-shop knew any more about Bessie's whereabouts than I did. Thus it is in the busy, workaday world. Nobody knows where you come from, and nobody knows where you go. Eunice suggested looking in the directory; but as we found forty of the same name, it seemed hopeless. I did happen to know, however, that her father had once been a cutter or tailor; and so out of the forty we selected all the likeliest names and began a general canvass. After five hours of weary search, and after climbing the stairs of more than a score of tenement-houses, without success, we turned at last into East Broadway, footsore and dusty. In this street, on the fifth floor of a baking tenement, we tapped at the door of Bessie's home. A little blonde woman answered the knock, and when we asked for Bessie she burst into sobs and pointed to a red placard on the door—the quarantine notice of the Board of Health, which we had not seen. And then Bessie's mother told us that four of her brood had been laid low with malignant diphtheria. The three younger ones were home, sick unto death, but they had yielded to the entreaties of the doctor and allowed him to take Bessie to Bellevue. Thither we hurried as fast as the trolley would take us, only to find the gates closed for the day. We were not relatives, we had no permits; and whether Bessie were dead or alive, we must wait until visiting-hours the next day to discover.

What we found out the next day, when we filed into the superintendent's office with the ill-dressed horde of anxious Sunday-afternoon visitors, was hardly a surprise. We expected nothing but what Eunice had predicted from the first. Bessie had died the night before—died murmuring about poppies, the young doctor told us.

"She 's better off where she is than she 'd be down at Wolff's," said Eunice, as we passed through the gates on to the street again. I made no comment, and we walked silently away from the big, ugly brick pile that holds such horrors for the poor. When we reached Third Avenue, Eunice stopped before a florist's window, and we looked in at a cluster of great white lilies. Neither spoke, however, and in a moment we passed on down Third Avenue, now brightly lighted and teeming with its usual gay Sunday night crowd. At last we turned into our own street, and were in front of the dark building we both called "home." Here Eunice caught my hand in hers, with a convulsive little motion, as might a child who was afraid of the dark. We climbed the stone steps together, and I pulled the bell, Eunice's grasp on my hand growing tighter and tighter.

"Good-by; it 's no use," she whispered suddenly, dropping my hand and moving away as we heard the matron fumbling at the lock; and before I could utter a word of protest, before I could reach forward and snatch her from some dread thing, I knew not what, she had disappeared among the shadows of the lamplit street.

"Where 's the other girl?" asked the matron.

"I don't know," I replied,—nor have I since been

able to find the faintest clue to her whereabouts, if living, or her fate, if dead. From that moment at the door-step when she said good-by, Eunice stepped out of my life as completely as if the earth had opened and swallowed her up. Is she dead or alive? Did the unhappy girl seek self-destruction that June night, or was she swept into that great, black whirl-pool, the name of which even a girl of the workaday world mentions always with bated breath? I do not know. I never expect to know the fate of Eunice. It is only in stories that such things are made clear, usually, and this was only an incident in real life.

XV

THE next day, Monday, they buried Bessie in a big, shabby Jewish cemetery out on Long Island. I did not follow my comrade to the grave. Nor did I go to work. All that long, beautiful June day was spent in fruitless search for poor Eunice.

This hopeless quest, begun on Monday, was continued for three days in the few hours that I could snatch between five o'clock, the closing-time at the shop, and ten o'clock, the curfew hour at the " home." On Wednesday the strain grew unbearable. All the associations of Wolff's were tinctured with memories of the dead Bessie and the lost Eunice. Under the counter, in the big pasteboard box, their checked-gingham aprons were still rolled up just as they had left them, with the scissors inside; and on the pine table under my eyes were their names and mine, scrawled in a lead-pencil by Bessie's hand,

and framed with heavy lines. Their high stools, which were on either side of mine, had been given over to two new-comers, also " lady-friends," who chewed gum vigorously and discussed beaux and excursions to Coney Island with a happy vivacity that made my secret misery all the harder to bear. That night I went to the desk and drew my money, tucked the two aprons away in a bundle with my own, and said good-by to Wolff's. The sum total of my capital now amounted to five dollars; and with this I felt that I could afford to spend the remainder of the week trying to find Eunice, and trust to luck to get taken back at Wolff's the following Monday morning.

After three days' systematic inquiry, I climbed the stairs to the dormitory late on Sunday night, no wiser than I had been a week before. My discouragement gave way to a thrill of joyous surprise when I descried a long, thin form stretched under the gray blanket of Eunice's cot. I sprang forward and laid an eager hand on the thin shoulder.

" Gr-r-r! Don't you try gettin' fresh, Susie Jane, er I 'll smash yer face! " snarled the angry voice of a new-comer, as she pulled the coverlet up to her eyes and rolled over on the other side.

Monday morning I presented myself at the jewel-case factory, and asked Miss Gibbs to take me back. But I was already adjudged a " shiftless lot," not steady, and was accordingly " turned down." Then once more I scanned the advertising columns.

" Shakers Wanted.—Apply to Foreman " was the first that caught my eye. I did n't know what a " shaker " was, but that did not deter me from forming a sudden determination to be one. The address took me into a street up-town—above Twenty-third Street—the exact locality I hesitate to give for reasons that shortly will become obvious. Here I found the " Pearl Laundry," a broad brick building, grim as a fortress, and fortified by a breastwork of laundry-wagons backed up to the curb and disgorging their contents of dirty clothes. Making my way as best I could through the jam of horses and drivers and baskets, I reached the narrow, unpainted pine door marked, " Employees' Entrance," and filed up the stairs with a crowd of other girls— all, like myself, seeking work.

At the head of the stairs we filed into a mammoth steam-filled room that occupied an entire floor. The foreman made quick work of us. Thirty-two girls I counted as they stepped up to the pale-faced, stoop-shouldered young fellow, who addressed each one as " Sally," in a tone which, despite its good-

natured familiarity, was none the less businesslike
and respectful.   At last it came my turn.

"Hello, Sally! Ever shook?"

"No."

"Ever work in a laundry?"

"No; but I 'm very handy."

"What did you work at last?"

"Jewel-cases."

"All right, Sally; we 'll start you in at three and
a half a week, and maybe we 'll give you four dollars
after you get broke in to the work.—Go over there,
where you seen them other ladies go," he called after
me as I moved away, and waved his hand toward a
pine-board partition.   Here, sitting on bundles of
soiled linen and on hampers, my thirty-two prede-
cessors were corralled, each awaiting assignment to
duty.   They were dressed, literally, "some in rags
and some in tags and some in velvet gowns."   Calico
wrappers brushed against greasy satin skirts, and
faded kimono dressing-jackets vied in filth and
slovenliness with unbelted shirt-waists.   A faded
rose bobbed in one girl's head, and on another's locks
was arranged a gorgeous fillet of pale-blue ribbon
of the style advertised at the time in every shop-
window in New York as the "Du Barry."   The
scene was a sorry burlesque on the boudoir and the

ball-room, a grim travesty on the sordid realities of
the kitchen on wash-day.

" Did yez come in the barber's wagon? " asked a
stupid Irish girl, looking at me curiously. I looked
blank, and she repeated the question.

" What does she mean? " I asked a more intelligent girl who was seated on a bundle in the corner.

" Did n't yez come in Tony's wagon? "

" No; who 's Tony? "

" Oh, Tony he 's a barber—a Ginny barber—that
goes out with a wagon when they run short of help,
and he picks up any girls he can find and hauls them
in. He brought three loads this morning. We
thought Tony picked you up. Me and her," pointing to a black-browed girl who was nodding to
sleep with her mouth wide open, " we come in the
barber's wagon."

The girl's face, fat, heavy, dough-colored, had
become suffused with amiability, and giving her
snoozing comrade a gentle push, she made room for
me on the bundle beside her.

" Ever worked at this job before? " she asked.

" No. Have you? "

She replied with a sharp laugh, and flinging back
the sleeve of her kimono, thrust out the stump of a
wrist. At my exclamation of horror, she grinned.

"Why, that 's nothing in this here business," she said. " It happens every wunst in a while, when you was running the mangles and was tired. That 's the way it was with me: I was clean done out, one Saturday night, and I jist could n't see no more; and first thing I know—Wo-o-ow! and that hand went right straight clean into the rollers. And I was jist tired, that 's all. I did n't have nothing to drink all that day, excepting pop; but the boss he swore I was drunk, and he made the foreman swear the same thing, and so I did n't try to get no damages. They sent me to the horspital, and they offered me my old job back again; but I jist got up my spunk and says if they can't pay me some damages, and goes and swears I was drunk when I did n't have nothing but rotten pop, I says, I can up and go some place else and get my four dollars a week."

Before I could ask what the poor creature would be able to do with only one hand, the foreman appeared in the door, and we trooped out at his heels. Down the length of the big room, through a maze of moving hand-trucks and tables and rattling mangles, we followed him to the extreme rear, where he deposited us, in groups of five and six, at the big tables that were ranged from wall to wall and heaped

234

high with wet clothes, still twisted just as they were turned out of the steam-wringer. An old woman with a bent back showed me the very simple process of " shaking."

" Jist take the corners like this,"—suiting the action to the word,—" and give a shake like this, and pile them on top o' one another—like this," and with that she turned to her own " shaking " and resumed gossip with her side-partner, another old woman, who was roundly denouncing the " trash " that was being thrust upon her as table-mates, and throwing out palpable insults to the " Ginnies " who stood vis-à-vis, and who either did n't hear or, hearing, did n't understand or care.

For the first half-hour I shook napkins bearing the familiar legend—woven in red—of a ubiquitous dairy-lunch place, and the next half-hour was occupied with bed-linen bearing the mark of a famous hostelry. During that time I had become fairly accustomed to my new surroundings, and was now able to distinguish, out of the steamy turmoil, the general features of a place that seethed with life and action. All the workers were women and girls, with the exception of the fifteen big, black, burly negroes who operated the tubs and the wringers which were ranged along the rear wall on a platform that ran parallel with and a little behind the shakers' tables. The negroes were stripped to the waist of all save a thin gauze undershirt. There was something demoniacal in their gestures and shouts as they ran about the vats of boiling soap-suds, from which they transferred the clothes to the swirling wringers, and then dumped them at last upon the big trucks. The latter were pushed away by relays of girls, who strained at the heavy load. The contents of the trucks were dumped first on the shakers' tables, and when each piece was smoothed out we— the shakers—redumped the stacks into the truck, which was pushed on to the manglers, who ironed it all out in the hot rolls. So, after several other dumpings and redumpings, the various lots were tied and labeled.

Meanwhile a sharp, incessant pain had grown out of what was in the first ten or fifteen minutes a tired feeling in the arms—that excruciating, nerve-torturing pain which comes as a result of a ceaseless muscular action that knows no variation or relaxation. To forget it, I began to watch the eight others at our particular table. There were four Italians, all stupid, uninteresting-looking girls, of anywhere from fifteen to twenty-five years old; there was a thin, narrow-chested girl, with delicate wrists

and nicely shaped hands, who seemed far superior to
her companions, and who might have been pretty had
it not been for the sunken, blue-black cavity where
one eye should have been; there was a fat woman of
forty, with a stiff neck, and of a religious temperament, who worked in a short under-petticoat and
was stolidly indifferent to the conversation round
her; the others were the two old dames—she who
had initiated me, and her sprightlier though not less
ancient crony, Mrs. Mooney. Both fairly bristled
with spite and vindictiveness toward everything in
general, and us new-comers in particular, and each
sustained her flagging energies with frequent
pinches of snuff and chunks of coffee-cake which
they drew from inexhaustible pockets. My attempts at conversation with these two having been
met with chilling silence, and as Mrs. Mooney had
given me several painful thrusts with her sharp
elbow when I happened to get too close to her, I took
care to keep a safe distance, puzzled as to wherein I
might have offended, and lapsing into a morbid interest in the gossip flying thick and fast around me.

The target of scandal was " the queen," a big,
handsome blonde girl of about twenty-five, who in a
different environment and properly corseted and
gowned would have been set down unquestionably

as " a voluptuous beauty." Here in the laundry, in stocking-feet and an unbelted black shirt-waist turned far in at the neck, she was merely " mushy," to use the adjective of her detractors. The queen owed her nickname to the boss, with whom she was said to " stand in," being " awful soft after him." She was a sort of assistant to the foreman, bossing the job when he was not around, and lending a hand in rush hours with true democratic simplicity such as only the consciousness of her prestige could warrant her in doing. Now she was assisting the black men load a truck, now helping a couple of girls push it across the floor, now helping us dump it on the table—laughing and joking all the while, but at the same time goading us on to the very limit of human endurance. She had been in the " Pearl " for seven years, slaved harder than any of us, and she looked as fresh and buoyant as if she never had known what work was. I rather liked the queen, despite the fact that I detected in her immediately a relentless task-master; everybody else seemed to like her, notwithstanding the malicious things they said about her.

" Tired? " asked the one-eyed girl. " Yes, it 's hard work, but it 's steady. You 're never out of a job if you 're a steady shaker that can be relied on."

There was cheerfulness in her tone, and both the old women stopped talking.

"Did yez come in the barber's wagon?" Mrs. Mooney asked. On being assured that we had not, she proceeded to establish amicable relations with the one-eyed girl and me by telling us she was glad we "were n't Ginnies, anyway."

"Whatever happened to yer eye?" inquired the other crone of my companion.

Unresentful of the blunt inquisitiveness, the girl responded cordially with her little story—glad, apparently, to have a listener.

"It was something I caught in the hospital when I had appendicitis three years ago. When I was discharged my appendicitis was well, but my eye had took sore. The doctor he says when he seen it, 'That eye 's too far gone, and it 's got to come out, or the poison 'll spread to the t'other eye, and then you won't have no eyes at all.' My mother she did n't know nothing about it till it was all over. She 'd have carried on awful if she 'd knowed it. But it did n't hurt a bit. I went under chloroform, and when I come out of it I jist thought I 'd been having a long sleep in a big brass bedstead, with hem-stitched sheets and things like that," and she pointed to the hotel linen we were all shaking.

"That 's the way with them hospitals," said Mrs. Mooney, sympathetically, and proffering the heroine of the story a chunk of spice-cake.

"You 'd been better to ha' stayed at home. Poor folks don't have no chanst in them high-toned places."

"Why don't you take off yer shoes like us, and let yer feet spread out?—it 'll rest them," suggested Mrs. Mooney, now passing me a peace-offering of coffee-cake, and tightening her mouth in a grim determination to be civil.

Indeed, the one-eyed girl's story had wrought a transformation in these two sullen old women. All that was human in them had been touched by the tale of physical suffering, and we now met on common ground—the common ground of brute sympathy which one animal feels for another in distress.

The work was now under full blast, and every one of the hundred and twenty-five girls worked with frenzied energy as the avalanche of clothes kept falling in upon us and were sent with lightning speed through the different processes, from the tubs to the packers' counters. Nor was there any abatement of the snowy landslide—not a moment to stop and rest the aching arms. Just as fast as the sweating negroes could unload the trucks into the tubs, more trucks came rolling in from the elevator, and the foaming tubs swirled perpetually, swallowing up, it would seem, all the towels and pillow-cases and napkins in Greater New York. Above the orchestra of noise I distinguished a faintly familiar voice, which I could not place until I heard:

"And it was nothing but pop I had that day—I had n't had nothing but rotten old pop all day!"

From the girl's argument it was hard to determine whether she was more grieved at not having had stronger potations than pop on that fatal occasion, or at the implied aspersions upon her character for sobriety. Looking up, I saw that she was in one of the truck-teams. She had her one hand and arm strained against the rear of the sodden load, which she was urging forward with her hip. The load happened to be for our table, and as we dumped it out I asked her if there was n't anything easier she could do. She responded cheerily:

"No. You 've got to have two hands to run the mangles, and you 've got to have two hands to shake, and you 've got to have two hands to tie up, but you can push a truck with one hand." Which statement of the case, combined with the cripple's optimism, made us laugh—all except the one-eyed girl, espy-

ing whom, the maimed girl suddenly changed the
tone of levity with which she treated her own misfortune, and asked in a lowered voice: " What 's
the matter with yer eye? " And the hospital infec-
tion tale was repeated.

Could a duchess have claimed greater grace than
that poor, unlettered, uncouth creature's delicate
perception of that subtle principle of courtesy,
which allowed her to jest over her own misfortunes,
but which prompted a gentle hesitation in speaking
to another about hers!

In the excruciating agony of the hours that followed, the trucks became a veritable anodyne for the
pains that shot through my whole body. Leaning
over their deep sides was a welcome relief from the
strained, monotonous position at the tables. The
one-eyed girl had likewise discovered the anodyne,
and remarked upon it once as we dived into the wet
freight.

" It 's so funny how one kind of pain sort of eases
up another," she said; " I always feel good every
time I see the truck coming, though trucking 's far
harder work than shaking if you had to do it steady.
I wonder why it is. It was the same way with my
eye. When it was getting better and just ached a
little bit, steady, all the time, I used to wish I could

have real hard jumping toothache, just for a change."

" God love ye, and it 's so," fervently exclaimed Mrs. Mooney.

The day was terrifically hot outdoors, and with the fearful heat that came up through the floor from the engine-room directly under us, combined with the humidity of the steam-filled room, we were all driven to a state of half-dress before the noon hour arrived. The women opened their dresses at the neck and cast off their shoes, and the foreman threw his suspenders off his shoulders, while the colored washers paddled about on the sloppy floor in their bare black feet.

" Don't any men work in this place except the foreman? " I asked Mrs. Mooney, who had toiled a long time in the " Pearl " and knew everything.

" Love of Mary! " she exclaimed indignantly; " and d' ye think any white man that called hisself a white man would work in sich a place as this, and with naygurs? "

" But we work here," I argued.

" Well, we be wimmin," she declared, drawing a pinch of snuff into her nostrils in a manner that indicated finality.

" But if it is n't good enough for a man, it is n't

good enough for us, even if we are women!" I persisted.

She looked at me half in astonishment, half in suspicion at my daring to question the time-honored order of things. Economics could make no appeal to her intelligence, and shooting a glance out of her hard old black eyes, she replied with a logic that permitted no gainsaying.

"Love of Mary! if yez don't like yer job, ye can git out. Sure and we don't take on no airs around here!"

At twelve the noise ceased, and a shrill whistle ushered in the half-hour's respite. The effect of that raucous shriek was as solemn, as awe-inspiring, for the first moment, as the ringing of the Angelus bell in a Catholic country-side. For one moment everybody stood motionless and mute, the women with arms akimbo on aching hips, the black washers with drooping, relaxed shoulders. Each tortured frame seemed to heave with an inaudible "Thank God!" and then we slowly scattered in all directions —some to the cloak-room, where the lunches were stored along with the wraps, some down the stairs into the street.

On this day the one-eyed girl and I found a bundle of clothes large enough for two to sit on, and shared our lunch. For half a ham sandwich she gave me a piece of cold sausage, and I gave her a dill pickle for a greasy doughnut. The inevitable bottle of " pop " neither of us was able to open until the foreman came along and lent his assistance. He lingered a moment to talk the usual inanities that pass between a democratic foreman and a couple of new girls. Under his jovial exterior there seemed to be a vein of seriousness, amounting almost to sadness when one looked at his well-modeled face and his steady gray eyes. Tall and pale and prematurely bent, he had a certain distinction, as if he had been cut out for better things. His manner had lost all the easy familiarity of a few hours before, and he asked us in the kindest tone possible how we liked the work, and heartened us with the assurance that it would n't be nearly so hard in a few days, telling us to " stand slack-like " and see if it did n't make the pain in our backs better. By slack-like he meant stoop-shouldered, as everybody grows sooner or later in a laundry.

The foreman's hygienic lecture was interrupted by the warning rumble of the awakening machinery, and we scurried back to our table to make practical test of his theory. We followed it to the letter, but, like every other palliative of pain, it soon lost its virtue, and the long afternoon was one of unspeakable agony. There were now not only aching backs and arms and legs, but feet parboiled to a blister on the burning floors. The air was rent with lamentations, and before long my side-partner and I had also shed our shoes. By four o'clock everybody had sunk into a state of apathetic quiet, and even the exuberant Queen lost something of her vivaciousness, and attended strictly to the business of goading us on to our tasks.

"We 're two days behind with them hospital sheets," she screamed to one relay; "S—— Hotel Barber Shop got to go out to-night," which information brought groans from Mrs. Mooney.

"Mother of God!" she cried. "Sure and that means nine o'clock to-night."

"Are n't we going to get out at six?" asked the one-eyed girl, while I glanced dismally at the never-ending train of trucks that kept rolling out upon the washers' platform, faster now than at any other time of the day.

"God love ye! dearie, no," returned Mrs. Mooney. "Ye 'll never get outside *this* shop at six any night, unless ye 're carried out dead. We 're in luck to get out as early as eight."

"Every night?"

"Sure, every night exceptin' Saturday, and then it 's twelve to half-past one."

"Oh, that 's not so bad if you have a half-holi-day."

"Half-holiday!" echoed Mrs. Mooney. "Will ye listen to that! A half-holiday, indeed!" Then the mocking voice grew kinder. "Sure and it 's every minute of twelve o'clock or a half-hour into Sunday mornin' afore you ever see the outside of this place of a Saturday in summer-time, with all the washin' and ironin' for the summer hotels and the big bugs as is at the sea-shore."

"Youse ain't got no kick coming," said one of the Ginney girls. "Youse gets six cents an hour over-time, and youse 'll be mighty glad to make that exter money!"

Mrs. Mooney glared viciously at the interlopers. "Yes, and if it was n't for the likes of yez Ginnies that 'll work for nothing and live in pig-pens, the likes of us white people would n't have to work nights."

"Well I made ninety-six cents' overtime last week," spoke up the silent fat woman in the under-petticoat, "and I was thankful to the Lord to get it."

Of the two hours or more that followed I have only

a hazy recollection of colored men bending over the pungent foam, of straining, sweating women dragging their trucks round and round the great steaming-room. I remembered nothing whatever of the moment when the agony was ended and we were released for the day. Up to a certain dim borderland I remember that my back ached and that my feet dragged heavily over the burning floor, two pieces of boiling flesh. I do remember distinctly, however, suddenly waking up on Third Avenue as I was walking past a delicatessen store, and looking straight into the countenance of a pleasant-faced woman. I must have walked right into her, for she seemed amused, and went on her way laughing at something —probably my look of surprise as the impact brought me suddenly to full consciousness. A clock was hanging in the delicatessen-store window, and the hour-hand stood at nine. A cooling sea-breeze was blowing up from the south, and as I continued my walk home I realized that I had just passed out of a sort of trance,—a trance superinduced by physical misery,—a merciful subconscious condition of apathy, in which my soul as well as my body had taken refuge when torture grew unbearable.

XVI

IN WHICH IT IS PROVED TO ME THAT THE DARKEST HOUR COMES JUST BEFORE THE DAWN

THE next morning I asked Mrs. Mooney what time it was when we left the laundry the evening before, and she said half-past eight. Then I recounted the strange experience of the trance, which did not arouse the interest I had expected.

"That's nothing. That's the way we all get sometimes," she declared. "If we did n't get into them trance-spells there'd be none of us workin' here at all, at all."

"Yes, indeed," said a prayerful voice. "Praise God, it's one of his blessid pervisions to help us bear our crosses."

"I don't think the Lord's got much to do with our breaking backs or feet, do you?" asked the one-eyed girl, as we turned to unload a truck. "Now I'm not an unbeliever, and I believe in God and

249

Jesus Christ, all right; but I sometimes think they
don't do all these things that the Methodists and Salvation Army says they do. Somehow, I don't believe God knows anything about my eye or that one-
armed girl's getting hurt in the roller. I used to
believe everything I heard the evangelist say, but I
don't think no more that religion is what it 's
cracked up to be." A few moments later she asked
if I was a Protestant, too, and receiving an affirmative, proceeded to express herself on the superior
merits of that form of faith as compared with the
Catholic, against which she had all the narrow-
minded ignorance and superstition which, strange
to say, only too often characterize the better element
of the class to which she belonged. This girl's unreasonable prejudice against something of which
she knew not the first thing presented a paradox
universal in her world. The Catholic Church as an
institution was her enemy, and the enemy of all
Protestants. " If they could kill you, and not be
found out by the law, they 'd do it just as quick as
wink, because the priest would bail them out of hell
for a dollar and a quarter." And yet, when it came
to the concrete and personal, she had to admit that
all the Catholics she had ever known were " just
about as good as Protestants."

THE LONG DAY

This religious discussion was carried on in a low voice, with many side-glances toward the Catholic side of the table, as if danger threatened were they to hear a word of it. I knew, however, that there was nothing to fear from that quarter. There was only one religious conscience there, and that belonged to the one-eyed girl herself. From innumerable other instances I had met with before I had come to this generalization: that bigotry and bitter prejudices in matters of faith, deplorable as they at first seem to be, mark a distinct step in the social evolution and moral development of the ignorant and degraded. Nobody else at that table was far enough along to worry herself with principles of faith.

"I think the Salvation Army 's a kind of good religion," she continued; "only they—" but I heard no more; we were interrupted by a flurry of interest in the front, which spread quickly to our region, as a portly man in an automobile coat and Panama hat made his way by the mangle-machines and the tables. The foreman, diffident and uncertain, was walking by his side; and from the peremptory and numerous instructions he was receiving, it became patent that his companion was the "boss." Everybody looked hastily, stealthily, at the Queen,

251

who hid her pleasure under a very transparent veil of dissembling, as she helped us unload a truck. Never before had I heard the queen laugh so merrily, and never before had I realized what a superb, handsome animal she was. There was a certain rhythmic movement as she raised and lowered her body over the truck. The excitement of the moment added a deeper color to her always splendid rose-and-white complexion, upon which the steam-laden atmosphere distilled perpetually that soft dewiness characteristic of the perfect complexion of young children or of goddesses. And like a goddess the queen appeared that moment,—an untidy, earth-chained goddess, mirthful, voluptuous.

" She thinks she 's mighty fine, don't she? " whispered my one-eyed friend.

The boss halted at the truck, and the queen looked up with ill-feigned surprise, as if she had n't known for five minutes that he was in the room. He seemed the personification of prosperous, ignorant vulgarity, and his manner, as he swept his eye carelessly over his queen's subjects, was one of good-natured insolence. He did n't tarry long, and if guilty of the gentle dalliance of which he was accused, it was plain to be seen that he did not allow it to interfere with the discipline of the " Pearl."

THE LONG DAY

At lunch-time the one-eyed girl and I went off to the same corner as before, and no sooner had we begun to divide our pickles and sandwiches than in sauntered the foreman, munching alternately from a cylinder of bologna sausage in one hand and a chunk of dry bread in the other.

"Well, how goes it?" he asked pleasantly, dropping his long, lank frame upon a bundle of hotel table-linen. "Did you try my advice about standin' slack-like?"

We replied to his question while the one-eyed girl carved a dill pickle and a sweet pickle each into three portions.

He related how he had come to the "Pearl" six years ago, and had worked himself up to his present job, which was not to be sneezed at, he said, considering that eighteen dollars a week was n't to be picked up every day—and steady work, too, no layoffs and no shut-downs. He emphasized the fact, evidently very important in his mind, that he was n't married, that he had not met any girl yet that would have him, which my companion insisted could n't possibly be true, or if it was, then none of the girls he had ever asked had any taste at all. He lived at home with his mother, whom he did n't allow to "work out" since he 'd been big enough to earn a living for her.   There was a sister, too, at home, who had a job in a near-by manufactory; but she was engaged, and going to be married in her " intended's " vacation.   Then, the foreman thought, he 'd have to get a wife himself, if he could find anybody to have him. And she would n't have to work, either—not on your tintype!   She would live at home with his mother, and darn his socks and sew on his buttons, and she 'd have no washing or ironing to do, as he got his all done for nothing in the " Pearl."   That perquisite went along with the eighteen dollars a week.   Oh, she 'd have things as nice as any hardworking young fellow could give her.

" Would she have to be purty? " asked the one-eyed girl, who seemed unusually interested in this hypothetical wife, and who took such a lively interest in the foreman and his plans that I felt my heart sink in pity for the poor maimed creature.   Was she hanging breathless on the foreman's reply to this question?   If so, there was a certain comfort in the gallant answer.

" No, I should say not," he replied, as I thought with gentle consideration of her to whom he was speaking; " I don't think I could ever trust a wife who was a ten-thousand-dollar beaut'.   She 'd want to gad too much.   I don't think looks count for much; and I 'd think she was pretty, anyway, if I was terrible stuck on her. Them things don't make much difference only in story-papers. But there 's one thing she would have to be, and that is handy at doing things. I would n't marry a lazy girl, and I would n't marry a girl that was n't a working girl."

The engines began to give out a warning rumble, and the foreman scrambled somewhat reluctantly to his feet, and stretching out his long arms, started off.

"Say, that feller 's clean, dead gone on you," remarked my companion, closing her hand over mine in a pressure that was full of congratulation and honest delight.

I scouted the idea, but nevertheless I became suddenly conscious of a complete change in his manner from the easy familiarity of the morning before. Instead of the generic name of "Sally," or the Christian name which on better acquaintance he applied to the other girls, he had politely prefixed a "Miss" to my surname. There had come, too, a peculiar feeling of trust and confidence in him—a welcome sensation in this horrible, degraded place; and it was with gratefulness that I watched him disappear in the steamy vista, throwing off his suspenders preparatory to plunging into the turmoil of the afternoon's work now under way.

"Sure thing he is, I'd bet my life on it," she insisted, as we, too, hurried back to the table and took up our towels and napkins once more. "There's no mistakin' them signs, and you'd be a little fool if you was n't to help him along. Men's all sort of bashful, some more 'n others, and it's a good thing to help along. I like the looks of that fellow—he'd be awful silly and soft with his wife."

There was gentle solicitude in the voice, and looking up, I was almost startled with the radiance of the girl's face—the face of a good woman who loves, and who takes a generous interest in the love affairs of another. As we leaned over the truck and began to haul out its wet freight, she whispered to me:

"I know all about it because I've been there myself. I've got a gentleman-friend, too, and he's awful nice to me. He's been going with me five years, and he did n't shake me when I lost my eye. Lots of fellows I know would have backed out. That's what I like about that foreman. I think he'd do just the same by a girl he loved as Jim did to me. We'd have been married this long time, only Jim's got his hands full with a crazy mother, and he says she'll never go to any asylum s' long 's he's able to keep her; and so Jim's aunt she lives with them and tends his mother, and it takes 'most all Jim makes, because his mother 's sick all the time, too, and has to have the doctor and be humored. But I like a man that 's good to his mother. Jim is n't overly strong, either, and is likely to break down."

Late in the afternoon my partner was overcome by an attack of sick-headache, and dropped with nausea and exhaustion. Mrs. Mooney and the Queen helped her to her feet.

" It 's them pickles and them rotten cold lunches you girls eat," declared Mrs. Mooney, who was fond of talking on the nutritious properties of food. " Now I says, the Lord only give me one stummick, and when that 's wore out he 'll never give me another, and I can't never buy one with no money, and I never put anything in that stummick at noon but a good cold beer and a good hot plate of soup, and that 's what you ought to do. Only cost you five cents for the both of them together, down to Devlin's place. We go there every day," jerking her head in the direction of her crony, " and you can go along if ye have a mind to."

In accordance with this invitation, we became patrons of Devlin's the very next day. Promptly at twelve we hurried out, sleeves still rolled up and our damp aprons unremoved. There was no time for making a toilet, Mrs. Mooney insisted, as Devlin's was three blocks away, and we had only a half-hour. Across Lexington, across Third Avenue, and down one block, we came to a corner saloon, and filed in the "ladies' entrance." The room was filled with workmen drinking beer and smoking at the little round tables, and when they saw us each man jumped up, and grabbing his glass, went out into the barroom. Commenting upon this to Mrs. Mooney, she explained as we seated ourselves:

"Sure, and what 'd ye expect! Sure, and it 's a proper hotel ye 're in, and it 's dacent wurrkin'-men that comes here, and they knows a lady when they see her, and they ups and goes!"

In response to Mrs. Mooney's vigorous order, "Six beers with the trimmin's!" a waiter appeared presently with a steaming tray.

"Now eat that, and drink that, and see if they don't go to the spot," cried the old woman, gaily, and we all fell to, with table manners more eager than elegant. Whatever the soup was made of, it seemed to me the best soup I had ever eaten in New York, and I instantly determined never again to blame a working man or woman for dining in a saloon in preference to the more godly and respectable dairy-lunch room. We all ate ravenously, and I, who never before could endure the sight or smell of beer, found myself draining my " schooner " as eagerly as Mrs. Mooney herself.

" My! but that braces me up," she declared, sighing deeply and licking the froth from her lips; " it 's almost as good as whisky." It was a propitious moment to ask questions, and I inquired how long she had worked at the " Pearl."

" Eighteen months, off and on. I gets the rheumatism and stay home sometimes. I believe in taking care of yer back. I says, I 've only got one back, and when that 's wore out the Lord ain't going to give me another. So I stay home; but it 's so lonesome I 'm always mighty glad to get to work ag'in."

The long, long days sped by, their torture relieved by such comfort as we could find in the gossip of the table, and in daily excursions to Devlin's, where I had become a regular patron. The foreman, too, added a little variety to the monotony by coming to our table sometimes, and shaking clothes for a few moments with us, while he gossiped with the one-eyed girl and me, which unusual proceeding filled her romantic soul with all sorts of happy anticipation. On Saturday morning, after he had come and gone, she whispered ecstatically: " That fellow is stuck on you, and I 'll bet he 'll be askin' you to go to the theayter with him—just see if he don't!"

But alas for woman's dreams! The next day we saw the boss coming across the floor, this time alone. He sauntered up to our table, began to fling jokes at us all in a manner of insolent familiarity, and asked the names of the new faces. When he came to me he lingered a moment and uttered some joking re- marks of insulting flattery, and in a moment he had grasped my bare arm and given it a rude pinch, walking hurriedly away. In a few moments the foreman came back and motioned me to go with him, and I followed to the front of the room, where the boss stood smoking and joking with the wrappers. The foreman retired a respectful distance, and the boss, after looking me over thoughtfully, informed me that I was to be promoted Monday morning to the wrappers' counter.

" And now run away, and be a good girl the rest of the day," he concluded, with a wave of the hand, and I rushed back to the table, more disgusted with the man and his manner than I was thankful to him for my promotion to a job that would pay me five dollars a week.

" Did n't I tell you so!" exclaimed my friend,

amid the excited comments and questions of the others at the table. " That 's some of the foreman's doing, and I 'm real glad for you—it 's nothing more than what I 've been expectin', though."

This opinion was not shared, however, by the rest of my companions, who repeated divers terrible tales of moral ruin and betrayal, more or less apocryphal, wherein the boss was inevitably the villain. I now found myself suddenly the cynosure of all eyes, the target of a thousand whispered comments, as I moved about the workroom. The physical agony of aching back and blistered feet was too great, though, for me to feel any mental distress over the fact—for the moment at least. In the awful frenzy of the Saturday-afternoon rush, greater than that of any other day of the week, I did not care much what they thought or said about the boss and me.

I was shaking my towels and napkins, and trying to look as indifferent as I believed I felt, when the foreman beckoned me again, and stepping aside, thrust a piece of yellow wrapping-paper into my hand.

" Read it when nobody 's looking," he said in a low voice; " and don't think wrong of me for meddling in what 's not my business "; and he was off again.

A few minutes later I read:

" You 'd better give up this job. It 's no place
for a girl that wants to do right. Come back Monday and get your money; and I would n't stay to-
night after six o'clock, if I was you, but go home and
rest. If you can't get a job as good as this inside
of a day or two, I think my sister can get one for
you in her place; but you won't stay here if you
take my advice.

" Yours truly,

" J. P.

" P. S. Please don't show this, or I 'd lose my job;
and be sure to come Monday evening for your
money."

I made at once for the cloak-room. When I
emerged, a moment later, it was to find the narrow
passage obstructed by one of the big soiled-linen
trucks, over which " J. P." bent industriously,
as if he had n't another thought in the world beyond
the sorting of table-cloths and napkins. Suddenly
he lifted up his lank frame, and seeing one of his
workpeople making her escape, he called out:

" It 's not six o'clock yet ! "

262

" I don't care if it is n't; I am going home," I replied promptly.

" What 's the matter? " he asked in a loud voice, and then, as he drew near, added in an undertone:

" You read my note? "

" Yes," I replied.

" S'pose you kind of wonder at me doing it? " he went on, moving with me toward the staircase.

" No; I guessed right away," I answered.

We had now reached the top of the stairs leading to the street door, and were out of ear-shot of the busy workroom. The curious faces and craning necks were lost to us through an interposing veil of steam. The foreman grasped my extended hand in a limp, hasty clasp as I began to move down the steps.

" You guessed part, but not all," he whispered, turning away.

I dragged myself to the end of the block and turned into Lexington Avenue just as the six-o'clock whistles began to blow. So much I remember very distinctly, but after that all is an indistinct blur of clanging street-cars, of jostling crowds. I do not know whether I had lost my senses from the physical agony I was enduring, though still able to perform the mechanical process of walking, or whether it was a case of somnambulism; but I know that I walked on, all unconscious of where I was going, or of my own identity, until I came in collision with some one, and heard a feminine voice beg my pardon. Then a little cry, and two arms were thrown about me, and I looked up into the smiling face of Minnie Plympton—Minnie Plympton as large as life and unspeakably stunning in a fresh shirt-waist and sailor-hat. She was smiling at me like a princess issuing from her enchantment in a rose-bush; and lest she should vanish as suddenly as she had appeared, I clutched wildly at her arm, trembling and sobbing at this delicious awakening from the horrible nightmare that had been my existence for so many days.

We were standing on the corner of Lexington Avenue and a cross-town thoroughfare, and ever after must that spot remain in my mind as the actual turning-point of my fortunes—indeed, the very turning-point of my whole life. As I look back upon that beautiful June evening, I again hear the rumble of the elevated trains in the street beyond, and again I hear the clang of the electric cars as they swirl out of the avenue into the street. Probably every man and woman who ever came a stranger to a great city has his or her own particular secret and holy place where angels came and ministered in the hour of need. I do not doubt it, but I do often wonder whether every such person visits his sacred place as often as I visit mine. I go to mine very often, especially in summer-time, about six o'clock, when, amid the roar and the turmoil and the banalities of the real and the actual, I recall the wondrous tale of the Burning Bush. For there God appeared to me that evening—the God who had hidden his face for so long.

"Why, you look as weak as a kitten—you look sick!" Minnie declared. "You need a good cup of tea and to be put to bed, and I 'm going to be the one to do it for you!"

I was half dazed as Minnie Plympton bundled me into a passing electric car; and then, with my head leaning comfortably on Minnie Plympton's plump shoulder, and with Minnie Plympton's strong arm about my aching body, I was jolted away somewhere into a drowsy happiness.

EPILOGUE

THREE years have elapsed since that last day in the " Pearl Laundry " and my providential meeting with Minnie Plympton. The events of those three years may be recounted in almost as few sentences, for prosperous working girls, like happy nations, have no history. And we have been very prosperous, Minnie Plympton and I. We, I say, because from the moment of our unforeseen meeting in the hurly-burly of that street corner, the interests of Minnie Plympton's life and of mine were to become, for the succeeding year, almost inseparable.

I said we have both been very prosperous. But Minnie Plympton has been more than that: she has been successful—successful in the only real way a woman can, after all, be successful. Minnie is married. She is the wife of an enterprising young business man, and the mother of a charming baby. She has been married nearly two years, and lives in a pretty cottage in a peaceful suburb. It was what the world would call a good match, and Minnie declares she is perfectly happy. And no doubt she is, else that honest creature would not be so bent upon making matches for everybody else.

As for myself, I have been merely prosperous—prosaically and uninterestingly, though none the less agreeably, prosperous. I do not know whether I am happy or not. I am still a working girl, and by all the portents of the dream-book I am foredoomed eternally to remain a wage-earner in spite of all Mrs. Minnie's good offices. For I was born on a Saturday; and " Saturday's child must work for its living."

Now, I do not care to be accused of a superstitious faith in dream-books, but I do want to say that I have found all sorts of inspiration in a philosophical acceptance of that oracle attaching to my unfortunate birthday. If Saturday's child must work for her living, why not make the best of it? Why not make the most advantageous terms possible with Fate? why not work with, and not against, that inexorable Forelady, in coöperation with her plans and along the lines of her least resistance?

This I have tried to do. How I have done it, and what the results have been, I shall now try to sketch with not more attention to tedious details than I feel justified in assuming may be of some help and encouragement to other strugglers.

I became a stenographer and typewriter, earning twenty dollars a week. I worked hard for my money, and the day was still a long day. I went to work at nine o'clock in the morning, and while I was supposed to get off at five, and sometimes did, I was often obliged to work till six or seven.

And this I called prosperity? Yes; for me this was prosperity, when I remembered the circumstances of my beginnings.

When I met Minnie Plympton on the street corner, that hot summer night, I was "dead broke," not only in purse, but in body and spirit as well. She took me home with her to the two small rooms where she was doing light housekeeping, and where we continued to live together until her marriage a year later broke up our happy domestic partnership. A few weeks after Minnie took me home with her I got a position in the notion department of one of the large stores. I received only four dollars a week; but, as our rent was small and our living expenses the very minimum, I was able to meet my half of the joint expenditure. I worked four months at selling pins and needles and thread and whalebone and a thousand and one other things to be found in a well-stocked notion department; and then, by a stroke of good luck and Minnie Plympton's assistance, I got a place as demonstrator of a new brand of tea and coffee in the grocery department of the same " emporium." My new work was not only much lighter and pleasanter, but it paid me the munificent salary of eight dollars a week.

But I did not want to be a demonstrator of tea and coffee all my life. I had often thought I would like to learn shorthand and typewriting. The demonstrator of breakfast foods at the next counter to mine was taking a night course in bookkeeping; which gave me the idea of taking a similar course in stenography. And then the Long Day began in earnest. I went to night-school five nights out of every week for exactly sixty weeks, running consecutively save for a fortnight's interim at the Christmas holidays, when we worked nights at the store. On Saturday night, which was the off night, I did my washing and ironing, and on Sunday night I made, mended, and darned my clothes—that is, when there was any making, mending, or darning to be done. As my wardrobe was necessarily slender, I had much time to spare. This spare time on Sunday nights I spent in study and reading. I studied English composition and punctuation, both of which

I would need later on when I should become a stenographer. I also brushed up on my spelling and grammar, in which, I had been informed—and correctly—the average stenographer is sadly remiss.

As for reading, which was the only recreation my life knew, it was of a most desultory, though always mercenary sort. I read every book I could get out of the circulating library which, from its title or general character as summarized in the newspaper reviews, I thought might help me to solve the problem of earning a good livelihood. The title of one book particularly attracted me—a book which was so much in demand that I had to wait a whole six months before I succeeded in getting it through the slow and devious process peculiar to circulating libraries. That book was "Up from Slavery," and it brought home to me as nothing else could have done what was the real trouble with myself and all the rest of the struggling, ill-paid, wretched working women with whom I had come in contact during my apprenticeship. What that trouble was I shall revert to later.

When I had thoroughly learned the principles of my trade and had attained a speed of some hundred and odd words a minute, the hardest task was yet before me. This task was not in finding a position, but in filling that position satisfactorily. My first position at ten dollars a week I held only one day. I failed to read my notes. This was more because of fright and of self-consciousness, however, than of inefficiency. My next paid me only six dollars a week, but it was an excellent training-school, and in it I learned self-confidence, perfect accuracy, and rapidity. Although this position paid me two dollars less than what I had been earning brewing tea and coffee and handing it over the counter, and notwithstanding the fact that I knew of places where I could go and earn ten dollars a week, I chose to remain where I was. There was method in my madness, however, let me say. I had a considerate and conscientious employer, and although I had a great deal of work, and although it had to be done most punctiliously, he never allowed me to work a moment overtime. He opened his office at nine in the morning, and I was not expected before quarter after; he closed at four sharp. This gave me an opportunity for further improving myself with a view to eventually taking not a ten-dollar, but a twenty-dollar position. I went back to night-school and took a three months' " speed course," and at the same time continued to add to my general education and stock of knowledge by a systematic reading of popular books of science and economics. I became tremendously interested in myself as an economic factor, and I became tremendously interested in other working girls from a similar point of view. Of science and economics I knew nothing when I started out to earn my living.

One day I answered an advertisement calling for the sort of stenographer I now believed myself to be. It brought a response signed with the name of a large religious publishing house. I got the position, beginning with a salary of fifteen dollars a week, which was to be increased to twenty dollars provided I could fill the position. That I should succeed in doing so, there was evident doubt in my employers' minds, and no wonder! For I was the fifth to attempt it.

My work consisted for the most part in taking dictation from the editor of the periodical published weekly by the house—letters to contributors, editorials, and special articles. Also, when it was found that I had some intelligent, practical knowledge of grammar and English—and here was where my studies of the preceding year bore fruit—I was intrusted with the revision and correction of the least important of the manuscripts, thus relieving the busy editors of one of their most irksome tasks.

THE LONG DAY

One day I had occasion to mention to the editor some of the strenuous experiences I had undergone in my struggle to attain a decent living. He was startled—not to say a little shocked—that a young woman of apparently decent birth and upbringing should have formed such an intimate acquaintance with the dark side of life. Inspired by his sympathetic interest, I boldly interviewed the editor of a well-known monthly magazine, with the result that I immediately prepared two papers on certain of my experiences; and, to my surprise and delight, they were accepted.

And, somehow, with the appearance of those two articles—the first fruits of authorship—part of the horror and loathing of that unhappy period of servitude fell away from me; the sordid suffering, the hurt to pride, the ineffaceable scar on heart and soul I felt had not been in vain. I can now look back upon the recent, still vivid past without a shiver; for there is comfort in the thought that what I have undergone is to be held up to others as a possible lesson and warning.

And now a word as to the verity of this narrative. Have I actually been through all that I have described? Yes, and more; and in other cities beside New York.

WOMEN AT WORK

Yet for the sake of unity the order of things has been somewhat changed; and no record is given of many weeks, and even months, when life flowed uneventfully, if not smoothly, on.

"But," says the thoughtful reader, "do your sordid experiences of some two or three years ago match conditions of to-day?" and I answer: Generally speaking, they do; because lately I reinforced memory by thorough investigation.

I went further than that: when it came to me to write this little book—that is so absolutely a transcript from real life—I voluntarily labored, a week here, a week there, at various trades allied to those that previously had been my sole means of livelihood, and all the time living consistently the life of the people with whom I was thus temporarily associated.

There were, of course, many little points that when I was a worker in earnest I had not eyes to see, but which my recent conscious study brought out in proper perspective.

Yet it was as a working girl that I learned to know most of the characters that people this book, and which give to it any value it may possess.

For obvious reasons, I have been obliged to give fictitious names to factories and shops in which I worked; and I have, in most cases, substituted for

274

the names of the streets where the factories were located the names of streets of like character.

The physical conditions, the sordid wretchedness of factory and workshop, of boarding- and lodging-house, I have not in any wise overstated.

As to moral conditions, I have not been in every instance so scrupulously truthful—that is, I have not told all the truth. For it is a truth which only too often will not bear even the suggestion of telling. Only in two or three instances—for example, in my account of Henrietta Manners—have I ventured to hint definitely at anything pertaining to the shame and iniquity underlying a discouragingly large part of the work-girls' world. In my magazine articles I was obliged to leave out all reference to this tabooed topic. The attitude of the public, especially the American public, toward this subject is a curious mixture of prudery and gallantry. It bridles at anything which impeaches the traditional honor and chastity of the working girl. The chivalry of American men—and my experience in workshop, store, and factory has proved to me how genuine and deep-rooted that chivalry is—combined with our inherent spirit of democracy, is responsible for the placing of the work-girl, as a class, in a light as false and ridiculous as that in which Don Quixote was wont to view the charms of his swineherd lady, Dulcinea. In the main, our notions of the woman who toils do more credit to our sentiments and to the impulses of our hearts than they do credit to our heads or to any serious desires we may cherish for her welfare. She has become, and is becoming more and more, the object of such an amount of sentimentality on the part of philanthropists, sociological investigators, labor agitators, and yellow journals—and a goodly share of journalism that prides itself upon not being yellow—that the real work-girl has been quite lost sight of. Her name suggests, according to their imaginations, a proud, independent, self-reliant, efficient young woman— a young woman who works for her living and is glad of it. One hardly dares criticize her, unless, indeed, it be to lecture her for an ever-increasing independence of her natural male protectors and an alleged aversion to babies.

That we should cling so tenaciously to this ideal is to our honor and glory. But fine words butter no parsnips; nor do our fine idealizations serve to reduce the quota which the working-girl ranks contribute to disreputable houses and vicious resorts. The factories, the workshops, and to some extent the stores, of the kind that I have worked in at least, are recruiting-grounds for the Tenderloin and the " red light " districts. The Springers and the " Pearl Laundries " send annually a large consignment of delinquents to their various and logical destinations. It is rare indeed that one finds a female delinquent who has not been in the beginning a working girl. For, sad and terrible though it be, the truth is that the majority of " unfortunates," whether of the specifically criminal or of the prostitute class, are what they are, not because they are inherently vicious, but *because they were failures as workers and as wage-earners.* They were failures as such, primarily, for no other reason than that they did not like to work. And they did not like to work, not because they are lazy—they are anything but lazy, as a rule—but *because they did not know how to work.*

Few girls know how to work when they undertake the first job, whether that job be making paper boxes, seaming corset-covers, or taking shorthand dictation. Nor by the term, " knowing how to work," do I mean, necessarily, lack of experience. One may have had no experience whatever in any line of work, yet one may know *how* to work—may understand the general principles of intelligent labor. These general principles a girl may learn equally well by means of a normal-school training or through familiarity with, and participation in, the domestic labor of a well-organized household. The working girl in a great city like New York does not have the advantage of either form of training. Her education, even at the best, is meager, and of housework she knows less than nothing. If she is city-born, it is safe to assume that she has never been taught how to sweep a room properly, nor how to cook the simplest meal wholesomely, nor how to make a garment that she would be willing to wear. She usually buys all her cheap finery at a cheap store, and such style and taste as she displays is " ready made."

Not having learned to work, either at school or at home, she goes to the factory, to the workshop, or to the store, crude, incompetent, and, worst of all, with an instinctive antagonism toward her task. *She cannot work, and she does not work. She is simply " worked."* And there is all the difference in the world between " working " and " being worked." To work is a privilege and a boon to either man or woman, and, properly regulated, it ought to be a pleasure. To be worked is degrading. To work is dignified and ennobling, for to work means the exercise of the mental quite as much as the physical self. But the average working girl puts neither heart nor mind into her labor; she is merely a machine, though the comparison is a libel upon the functions of first-class machinery.

The harsh truth is that, hard as the working girl is "worked," and miserable as her remuneration is, she is usually paid quite as much as she is worth.

For her incompetency she is not entirely to blame; rather is it a matter of heredity and environment. Being a girl, it is not natural to her to work systematically. The working woman is a new product; in this country she is hardly three generations old. As yet she is as new to the idea of what it really means to work as is the Afro-American citizen. The comparison may not be flattering to our vanity, but, after a reading of Booker Washington's various expositions of the industrial abilities of the negro, I cannot but be convinced that the white working woman is in a corresponding process of evolution, so far as her specific functions for labor have been developed.

Conditions in the "Pearl," from the view-point of mere physical labor, were the most brutal in all my experience; but, from what I can learn, the "Pearl" is no worse than many other similar establishments. Young women will work in such places only as a last resort, for young women cannot work long under conditions so detrimental to bodily health. The regular workers are old women —women like Mrs. Mooney and her cronies. The steady workers at the " Pearl " were, with the exception of the " queen," all old women. Every day saw the arrival of a new force of young hands who were bound to " play out " at the end of three or four days' apprenticeship, if not sooner. I played out completely: I did n't walk a step for a week after I went home with Minnie Plympton that Saturday night. Which was all in accord with Mrs. Mooney's prediction the first day: " You won't last long, mind ye; you young uns never do. If you ain't strong as an ox it gits in your back and off ye go to the 'orspital; and if you 're not able to stand the drivin', and thinks you 're good-lookin', off you goes to the bad, sooner 'n stay here."

I would like to dwell for a moment upon the character and personality of her whom I have more than once referred to as the " queen." The queen had worked, I was told, for seven years in the laundry, and she was, as I saw and knew her in those days, as fresh as the proverbial daisy. She seemed the very embodiment of blithesome happiness. In the chapter dealing with the laundry I had occasion to speak of her voluptuous beauty. Her long years of

280

hard labor—and she labored harder than any one else there—seemed to have wrought no effect upon her handsome, nerveless body. Her lovely eyes, her hair, her dazzling complexion and perfect features, were all worthy the reputation of a stage beauty. She was kind; in her rough, uncouth way, she was kind to everybody—so kind, in fact, that she was generally popular, though envied as enjoying the boss's favor. And, as may be imagined, her influence, during those seven years, upon the underfed, underpaid, ignorant, unskilled green hands who streamed into the " Pearl " every morning must have been endless for evil.

On the subject of morality I am constrained to express myself with apparent diffidence, lest I be misinterpreted and charged with vilifying the class to which I once belonged. And yet behind my diffidence of expression I must confess to a very honest and uncompromising belief, founded upon my own knowledge and observation, that the average working girl is even more poorly equipped for right living and right thinking than she is for intelligent industrial effort. One of the worst features of my experience was being obliged to hear the obscene stories which were exchanged at the work-table quite as a matter of course; and, if not a reflection of

vicious minds, this is at least indicative of loose
living and inherent vulgarity. The lewd joke, the
abominable tale, is the rule, I assert positively, and
not the exception, among the lower class of working
girls with whom I toiled in those early months of
my apprenticeship. The flower-manufactory in
Broadway was the one glorious exception. I do
not attempt to account for this exception to the general rule, unless it be explainable upon the logical
theory that the skill necessary for the making of
artificial flowers is found only in a vastly superior
class of girls. The flower-girls I met at Rosenberg's
were, without exception, wholesome-minded and
pure-hearted. They knew how to cook, as they had
ample opportunity of proving at our luncheons and
dinners during those four busy, happy weeks. I
never met factory-girls in any other line of employment who knew how to make a cup of tea or coffee
that was fit to drink. The flower-girls gave every
evidence of having come from homes which, humble
though many of them must have been, were nevertheless well-ordered and clean. The girls I met in
other places seemed never to have lived in homes at
all.

In the telling of the obscene story, Jew and Gen-
tile, Catholic and Protestant, were equally guilty.

THE LONG DAY

That the responsibility for these conditions of moral as well as physical wretchedness is fundamentally attributable to our present socio-economic system is a fact that has been stated so often before, and by writers who by right of specialized knowledge and scientific training are so much better equipped to discuss social economics than I may ever hope to be, that I need not repeat the axiom here. Nor would it be any more becoming for me to enter into any discussion of the various theories upon which the economists and the social reformers base their various projects for the reconstruction of the present system. Personally I have a strong prejudice in favor of the trades-union. I believe that working women should awaken as quickly as possible to the advantages to be derived from organization of the industries in which they are employed. But I seem to be alone in my cherished desire. The women and girls I have worked with in New York do not view the trades-union as their more progressive and enlightened sisters of Chicago and the West generally choose to regard it. Chicago alone shows a roster of nearly forty thousand women and girls who are organized into unions of their own, officered by themselves and with their own feminine " walking delegates." I recently spent four weeks among these

trades-unions, numbering thirty-five distinct women's organizations, and I found, everywhere I
went, the same enthusiasm for, and the same superior
degree of intelligence regarding, the aim and object
of the organization idea.

As for the working women of New York, they
have so far refused to countenance the trades-
union. New York has no woman's trades-union.
A small percentage of women workers belong to
labor organizations, it is true; but it is merely as
auxiliaries to the men's unions, and where they work
at trades that have been thoroughly organized for
the benefit of the men workers. They belong to
these unions always under protest, not of their own
volition; because they are obliged to do so in order
to be permitted to work at their trades in competition with men who are organized.

For this reason, owing to the blindness of the
workwoman to the benefits to be derived from organization,—and because, moreover, it has not yet been
proved that the trades-union, carried to its logical
conclusion, is likely to be a panacea for the industrial woes of the sex which does favor and support
it—it seems to me rather idle to urge its wider
adoption under the protest of those most vitally con-

cerned—the women workers themselves. The idea of organized labor will have to grow among the ranks of women workers just as the idea has grown into the consciousness of her father and brother.

We have a great and crying need for two things —things which it is entirely within the power of a broad-minded philanthropy to supply. The most urgent of these needs is a very material and unpoetic one. We need a well-regulated system of boarding- and lodging-houses where we can live with decency upon the small wages we receive. We do not want any so-called " working girls' homes "—God forgive the euphemism!—which, while overcharging us for the miserable accommodations, at the same time would put us in the attitude of charity dependants. What the working girl needs is a cheap hotel or a system of hotels—for she needs a great many of them—designed something after the Mills Hotels for working-men. She also needs a system of well-regulated lodging-houses, such as are scattered all over the city for the benefit of men. My experience of the working girls' home in which I lived for many weeks, and from my observation and inquiries regarding a number of similar " homes " which I have since visited, justifies me in making a few suggestions regarding the general plan and conduct of the ideal philanthropic scheme which I have in mind.

First and most important, there must be no semblance of charity. Let the working girls' hotel and the working girls' lodging-house be not only self-supporting, but so built and conducted that they will pay a fair rate of interest upon the money invested. Otherwise they would fail of any truly philanthropic object.

As to their conduct as institutions there should be no rules, no regulations which are not in full operation in the Waldorf-Astoria or the Hotel St. Regis. The curse of all such attempts in the past has been the insistence upon *coercive morality*. Make them not only non-sectarian, but non-religious. There is no more need of conducting a working girls' hotel or lodging-house in the name of God or under the auspices of religious sentiment than there is necessity for advertising the Martha Washington Hotel or any fashionable bachelor-apartment house as being under divine guidance.

A clean room and three wholesomely cooked meals a day *can* be furnished to working girls at a price such as would make it possible for them to live honestly on the small wage of the factory and store.

THE LONG DAY

We do not ask for luxuries or dainties. We do not get them in the miserable, dark warrens where we are now obliged to sleep, and we do not get them at the unappetizing boarding-house tables where countless thousands of us find sustenance. I do not know—I suppose nobody does know—how many working girls in New York City live in lodging- and boarding-houses. But they are legion, and very few of them are contented with that life.

The most important necessity of the model working woman's hotel or lodging-house would be, not a luxurious table, not a dainty sleeping-room, but a parlor! The number of young girls who go wrong in a great city like this for want of the various necessities of a parlor must make the angels in heaven weep. The houses where the poorly paid girl lives have no accommodations for the entertainment of her male friends. If the house is conducted with any respect for the conventions, the girl lodger must meet her young man on the " stoop " or on the street corner. As the courtship progresses, they must have recourse either to the benches of the public parks, provided the weather be favorable, or else to the light and warmth of the back room of a saloon. The average cheap lodging-house is usually conducted, however, with but scant regard for the conventions, and the girl usually is forced to adopt the more convenient and, as it would seem to her, really more self-respecting habit of receiving her company in her room. And either one of these methods of courtship, it is evident, cannot but be in the end demoralizing and degrading to thoughtless young people, however innocent they may be of any deliberate wrong-doing. In the model lodging-house there should be perfect liberty of conduct and action on the part of guests—who will not be " inmates " in any sense of the word. Such guests should have perfect liberty to go and come when they please at any hour of the day or night; be permitted to see any person they choose to have come, without question or challenge, so long as the conventions of ordinary social life are complied with. Such an institution, conducted upon such a plan and managed so that it would make fair returns to its promoters, cannot fail to be welcomed; and would be of inestimable benefit as an uplifting and regenerative force with those for whom it is designed.

The other need is for a greater interest in the workwoman's welfare on the part of the church, and an effort by that all-powerful institution to bring about some adjustment of her social and economic difficulties. I am old-fashioned enough to believe in the supreme efficacy of organized religion in relation to womanhood, and all that pertains to womanhood. I believe that, in our present state of social development, the church can do more for the working girl than any of the proposed measures based upon economic science or the purely ethical theory. Working women as a class are certainly not ripe for the trades-union, as I have already intimated; and the earnest people of the " settlements " are able to reach but a small part of the great army of women marching hopelessly on, ungeneraled, untrained, and, worst of all, uncaring.

Few are they who, like Tolstoi, can gracefully stoop to conquer; and those who shall be ordained to revolutionize conditions will rise from the ranks, even as did Booker T. Washington. This, of course, is the ultimate object of settlement work: to prepare the leaven for the loaf.

But a live and progressive church—a church imbued with the Christian spirit in the broadest and most liberal interpretation of the term—can do for us, and do it quickly and at once, more than all the college settlements and all the trades-unions that can be organized within the next ten years could hope to do. And for this reason: the church has all the machinery ready, set up and waiting only for the proper hand to put it in motion to this great end. The Christian church has a vast responsibility in the solution of all problems of the social order, and none of those problems is more grave or urgent than the one affecting the economic condition of the wage-earning woman. It is curious that the church, in this age, should choose to regard its primary function with such evident apathy. The first business of the church in the past was the adjustment of social difficulties. The gospel of Jesus Christ was preëminently a social gospel, and when the church ceases to be a social force it will have outlived its usefulness.

There are those who believe that the church *has* outlived that primal usefulness. I do not believe so. For men, perhaps, it has; but not for women—certainly not for working women. We do not as a sex, we do not as a class, flatter ourselves that we have got along so far in race development that we have no further need of organized religion. In all my experience of meeting and talking, often becoming intimately acquainted, with girls and women of all sorts, I have never known one, however questionable, to whom the church was not, after all, held in respect as the one all-powerful human institution.

And yet, unless they were Catholics, mighty few

went to church at all, and most of them were resentful, often bitter, toward the church and hostile toward all kinds of organized religion. They accused the church of not doing its duty toward them, and they declared that organized religion was a sham and a hypocrisy.

The only activity exerted by the church in the direction indicated partakes too strongly of the eleemosynary nature to make it acceptable to any save the most degraded—the weak-chinned, flabby-natured horde of men and women who rally instinctively to the drum-taps of the street-corner Salvationist, or seek warmth and cheer on cold winter nights, and if possible more substantial benefits, from the missions and " church houses."

I have no quarrel to pick with the Salvation Army, nor with the city missions, as institutions. Both have done too much good for that " ninety and nine " which the church forgets. But it is a pity that the work of the Salvation Army and of the city missions is sometimes relegated to the control of such incompetent and unworthy persons as Henrietta Manners and " Brother " Mason. Since my brief acquaintance with those aspiring reformers, I have investigated and found that both were prominent workers and " guides " in the respective religious movements to which they claimed allegiance; I also found that there were other Henrietta Mannerses and not a few "Brother" Masons interested in the same good work. It is the part of charity and justice to assume that their superior officers were totally ignorant of their real characters.

But why should these sacred duties be relegated to the Henrietta Mannerses and the "Brother" Masons? Are there not enough intelligent, conscientious Christian men and women among the churches who would consider it not only a duty, but a precious privilege, to carry the gospel of Jesus Christ into the dark places? It is not wise to set a thief to catch a thief, and it is worse than useless to encourage the weak, not to say the depraved, to carry the gospel to their kind.

In the days when I could see no silver lining to the clouds I tried going to a Protestant church, but I recognized very shortly the alienation between it and me. Personally, I do not like to attend Salvation meetings or listen to the mission evangelists. So I ceased any pretension of going to church, thus allying myself with that great aggregation of non-church-going Protestant working women who have been forced into a resentful attitude against that which we should love and support. It is encouraging, however, to find that the church itself has, at last, begun to heed our growing disaffection and alienation:

" The fact must be admitted that the wage-workers of this country are largely outside the churches. This breach has been steadily widening; conditions are worse now than they were ten years ago. One of the strongest reasons for this is the fact that the churches have not recognized so clearly as they ought the equities of this conflict. It is a grave failure. They ought never to have suffered such an alienation to occur between themselves and the people who constitute the very bone and sinew of our civilization," says a prominent preacher and reformer.

" How can the Christian church clear herself of the charge that the very people who heard her Lord gladly turn in multitudes from her threshold? There is need of sober thought and deep humiliation, that this most grave social problem may find a solution which shall bring honor to the church and peace to society." [1]

Obviously the fundamental need of the worker of

[1] " The Church and Social Problems," by Rev. Washington Gladden, D.D. (" International Quarterly.")

either sex is education. She needs to be educated, this work-girl. She does not need a fancy education; but she does need a good education, so that upon her entrance into the workshop she will be able to read and write and add up a column of figures correctly and with ease. This she seems not to be able to do under present conditions. And there are other things, even more important than the " three R's," which she should be taught. She should be taught how to work—how to work *intelligently*. She should be trained young in the fundamental race activities, in the natural human instinct for making something with the hands, or of doing something with the hands, and of taking an infinite pleasure in making it perfect, in doing it well.

I have no technical knowledge of pedagogics; I must admit that. My criticism of the public-school system I base entirely upon the results as I have seen them in the workshops, the factories, and the store in which I worked. During this period I had opportunity for meeting many hundreds of girls and for becoming more or less acquainted with them all. Now, of all these I have not yet discovered one who had not at some time in her earlier childhood or girlhood attended a public school. Usually the girl had had at least five years' continuous schooling, but often it was much more. But, great or small as the period of her tuition had been, I never met one whose knowledge of the simplest rudiments of learning was confident and precise. Spelling, geography, grammar, arithmetic, were never, with them, positive knowledge, but rather matters of chance and guess. Even the brightest girls showed a woeful ignorance of the "three R's." In only one thing did I find them universally well taught, and that was in handwriting. However badly spelled and ungrammatical their written language might be, it was invariably neatly and legibly—often beautifully—executed. But if these girls, these workmates of mine, learned to write clear and beautiful hands, why were they not able also to learn how to spell, why were they not able to learn the principles of grammar and the elementary knowledge of arithmetic as far at least as long division? That they did not have sufficient "apperceiving basis" I cannot believe, for they were generally bright and clever.

It is true that the public schools are already teaching manual training, and that kindergartens have enormously increased lately. These facts I know very well. I also know how much ignorance and senseless prejudice the pioneers of these educational reforms have had to overcome in the introduction of the newer and better methods. The point I wish to make carries no slur upon the ideal which the best modern pedagogy is striving for; it is, on the contrary, an appeal for the support and furtherance of that ideal on the part of intelligent citizenship generally, and of conscientious parenthood particularly. I believe firmly in the kindergarten; I believe that the child, whether rich or poor, who goes to kindergarten in his tender years has a better chance in life, all else being equal, than the child who does not. I do not know how long the free kindergarten system has obtained to any degree in New York City, but I do know that I have as yet found only one working girl who has had the benefit of any such training in childhood. She was " Lame Lena " at Springer's box-factory; and in spite of her deformity, which made it difficult for her to walk across the floor, she was the quickest worker and made more money than any other girl in the shop.

Tersely put, and quoting her own speech, the secret of her success was in " knowing how to kill two birds with one stone," and, again, " makin' of your cocoanut save your muscle." These formulæ were more or less vague until further inquiry elicited the interesting fact that " lame Lena," had had in childhood the privilege of a kindergarten training in a class maintained by some church society when the free kindergarten was not so general as it is now.

It is not unreasonable to suppose that had this lame girl's workmates enjoyed the privilege of the same elementary training, they might have shown an equal facility in the humble task of pasting and labeling and tissuing paper boxes. "Lame Lena" knew how to work; she knew how to husband every modicum of nervous energy in her frail, deformed body; and thus she was able to make up—more than make up—for her physical inferiority. "Lame Lena" brought to her sordid task a certain degree of organizing faculty; she did the various processes rhythmically and systematically, always with the idea in view of making one stroke of the arm or the hand do, if possible, a double or a triple duty. The other girls worked helter-skelter; running hither and thither; taking many needless journeys back and forth across the floor; hurrying when they were fresh to the task, dawdling when they were weary, but at all times working without method and without organization of the task in hand, and without that coördination of muscular and mental effort which the kindergarten might have taught them, just as it had certainly taught "Lame Lena."

The free kindergarten movement is not yet old

enough to begin to show its effects to any perceptible
degree in the factory and workshop. Henrietta
Manners and Phœbe Arlington and little Angelina
were born too soon: they did not know the joy of the
kindergarten; they did not know the delight of sitting in a little red chair in a great circle of other
little red chairs filled with other little girls, each and
all learning the rudimentary principles of work under the blissful delusion that they were at play.
These joys have been reserved for their little sisters,
who, sooner or later, will step into their vacant places
in the box-factory. What was denied Angelina it is
the blessed privilege of Angelina's baby to revel in.

Angelina's baby—the little baby that she kept in
the day-nursery when we worked together at Springer's—now goes to a free kindergarten. I happen
to know this because not long ago I met Angelina.
She did not recognize me—indeed, she had difficulty
in recalling vaguely that I had worked with her
once upon a time; for Angelina's memory, like that
of a great majority of her hard-worked class, is
very poor,—a fact I mention because it is very much
to the point right here. My solicitous inquiry for
the baby brought forth a burst of Latin enthusiasm
as to the cunningness and sweetness of that incipient
box-maker, who, Angelina informed me, goes to kin-

dergarten in a free hack along with a crowd of other babies. But Angelina, bless her soul! is down on the kindergarten. She says, with a pout and a contemptuous shrug, "they don't teach you 're kid nothing but nonsense, just cutting up little pieces of paper and singing fool songs and marching to music." Angelina admitted, however, that her *bambino* was supremely happy there,—so happy, in fact, that she had n't the heart to take her away, even though she does know that it is all "tomfoolishness" the "kid" is being taught by a mistaken philanthropy.

It is fair to suppose that in the factory and workshop of every description the kindergarten is bound to work incalculable results. Indeed, I sometimes wonder if the kindergarteners themselves can quite realize how well they are building—can fully comprehend the very great need in the working woman of the identical principles which they are so patiently and faithfully inculcating into the tender minds of these forlorn babies gathered up in the courts and alleys.

Another important thing looking to the well-being of the working girl of the future would be the wide dissemination of a better literature than that with which she now regales herself. I have already outlined at some length the literary tastes of my workmates at the box-factory. The example cited is typical of other factories and other workshops, and also of the department-store. A certain down-town section of New York City is monopolized by the publishers and binders of " yellow-backs," which are turned out in bales and cart-loads daily. Girls fed upon such mental trash are bound to have distorted and false views of everything. There is a broad field awaiting some original-minded philanthropist who will try to counteract the maudlin yellow-back by putting in its place something wholesome and sweet and sane. Only, please, Mr. or Mrs. Philanthropist, don't let it be Shakspere, or Ruskin, or Walter Pater. Philanthropists have tried before to reform degraded literary tastes with heroic treatment, and they have failed every time.

That is sometimes the trouble with the college-settlement folk. They forget that Shakspere, and Ruskin, and all the rest of the really true and great literary crew, are infinite bores to every-day people. I know personally, and love deeply and sincerely, a certain young woman—a settlement-worker —who for several years conducted an evening class in literature for some girl " pants-makers." She gave them all the classics in allopathic doses, she gave them copies of " A Crown of Wild Olive "

300

and " The Ethics of the Dust," which they read dutifully, not because they liked the books, which were meaningless to their tired heads, but because they loved Miss —— and enjoyed the evenings spent with her at the settlement. But Miss —— did not succeed in supplanting their old favorites, which undoubtedly she could have done had she given them all the light, clean present-day romance they could possibly read. It is a curious fact that these girls will not read stories laid in the past, however full of excitement they may be. They like romance of the present day, stories which have to do with scenes and circumstances not too far removed from the real and the actual. All their trashy favorites have to do with the present, with heroes and heroines who live in New York City or Boston or Philadelphia; who go on excursions to Coney Island, to Long Branch, or to Delaware Water Gap; and who, when they die, are buried in Greenwood over in Brooklyn, or in Woodlawn up in Westchester County. In other words, any story, to absorb their interest, must cater to the very primitive feminine liking for identity. This liking, this passion, their own special authors have thoroughly comprehended, and keep it constantly in mind in the development of their plots.

This taste for better literature could be helped

along immeasurably if still another original-minded philanthropist were to make it his business that no tenement baby should be without its "Mother Goose" and, a little later, its "Little Women," "Uncle Tom's Cabin," "Robinson Crusoe," and all the other precious childhood favorites. As it is, the majority know nothing about them.

But, after all, the greatest factor in the ultimate development of the working girl as a wage-earning unit—the most potent force for the adjustment of all the difficulties besetting her at every turn, and for the righting of all her wrongs, social, economic, or moral—will be the attitude which she herself assumes toward the dispassionate consideration of those difficulties to be adjusted, and of those wrongs to be righted.

At the present time there is nobody so little concerned about herself and her condition as the working woman herself. Taking everything into consideration, and in spite of conditions which, to the observer viewing them at a distance great enough to get a perspective, seem irreconcilably harsh and bitter—in the face of all this, one must characterize the working woman as a contented, if not a happy woman. That is the great trouble that will have to be faced in any effort to alleviate her condition. She is too contented, too happy, too patient. But not wholesomely so. Hers is a contentment, a happiness, a patience founded, not in normal good health and the joy of living and working, but in apathy. Her lot is hard, but she has grown used to it; for, being a woman, she is patient and long-suffering. She does not entirely realize the tragedy of it all, and what it means to herself, or to her children perhaps yet to be born.

In the happy future, the working girl will no longer be content to be merely " worked." Then she will have learned to work. She will have learned to work intelligently, and, working thus, she will begin to think—to think about herself and all those things which most vitally concern her as a woman and as a wage-earner. And then, you may depend upon it, she will settle the question to please herself, and she will settle it in the right way.

INSIDE THE NEW YORK TELEPHONE COMPANY

by Elinor Langer

(1970)

INSIDE THE NEW YORK
TELEPHONE COMPANY

F ROM October to December 1969 I worked for the
New York Telephone Company as a Customer's
Service Representative in the Commercial Department. My office was one of several in the Broadway–City
Hall area of lower Manhattan, a flattened, blue-windowed
commercial building in which the telephone company oc-
cupies three floors. The room was big and brightly lit—like
the city room of a large newspaper—with perhaps one hundred desks arranged in groups of five or six around the desk
of a Supervisor. The job consists of taking orders for new
equipment and services and pacifying customers who com-
plain, on the eleven exchanges (although not the more complex business accounts) in the area between the Lower East
Side and 23rd Street on the North and bounded by Sixth
Avenue on the West.

WOMEN AT WORK

My Supervisor is the supervisor of five women. She reports to a Manager who manages four supervisors (about twenty women) and he reports to the District Supervisor along with two other managers. The offices of the managers are on the outer edge of the main room separated from the floor by glass partitions. The District Supervisor is down the hall in an executive suite. A job identical in rank to that of the district supervisor is held by four other men in Southern Manhattan alone. They report to the Chief of the Southern Division, himself a soldier in an army of division chiefs whose territories are the five boroughs, Long Island, Westchester, and the vast hinterlands vaguely referred to as " Upstate." The executives at——Street were only dozens among the thousands in New York Tel alone.

Authority in their hierarchy is parceled out in bits. A Representative, for example, may issue credit to customers up to, say, $10.00; her supervisor, $25.00; her manager, $100.00; his supervisor, $300.00; and so forth. These employees are in the same relation to the centers of power in AT&T and the communications industry as the White House guard to Richard Nixon. They all believe that " The business of the telephone company is Service " and if they have ever heard of the ABM or AT&T's relation to it, I believe they think it is the Associated Business Machines, a particularly troublesome customer on the Gramercy-7 exchange.

I brought to the job certain radical interests. I knew I would see " bureaucratization," " alienation," and " exploi-

THE TELEPHONE COMPANY

tation." I knew that it was " false consciousness " of their true role in the imperialist economy that led the " workers " to embrace their oppressors. I believed those things and I believe them still. I know why, by my logic, the workers should rise up. But my understanding was making reality an increasing puzzle: Why didn't people move? What things, invisible to me, were holding them back? What I hoped to learn, in short, was something about the texture of the industrial system: what life within it meant to its participants.

I deliberately decided to take a job which was women's work, white collar, highly industrialized and bureaucratic. I knew that New York Tel was in a management crisis notorious both among businessmen and among the public and I wondered what effect the well-publicized breakdown of service was having on employees. Securing the position was not without hurdles. I was " overqualified," having confessed to college; I performed better on personnel tests than I intended to do; and I was inspected for symptoms of militance by a shrewd but friendly interviewer who noticed the several years' gap in my record of employment. " What have you been doing lately? " she asked me. " Protesting? " I said: " Oh, no, I've been married," as if that condition itself explained one's neglect of social problems. She seemed to agree that it did.

My problem was to talk myself out of a management traineeship at a higher salary while maintaining access to the job I wanted. This, by fabrications, I was able to do.

WOMEN AT WORK

I said: "Well, you see, I'm going through a divorce right now and I'm a little upset emotionally, and I don't know if I want a career with managerial responsibility." She said: "If anyone else said that to me, I'm afraid I wouldn't be able to hire them," but in the end she accepted me. I had the feeling it would have been harder for her to explain to her bosses why she had let me slip away, given my qualifications, than to justify to them her suspicions.

I nonetheless found as I began the job that I was viewed as "management material" and given special treatment. I was welcomed at length by both the District Supervisor and the man who was to be my Manager, and given a set of fluffy feminist speeches about "opportunities for women" at New York Tel. I was told in a variety of ways that I would be smarter than the other people in my class; "management" would be keeping an eye on me. Then the Manager led me personally to the back classroom where my training program was scheduled to begin.

The class consisted of five students and an instructor. Angela and Katherine were two heavy-set Italian women in their late forties. They had been promoted to Commercial after years of employment as clerks in the Repair Department where, as Angela said, "they were expected to be robots." They were unable to make the transition to the heavier demands of the Representative's job and returned to Repair in defeat after about a week.

Billy was a high-school boy of seventeen who had somehow

310

been referred by company recruiters into this strange women's world. His lack of adult experience made even simple situations difficult for him to deal with: he could not tell a customer that she had to be in the apartment when an installer was coming without giggling uncontrollably about some imaginary tryst. He best liked " drinking with the boys," a pack of Brooklyn high schoolers whose alcoholism was at the Singapore Sling stage; he must have belonged to one of the last crowds in Brooklyn that had never smoked dope.

Betty was a pretty, overweight, intelligent woman in her mid-twenties who had been a Representative handling " Billing " and was now being " cross-trained " (as they say in the Green Berets) in Orders. She was poised, disciplined, patient, ladylike, competent in class and, to me, somewhat enigmatic outside it: liberal about Blacks, in spite of a segregated high-school education, but a virtual Minuteman about Reds, a matter wholly outside her experience. By the end of the class Betty and I had overcome our mutual skepticism enough to be almost friends and if there is anyone at the phone company to whom I feel slightly apologetic—for having listened always with a third ear and for masquerading as what I was not—it is Betty.

Sally, the instructor, was a pleasant, stocky woman in her early thirties with a frosted haircut and eyes made up like a raccoon. She had a number of wigs, including one with strange dangling curls. Sally's official role was to persuade us of the rationality of company policies and practices, which she did skillfully and faithfully. In her private life, however, she was a believer in magic, an aficionado rather than a practitioner only because she felt that while she understood how to conjure up the devil, she did not also know how to make him go away. To Sally a disagreeable female customer was not oppressed, wretched, impoverished in her own life, or merely bitchy: she was—literally—a witch. Sally explained to herself by demonology the existence of evils of which she was far too smart to be unaware.

The Representative's course is " programmed." It is apparent that the phone company has spent millions of dollars for high-class management consultation on the best way to train new employees. The two principal criteria are easily deduced. First, the course should be made so routine that any employee can teach it. The teacher's material—the remarks she makes, the examples she uses—are all printed in a loose-leaf notebook that she follows. Anyone can start where anyone else leaves off. I felt that I could teach the course myself, simply by following the program. The second criterion is to assure the reproducibility of results, to guarantee that every part turned out by the system will be interchangeable with every other part. The system is to bureaucracy what Taylor was to the factory: it consists in breaking down every operation into discrete parts, then making verbal the discretions that are made.

At first we worked chiefly from programmed booklets organized around the principle of supplying the answer, then rephrasing the question. For instance:

It is annoying to have the other party to a conversation leave the line without an explanation.

Before leaving, you should excuse yourself and _____ what you are going to do.

Performing skillfully was a matter of reading, and not actual comprehension. Katherine and Angela were in constant difficulty. They "never read," they said. That's why it was hard for them.

Soon acting out the right way to deal with customers became more important than self-instruction. The days were organized into Lesson Plans, a typical early one being: How to Respond to a Customer If You Haven't Already Been Trained to Answer His Question, or a slightly more bureaucratic rendering of that notion. Sally explained the idea, which is that you are supposed to refer the call to a more experienced Representative or to the Supervisor. But somehow they manage to complicate this situation to the point where it becomes confusing even for an intelligent person to handle it. You mustn't say: " Gosh, that's tough. I don't know anything about that, let me give the phone to someone who does," though that in effect is what you do. Instead when the phone rings, you say: " Hello. This is Miss Langer.

May I help you? " (The Rule is, get immediate " control of the contact " and hold it lest anything unexpected happen, like, for instance, a human transaction between you and the customer.)

He says: " This is Mr. Smith and I'd like to have an additional wall telephone installed in my kitchen."

You say: " I'll be very glad to help you, Mr. Smith (Rule the Second: Always express interest in the Case and indicate willingness to help), but I'll need more information. What is your telephone number? "

He tells you, then you confess: " Well, Mr. Smith, I'm afraid I haven't been trained in new installations yet because I'm a new representative, but let me give you someone else who can help you." (Rule the Third: You must get his consent to this arrangement. That is, you must say: *May* I get someone else who can help you? *May* I put you on hold for a moment?)

The details are absurd but they are all prescribed. What you would do naturally becomes unnatural when it is codified, and the rigidity of the rules makes the Representatives in training feel they are stupid when they make mistakes. Another lesson, for example, was: What to Do If a Customer Calls and Asks for a Specific Person, such as Miss Smith, another Representative, or the Manager. Whatever the facts, you are to say " Oh, Miss Smith is busy but I have access to your records, may I help you? " A customer is never allowed to identify his interests with any particular employee.

THE TELEPHONE COMPANY

During one lesson, however, Sally said to Angela: "Hello, I'd like immediately to speak to Mrs. Brown," and Angela said, naturally, "Hold the line a minute, please. I'll put her on." A cardinal sin, for which she was immediately rebuked. Angela felt terrible.

Company rhetoric asserts that this rigidity does not exist, that Representatives are supposed to use "initiative" and "judgment," to develop their own language. What that means is that instead of using the precise words "Of course I'll be glad to help you but I'll need more information," you are allowed to "create" some individual variant. But you must always (1) express willingness to help and (2) indicate the need for further investigation. In addition, while you are doing this, you must always write down the information taken from the customer, coded, on a yellow form called a CF-1, in such a way as to make it possible for a Representative in Florida to read and translate it. "That's the point," Sally told us. "You are doing it the same way a rep in Illinois or Alaska does it. We're one big monopoly."

The logic of training is to transform the trainees from humans into machines. The basic method is to handle any customer request by extracting "bits" of information: by translating the human problem he might have into bureaucratic language so that it can be processed by the right department. For instance, if a customer calls and says: "My wife is dying and she's coming home from the hospital today and I'd like to have a phone installed in her bedroom right away," you *say*, "Oh, I'm very sorry to hear that sir, I'm sure I can help you, would you be interested in our Princess model? It has a dial that lights up at night," meanwhile *writing* on your ever-present CF-1: "Csr wnts Prn inst bdrm immed," issuing the order, and placing it in the right-hand side of your work-file where it gets picked up every fifteen minutes by a little clerk.

The knowledge that one is under constant observation (of which more later) I think helps to ensure that contacts are handled in this uniform and wooden manner. If you varied it, and said something spontaneous, you might well be overheard; moreover, it is probably not possible to be especially human when you are concentrating so hard on extracting the bits, and when you have to deal with so many bits in one day.

Sometimes the bits can be extraordinarily complicated. A customer (that is, a CSR) calls and says rapidly, "This is Mrs. Smith and I'm moving from 23rd Street to 68th Street, and I'd like to keep my green Princess phone and add two white Trimlines and get another phone in a metallic finish and my husband wants a new desk phone in his study." You are supposed to have taken that all down as she says it. Naturally you have no time to listen to how she says it, to strike up a conversation, or be friendly. You are desperate to get straight the details.

The dehumanization and the surprising degree of complication are closely related: the number of variables is large, each variable has a code which must be learned and manipulated, and each situation has one—and only one—correct answer. The kind of problem we were taught to handle, in its own language, looks like this:

A CSR has: IMRCV EX CV GRN BCHM IV
He wants: IMRCV WHT EX CV WHT BCHM IV

This case, very simplified, means only that the customer has regular residential phone service with a black phone, a green one, and an ivory bell chime, and that he wants new service with two white phones and a bell chime. Nonetheless, all these items are charged at differing monthly rates which the Representative must learn where to find and how to calculate; each has a separate installation charge which varies in a number of ways; and, most important, they represent only a few of the dozens of items or services a customer could possibly want (each of which, naturally, has its own rates and variables, its own codes).

He could want a long cord or a short one, a green one or a white one, a new party listed on his line, a special headset for a problem with deafness, a Touchtone phone, and on and on and on. For each of the things he could possibly want there would be one and only one correct charge to quote to him, one and only one right way to handle the situation.

It is largely since World War II that the Bell System abandoned being a comparatively simple service organization and began producing such an array of consumer products as to rival Procter and Gamble. It is important to realize what contribution this proliferation makes both to creating the work and to making it unbearable. If the company restricted itself to essential functions and services—standard telephones and standard types of service—whole layers of its bureaucracy would not need to exist at all, and what did need to exist could be both more simple and more humane. The pattern of proliferation is also crucial, for, among other things, it is largely responsible for the creation of the " new "—white collar— " working class " whose job is to process the bureaucratic desiderata of consumption.

In our classroom, the profit motivation behind the telephone cornucopia is not concealed and we are programmed to repeat its justifications: that the goods were developed to account for different " tastes " and the " need of variation." Why Touchtone Dialing? We learn to say that " it's the latest thing," " it dials faster," " it is easier to read the letters and numbers," and " its musical notes as you depress the buttons are pleasant to hear." We learn that a Trimline is a " space-saver," that it has an " entirely new feature, a recall button that allows you to hang up without replacing the receiver," and that it is " featured in the Museum of Modern Art's collection on industrial design." Why a night-light? we were asked. I considered saying, " It would be nice to make love by a small sexy light," but instead helped to contribute the expected answers: " It gives you

318

security in the bedroom," " it doesn't interfere with the TV."

One day a woman named Carol Nichols, whose job it is to supervise instruction, came to watch our class. Carol is a typical telephone company employee: an aging, single woman who has worked her way up to a position of modest authority. In idle conversation I inquired into the origins of our programmed instruction. Carol said it was all prepared under centralized auspices but had recently benefited from the consultation of two Columbia professors. One, she believed, was the chairman of the English department; another, an English professor. Their principal innovation, I gathered, was to suggest formal quizzes in addition to role-playing.

Carol took the content of the work very seriously. She was concerned to impress on us the now familiar Customer's Service Ideology that We Do Help the Customer no matter what his problem. She said: " If the customer tells you to drop dead, you say 'I'll be very glad to help you, sir.' " I couldn't resist raising the obvious question, wondering what is the Rule covering obscene propositions, but saying innocently, " Gee, I can think of things a customer might say that you wouldn't want to help him with." Carol looked very tough and said: " Oh. We don't get *those* kind of calls in the Commercial Department."

Carol threw herself into role-playing tests with gusto. In one of the tests she pretended to be a Mrs. Van Der Pool from Gramercy Park South, whose problem was that she had four dirty white phones that needed cleaning and one gold phone that was tarnishing. Carol enjoyed playing the snotty Mrs. VDP to the hilt, and what sense of identity, projection, or simple resentment went into her characterization it is hard to say. On the other hand, despite her caricatured and bossy airs, Carol was very nice to the women in the class. At the end, when Angela and Katherine were complaining that they were doing so poorly, Carol gave them a little pep talk in which she said that she had been miserable on her first day as a Rep, had cried, but had just made up her mind to get through it, and had been able to do so.

" Many have passed this way and they all felt the way you do," she told them. " Just keep at it. You can do it." Angela and Katherine were very grateful to Carol for this. Later in the week when, frustrated and miserable, Katherine broke down and cried, Sally too was unobtrusive, sympathetic, encouraging.

Selling is an important part of the Representative's job. Sally introduced the subject with a little speech (from her program book) about the concept of the " well-telephoned home," how that was an advance from the old days when people thought of telephone equipment in a merely functional way. Now, she said, we stress " a variety of items of beauty and convenience." Millions of dollars have been spent by the Bell System, she told us, to find out what a customer wants and to sell it to him. She honestly believed that good selling is as important to the customer as it is to the company: to the company because " it makes additional and

THE TELEPHONE COMPANY

worthwhile revenue," to the customer because it provides
services that are truly useful. We are warned not to attempt
to sell when it is clearly inappropriate to do so, but basically
to use every opportunity to unload profitable items. This
means that if a girl calls up and asks for a new listing for a
roommate, your job is to say: " Oh. Wouldn't your roommate
prefer to have her own extension? "

The official method is to avoid giving the customer a choice
but to offer him a total package which he can either accept
or reject. For instance, a customer calls for new service.
You find out that he has a wife, a teen-age daughter, and a
six-room apartment. The prescription calls for you to get
off the line, make all the calculations, then come back on and
say all at once: " Mr. Smith, suppose we installed for you a
wall telephone in your kitchen, a Princess extension in your
daughter's room and one in your bedroom, and our new
Trimline model in your living room. This will cost you only
X dollars for the installation and only Y dollars a month."

Mr. Smith will say, naturally, " That's too many telephones for a six-room apartment," and you are supposed to
" overcome his objections " by pointing out the " security "
and " convenience " that comes from having telephones all
over the place.

Every Representative is assigned a selling quota—so many
extensions, so many Princesses—deduced and derived in some
way from the quota of the next largest unit. In other words,
quotas are assigned to the individual because they are first

assigned to the five-girl unit; they are assigned to the unit because they are assigned to the twenty-girl section; and they are assigned to the section because they are assigned to the district: to the manager and the district supervisor. The fact that everyone is in the same situation—expected to contribute to the same total—is one of the factors that increase management-worker solidarity.

The women enact the sales ritual as if it were in fact in their own interest and originated with them. Every month there is a sales contest. Management provides the money— $25.00 a month to one or another five-girl unit—but the women do the work: organizing skits, buying presents, or providing coffee and doughnuts to reward the high sellers. At Thanksgiving the company raffled away turkeys: the number of chances one had depended on the number of sales one had completed.

As the weeks passed our training grew more and more rigid. For each new subject we followed an identical Army-like ritual beginning with " Understanding the Objectives " and ending with " Learning the Negotiation." The Objectives of the " Lesson on Termination of Service," for instance, were:

1. To recognize situations where it is appropriate to encourage users to retain service.
2. To be able to apply " Save effort " successfully.
3. To negotiate orders for Termination.
4. To offer " Easy Move."

THE TELEPHONE COMPANY

5. To write Termination orders.

Or, for example, Cords. It is hard to believe such a subject could be complicated but in fact it is: cords come in different sizes, standard and special, and have different costs, different colors, and different installation intervals. There is also the weighty matter of the distinction between the handset cord (connecting the receiver to the base) and the mounting cord (connecting the base to the wall or floor). The ritual we were taught to follow when on the telephone with a customer goes like this, and set up on our drawing board it looked like this as well:

Fact-finding:
1. Business or residence.
2. New or existing service.
3. Reason for request
   a. handset or mounting cord
   b. approximate length
4. Type of set or location.
5. Other instruments in the household and where located.
6. Customer's phone number.

Then you get:

Off the line, where you
1. Get Customer's records.
2. Think and plan what to do.
3. Check reference materials.
4. Check with supervisor if necessary.

Then you return to the line with a:

Recommendation:
1. Set stage for recommendation.
2. Suggest alternative where appropriate or
3. Accept order for cord.
4. Suggest appropriate length.
   a. Verify handset or mounting.
5. Present recommendation for suitable equipment that " goes with " request including monthly rental (for instance, an extension bell).
6. Determine type of instrument and color.
7. Quote total non-recurring charges.
8. Arrange appointment date, access to the apartment, and whom to see.

On the floor, substantial departure from this ritual is an Error (more later). This pattern of learning became so intolerable that, one day, while waiting for Sally to return from lunch, the class invented a lesson of its own. We called it Erroneous Disconnections. The Objectives were:
1. To identify situations in which it is appropriate to disconnect Customer.
2. To apply the necessary techniques so that disconnects can be accomplished with minimum irritation to the Representative.
3. To accomplish these ends without being observed.
We then identified a variety of situations in which our natural response would be to disconnect. I was surprised by

how deeply Billy and Betty were caught up in our parody, and I thought it represented an ability to dissociate from the company, which most of the time was very little in evidence; it seemed to me somehow healthy and promising.

As the weeks wore on our classes became in some ways more bizarre. On several afternoons we were simultaneously possessed by the feeling that we simply couldn't bear it and—subtly at first but with increasing aggression as time passed—we would simply stop work: refuse to learn any more. At these times all kinds of random discussions would take place. On one occasion we spent an entire afternoon discussing the Seven Wonders of the Ancient World and calling up information services of newspapers to find out what they were; on another afternoon Sally explained at great length her views on magic.

At first I believed that these little work stoppages were spontaneous but later, as we completed our class work close to schedule, I came to believe that this was not so: that they were a part of our program and were meant to serve as an opportunity for the instructor to discover any random things about our views and attitudes the company might find it useful to know. In any event, partly because of these chats and partly because of the intensity of our training experience, by the end of the class we were a fairly solid little unit. We celebrated our graduation with perfume for Sally, a slightly alcoholic and costly lunch, and great good feeling all around.

II

Observers at the phone company. They are everywhere. I became aware of a new layer of Observation every day. The system works like this. For every five or six women there is, as I have said, a Supervisor who can at any moment listen in from the phone set on her desk to any of her Representatives' contacts with a customer. For an hour every day, the Supervisor goes to a private room off the main floor where she can listen (herself unobserved) to the conversations of any of her " girls " she chooses. The women know, naturally, *when* she is doing this but not *whose* contact she is observing.

Further off the main floor is a still more secret Observing Room staffed by women whose title and function is, specifically, Observer. These women " jack in " at random to any contact between any Representative and a customer: their job is basically to make sure that the Representatives are giving out correct information. Furthermore, these Observers are themselves observed from a central telephone company location elsewhere in the city to make sure that they are not reporting as incorrect information which is actually correct. In addition the Observers make " access calls " by which they check to see that the telephone lines are open for the customers to make their connections. This entire structure of observation is, of course, apart from the formal representative-supervisor-manager–district supervisor–division head

326

THE TELEPHONE COMPANY

chain of managerial command. They are, in effect, parallel hierarchical structures.

One result of the constant observation (the technology being unbounded) is that one can never be certain where the observation stops. It is company policy to stress its finite character, but no one ever knows for sure. Officials of the Communications Workers of America have testified, for instance, that the company over-indulged in the wired-Martini stage of technology, bugging the pen sets of many of its top personnel. At——Street there were TV cameras in the lobby and on the elevators. This system coexists with the most righteous official attitude toward wiretapping. Only supervisors and managers can deal with wiretap complaints; Federal regulations about the sanctity of communications are posted; and the overt position toward taps, in the lower managerial echelons, is that they are simply illegal and, if they exist, must be the result of private entrepreneurship (businesses bugging one another) rather than Government policy.

" If someone complains about a tap," Sally said, " I just ask them: Why would anyone be tapping your phone? " Consciousness of the Government's " internal security " net is simply blacked out. Nonetheless, the constant awareness of the company's ability to observe creates unease: Are the lounge phones wired into the Observing structure? Does the company tap the phones of new or suspicious personnel? Is union activity monitored? No one can say with confidence.

WOMEN AT WORK

Sally had two voices, one human, one machine, and in her machine voice on the very first day she explained the justification for Observation. "The thing about the phone company," she said, "is that it has No Product except the Service it Gives. If this were General Motors we would know how to see if we were doing a good job: we could take the car apart and inspect the parts and see that they were all right and that it was well put together. But at the phone company we can't do that. All we can do is check ourselves to see that we are doing a good job."

She took the same attitude toward "access calls," explaining that a completed access call is desirable because it indicates to the manager and everyone up the line that the wires are open and the system is working as it should. The position toward Observers she attempted to inculcate was one of gratitude: Observers are good for you. They help you measure your job and see if you are doing well.

The system of Observers is linked with the telephone company's ultimate weapon, the Service Index by which Errors are charted and separate units of the company rated against each other. Through training—in class and in our days on the floor—hints of the monumental importance of the Index in the psychic life of the employees continually emerged. "Do you know how many Errors you're allowed?" Sally would ask us. "No Errors"—proud that the standard was so high. Or: "I can't afford an Error"—from my supervisor, Laura, on the floor, explaining why she was keeping

328

me roped in on my first days on the job. But the system was not revealed in all its parts until the very end of training when as a *pièce de résistance* the manager, Y, came in to give a little talk billed as a discussion of " Service " but in fact an attempt to persuade the class of the logic of observation.

Y was a brooding, reserved man in his mid-twenties, a kind of Ivy League leftover who looked as if he'd accidentally got caught in the wrong decade. His talk was very much like Sally's. " We need some way to measure Service. If a customer doesn't like Thom McAn shoes he can go out and buy Buster Brown. Thom McAn will know something is wrong. But the phone company is a monopoly, people can't escape it, they have no other choice. How can we tell if our product, Service, is good? " He said that observation was begun in 1924 and that, although the company had tried other methods of measuring service, none had proved equally satisfactory. Specifically, he said, other methods failed to provide an accurate measure of the work performance of one unit as opposed to another.

Y's was a particularly subtle little speech. He used the Socratic method, always asking us to give the answers or formulate the rationales, always asking, Is it right? Is it fair? (I'm certain that if we did not agree it was right and fair, he wanted to know.) He stressed the limited character of observation. His units (twenty " girls "), he said, took about 10,000 calls per month; of these only about 100 were observed, or about five observations per woman per month. He emphasized that these checks were random and anonymous. He explained that the Index has four components which govern what the observers look for:

Contact Performance Defects (CPD)
Customer Waiting Interval (CWI)
Contacts Not Closed (CNC)
Business Office Accessibility (BOA)

The CPD is worth 70 per cent of the Index, the other factors 10 per cent each. The elements of CPD are, for example, incomplete or incorrect information, making inadequate arrangements, or mistreating a customer; the elements of BOA are the amount of time it takes a customer to reach the central switchboard, and the promptness of the Representative in answering the phone after the connection has been made. Points are assigned on a scientific basis, based on the number of errors caught by the observers. Charts are issued monthly, rating identical units of the company against each other. Y's unit (mine) was the top unit in Manhattan, having run for the preceding three months or so at about 97 or 98 per cent. While I was there, there was a little celebration, attended by high company officials, in which Y was awarded a plaque and the women on the floor given free " coffee and danish."

Now, a number of things about this system are obvious. First, demeaning and demanding as it is, it clearly provides management with information it believes it has a desperate need to know. For instance, there was a unit on the East Side of Manhattan running at about an 85 per cent level. The mathematics of it are complicated but it basically means that about 12,000 people every month were getting screwed by the department in one form or another: they asked for a green phone and the Representative ordered a black one; they arranged to be home on the 24th and the woman told the installer to come on the 25th; they were told their service would cost $10.00 and it actually cost $25.00, and so forth. Management has to know which of its aspirants, scrambling up the ladder, to reward and which to punish.

On the other hand, their official justifications for observation are a lie for two reasons. First, the Index does not measure actual service: our unit could run at 98 per cent while half the phones in our area were out of service because the Index does not deal with the service departments of the company which are, in fact, where its troubles are. The angriest customer in Manhattan would not show up as an error on the Index if he were treated politely and his call transferred: the Commercial Index is a chimera capable of measuring only its internal functioning, and that functioning, being simply bureaucratic, is cut off from the real world of telephone service and servicing. Secondly, it is a lie because it does not spring from the root that management claims—that is, the absence of a tangible physical product (observation is in fact commonplace in industry where the nonexistence of a product is not an issue) but from another root: the need to control behavior. That is, if the system is technically linked to measurement of service it is functionally linked to control.

Furthermore, it works: it absolutely controls behavior. On December 24, the one day of the year when there is no observation (and no contribution to the Index) the concept of service utterly disappeared. The women mistreated the customers and told them whatever came into their minds. Wall lights whose flickering on a normal day indicates that customers are receiving busy signals were flashing wildly; no one cared about the BOA.

But on a normal day, the Index is King. It is a rule, for instance, that if one Representative takes over a call for another, the first must introduce the second to the customer, saying " Sir, I'm going to put Miss Laramie on the line. She'll be able to help you." " Don't forget to introduce me," said Miss L. anxiously to me one day. " An observer might be listening." Or: we were repeatedly told *never* to check the box labeled " Missed on Regular Delivery " on the form authorizing delivery of directories. " It will look as if Commercial made an Error," Sally told us, " when the Error is really Directory's. " This awareness of observers and Errors is constant not because of fear of individual reprisal—there is none—but because of block loyalty: first to the immediate unit of five women, then to the twenty-women unit, then to the still larger office.

The constant weighing, checking, competition also binds

the managers to the women and is another source of the overwhelmingly paternalistic atmosphere: the managers are only as good as their staffs and they are rated by the same machine. The women make, or don't make, the Errors; the managers get, or don't get, the plaques and the promotions.

What the system adds up to is this: if we count both supervisors and observers, at least three people are responsible for the correct performance of any job, and that is because the system is based on hiring at the lowest level, keeping intelligence suppressed, and channeling it into idiotic paths. The process is circular: hire women who are not too talented (for reasons of social class, limited educational opportunities, etc.); suppress them even further by the " scientific " division of the job into banal components which defy initiative or the exercise of intelligence; then keep them down by the institutionalization of pressures and spies.

Surely it would be better if the jobs' horizons were broadened—a reformist goal—if women were encouraged to take initiative and responsibility, and then left on their own. And it would be better yet if those aspects of the work directly tied to the company's profit-oriented and " capitalistic " functions—the Princess and Trimline phones and all the bureaucratic complications that stem from their existence— were eliminated altogether and a socialized company concentrated on providing all the people with uniform and decent service. But . . .

III

Daily life on the job at the New York Telephone Company consists largely of pressure. To a casual observer it might appear that much of the activity on the floor is random, but in fact it is not. The women moving from desk to desk are on missions of retrieving and refiling customers' records: the tête-à-têtes that look sociable are anxious conferences with a Supervisor in which a Representative is Thinking and Planning What to Do Next. Of course the more experienced women know how to use the empty moments that do occur for social purposes. But the basic working unit is one girl-one telephone, and the basic requirement of the job is to answer it, perhaps more than fifty times a day.

For every contact with a customer, the amount of paperwork is huge: a single contact can require the completion of three, four, or even five separate forms. No problems can be dispensed with handily. Even if, for example, you merely transfer a customer to Traffic or Repair you must still fill out and file as CF-1. At the end of the day you must tally up and categorize all the services you have performed on a little slip of paper and hand it in to the Supervisor, who completes a tally for the unit: it is part of the process of " taking credit " for services rendered by one unit vis-à-vis the others.

A Representative's time is divided into " open " and " closed " portions, according to a recent scientific innova-

334

tion called **FADS** (for Force Administration Data System), of which the company is particularly proud; the innovation consists in establishing how many Representatives have to be available at any one moment to handle the volume of business anticipated for that month, that day, and that hour. Under this arrangement the contact with the customer and the processing of his request are carried out simultaneously: that is, the Representative does the paperwork needed to take care of a request while she is still on the line. For more complex cases, however, this is not possible and the processing is left for " closed " time: a time when no further calls are coming in.

This arrangement tends to create a constant low-level panic. There is a kind of act which it is natural to carry to its logical conclusion: brushing one's teeth, washing a dish, or filling out a form are things one does not leave half done. But the company's system stifles this natural urge to completion. Instead, during " open " time, the phone keeps ringing and the work piles up. You look at the schedule and know that you have only one hour of " closed " time to complete the work, and twenty minutes of that hour is a break.

The situation produces desperation: How am I to get it done? How can I call back all those customers, finish all that mail, write all those complicated orders, within forty minutes? Occasionally, during my brief time at the job, I would accidentally press the wrong button on my phone and it would become " open " again. Once, when I was feeling particularly desperate about time, I did that twice in a row and both times the callers were ordering new telephone service—a process which takes between eight and ten minutes to complete.

My feeling that time was slipping away, that I would never be able to " complete my commitments " on time was intense and hateful. Of course it was worse for me than for the experienced women—but not much worse. Another situation in which the pressure of time is universally felt is in the minutes before lunch and before five o'clock. At those times, if your phone is open, you sit hoping that a complex call will not arrive. A " new line " order at five minutes to five is a source of both resentment and frustration.

Given the pressure, it becomes natural to welcome the boring and routine—the simple suspensions or disconnections of service—and dread the unusual or complex. The women deal with the pressure by quietly getting rid of as many calls as they can, transferring them to another department although the proper jurisdiction may be a borderline matter. This transferring, the lightening of the load, is the bureaucratic equivalent of the " soldiering " that Taylor and the early scientific managers were striving to defeat. It is a subtle kind of slowdown, never discussed, but quickly transmitted to the new Representative as legitimate. Unfortunately, it does not slow things down very much.

As Daniel Bell points out in his extraordinary essay, " Work

THE TELEPHONE COMPANY

and Its Discontents," the rhythm of the job controls the time spent off the job as well: the breaks, the lunches, the holidays; even the weekends are scarcely long enough to re-establish a more congenial or natural path. The work rhythm controls human relationships and attitudes as well. For instance: there was a Puerto Rican worker in the Schrafft's downstairs whose job was to sell coffee-to-go to the customers: he spent his day doing nothing but filling paper cups with coffee, fitting on the lids, and writing out the checks. He was very surly and very slow and it looked to me as if the thoughts swirling in his head were those of an incipient murderer, not an incipient revolutionary. His slowness was very inconvenient to the thousands of workers in the building who had to get their coffee, take it upstairs, and drink it according to a precise timetable. We never had more than fifteen minutes to get there and back, and buying coffee generally took longer. The women resented him and called him " Speedy Gonzales," in tones of snobbery and hate. I know he hated us.

IV

The women of the phone company are middle class or lower middle class, come from a variety of ethnic backgrounds (Polish, Jewish, Italian, Irish, black, Puerto Rican), mainly high-school graduates or with a limited college education. They live just about everywhere except in Manhattan: the

WOMEN AT WORK

Bronx, Brooklyn, Staten Island, or Queens. Their leisure time is filled, first of all, with the discussion of objects. Talk of shopping is endless, as is the pursuit of it in lunch hours, after work, and on days off. The women have a fixation on brand names, and describe every object that way: it is always a London Fog, a Buxton, a White Stag. This fixation does not preclude bargain-hunting: but the purpose of hunting a bargain is to get the brand name at a lower price. Packaging is also important: the women will describe not only the thing but also the box or wrapper it comes in. They are especially fascinated by wigs. Most women have several wigs and are in some cases unrecognizable from day to day, creating the effect of a continually changing work force. The essence of wiggery is escapism: the kaleidoscopic transformation of oneself while everything else remains the same. Anyone who has ever worn a wig knows the embarrassing truth: it *is* transforming.

Consumerism is one of the major reasons why these women work. Their salaries are low in relation to the costs of necessities in American life, ranging from $95.00 to $132.50 *before* taxes: barely enough, if one is self-supporting, to pay for essentials. In fact, however, many of the women are not self-supporting, but live with their families or with husbands who also work, sometimes at more than one job. Many of the women work overtime more than five hours a week (only for more than five extra hours do they get paid time and a half) and it seems from their visible spending that it is

338

simply to pay for their clothes, which are expensive, their wigs, their color TV's, their dishes, silver, and so forth.

What the pressures of food, shelter, education, or medical costs contribute to their need to work I cannot tell, but it seems to me the women are largely trapped by their love of objects. What they think they need in order to survive and what they endure in order to attain it is astonishing. Why this is so is another matter. I think that the household appliances play a real role in the women's family lives: helping them to run their homes smoothly and in keeping with a (to them) necessary image of efficiency and elegance. As for the clothes and the wigs, I think they are a kind of tax, a tribute exacted by the social pressures of the work-place. For the preservation of their own egos against each other and against the system, they had to feel confident of their appearance on each and every day. Outside work they needed it too: to keep up, to keep their men, not to fall behind.

The atmosphere of passionate consuming was immeasurably heightened by Christmas, which also had the dismal effect of increasing the amount of stealing from the locker room. For a period of about three weeks nothing was safe: hats, boots, gloves. The women told me that the same thing happens every year: an overwhelming craving, a need for material goods that has to find an outlet, even in thievery from one another.

The women define themselves by their consumerism far more than by their work, as if they were compensating for their exploitation as workers by a desperate attempt to express their individuality as consumers. Much of the consuming pressure is generated by the women themselves: not only in shopping but in constant raffles, contests, and so forth in which the prize is always a commodity—usually liquor. The women are asked to participate in these raffles at least two or three times a week.

But the atmosphere is also deliberately fostered by the company itself. The company gave every woman a Christmas present: a little wooden doll, about four inches tall, with the sick-humor look that was popular a few years ago and still appears on greeting cards. On the outside the doll says " Joy is . . . " and when you press down the springs a little stick pops up that says " Extensions in Color " (referring to the telephone extensions we were trying to sell). Under that label is another sticker, the original one, which says " Knowing I wuv you." The doll is typical of the presents the company distributes periodically: a plastic shopping bag inscribed with the motto " Colorful Extensions Lighten the Load "; a keychain with a plastic Princess telephone saying " It's Little, It's Lovely, It Lights "; plastic rain bonnets with the telephone company emblem, and so forth.

There were also free chocolates at Thanksgiving and, when the vending machine companies were on strike, free coffee for a while in the cafeteria. The women are disgusted by the company's gift-giving policies. Last year, I was told, the Christmas present was a little gold-plated basket filled with velour fruit and adorned with a flag containing a company motto of the " Extensions in Color " type. They think it is a cheap trick—better not done at all—and cite instances of other companies which give money bonuses at Christmas.

It is obvious that the gifts are all programmed, down to the last cherry-filled chocolate, in some manual of Personnel Administration that is the source of all wisdom and policy; it is clear from their frequency that a whole agency of the company is devoted to devising these gimmicks and passing them out. In fact, apart from a standard assortment of insurance and pension plans, the only company policy I could discover which offers genuine advantage to the employees and which is not an attempt at manipulation is a tuition support program in which the company pays $1,000 out of $1,400 of the costs of continuing education.

Going still further, the company, for example, sponsors a recruiting game among employees, a campaign entitled " People Make the Difference." Employees who recruit other employees are rewarded with points: 200 for a recommendation, an additional thousand if the candidate is hired. Employees are stimulated to participate by the circulation of an S&H-type catalogue, a kind of encyclopedia of the post-scarcity society. There you can see pictured a GE Portable Color Television with a walnut-grained polystyrene cabinet (46,000 points), a Silver-Plated Hors d'Oeuvres Dish by Wallace (3,900 points), and a staggering assortment of mass-produced candelabra, linens, china, fountain pens, watches, clothing, luggage, and—for the hardy—pup tents, power tools, air mattresses.

Similarly, though perhaps less crudely, the company has institutionalized its practice of rewarding employees for longevity. After every two years with the company, the women receive a small gold charm, the men a " tie-tac." These grow larger with the years and after a certain period jewels begin to be added: rubies, emeralds, sapphires, and eventually diamonds and bigger diamonds. The tie-tac evolves over the years into a tie-clasp. After twenty-five years you may have either a ceremonial luncheon or an inscribed watch: the watches are pre-fixed, pre-selected, and pictured in a catalogue.

The company has " scientifically structured " its rewards just as it has " scientifically structured " its work. But the real point is that the system gets the women as consumers in two ways. If consumption were less central to them, they would be less likely to be there in the first place. Then, the company attempts to ensnare them still further in the mesh by offering as incentives goods and images of goods which are only further way stations of the same endless quest.

V

Another characteristic of the telephone company is a kind of programmed " niceness " which starts from the top down but which the women internalize and mimic. For management the strategy is clear (the Hawthorne experiments, after all, were carried out at Western Electric): it is, simply, make the employees feel important. For trainees this was accomplished by a generous induction ceremony complete with flowers, films, a fancy buffet, and addresses by top division representatives, all of which stressed the theme: the company cares about you.

The ceremonies had another purpose and effect: to instill in the minds of new employees the image the company would like the public to have of it, that it is a goodhearted service organization with modest and regulated profits. A deliberate effort was made to fend off any free-floating negative ideas by explaining carefully, for instance, why AT&T's monopolistic relationship with Western Electric was a good thing. The ideology of Service, embraced without much cynicism by the low-level managers who are so abundant, is in that way—and others—passed along.

The paternalism, the " niceness," filters down and is real. Employees are on a first-name basis, even the women with the managers. The women are very close to one another, sharing endless gossip, going on excursions together, and continually engaging in ceremonial celebration of one another's births, engagements, promotions. The generosity even extends to difficult situations on the job. I have, for example, seen women voluntarily sharing their precious closed time when one of them was overcommitted and the other slightly more free. Their attitude toward new employees was uniformly friendly and helpful. When I first went out on the floor my presence was a constant harassment to the other women in my unit: I didn't know what to do, had to ask a lot of questions, filed incorrectly. As a newcomer, I made their already tense lives far more difficult. Nonetheless I was made to feel welcome, encouraged. " Don't feel bad," one or another would say at a particularly stupid error. " We were all new once. We've all been through it. Don't worry. You'll catch on." In the same way I found them invariably trying to be helpful in modest personal crises: solicitous about my health when I faked a few days of illness, comforting in my depression when a pair of gloves was stolen, always friendly, cheering me (and each other) on.

This " niceness " is carefully preserved by the women as a protection against the stress of the work and the hostility of customers. " We have to be nice to each other," Sally told me once. " If we yelled at each other the way the customers yell at us, we'd go crazy. " At the same time it is a triumph of their spirit as well. There is some level on which they are too proud to let the dehumanization overtake them; too decent to let the rat race get them down.

On the job, at least, the women's sense of identification with the company is absolute. On several occasions I tried to bring up issues on which their interests—and the public's—diverged from that of the company, and always I failed to make my point. It happened, for example, on the issue of selling, where I told my class frankly that I couldn't oversell, thought it was wrong, and that people needed far fewer telephones than we were giving them. Instead of noticing that I was advocating a position of principle, my class thought that, because I was so poor myself (as measured by having only one black telephone) I just somehow couldn't grasp the concept of the " well-telephoned home, " but that I would catch on when I became convinced that the goods and services in question were truly valuable and desirable.

It happened again during a discussion of credit ratings when, because welfare women are always put in the lowest category, I said I thought credit rested on racist assumptions. The class explained to me that " if you worked in Billing and knew how hard it is to collect from those people " I wouldn't feel that way. And it happened another time during a particularly macabre discussion over coffee when the women were trading horror stories about tragic cases where telephone service had to be cut off because people weren't paying their bills: they were grotesque tales about armless veterans and blind old ladies of eighty-five.

I kept saying that terminating those services was intolerable, that some way should be found for people to have services free. Instead of thinking that was an odd position, the women reported that " every new representative feels that way," that they used to feel that way themselves, but they'd gotten over it. In other words they began their jobs with all the feelings any decent (never mind radical) person would have, and gradually learned to overcome them, because of the creeping identification with the company produced by their having to act out daily a company-defined role. Their basic belief in the legitimacy of the " make a buck " system established in their minds a link between company revenue and their own paychecks. " That's where your money comes from " was a common conclusion to these discussions.

The women have a strangely dissociated attitude toward company operations that aren't working well. What company *policy* is—that is, the way they learn things are supposed to be—gets pressed into their heads so much that they get a little confused by their simultaneous understanding that it isn't really working that way at all. I pointed that out a lot, to see what would happen. For instance our lesson books say: " Customers always get Manhattan directories delivered with their regular installations." I said, in class: " Gee, that's funny, Sally, I had a telephone installed recently and I didn't get any phone books at all." Sally would make sure not to lose control and merely repeat: " Phone books are delivered with the regular installations."

It was the same with installation dates, which, in the company's time of troubles, are lagging behind. Company *policy* is that installations are made two days from the date they are requested. In reality we were making appointments for two, three, or even four weeks in advance. There are explanations for these lapses—everyone knows that things go wrong all the time—but there are no reasonable explanations which do not undermine the basic assumption that the company has everything " scientifically " under control. Thus the " policy " is that they are not happening at all.

The effect of the pressure of work and the ethos of niceness is to defuse political controversy. There is a kind of compact about tolerance, a governing attitude which says, " Let's not talk about religion or politics." During the time I was there I heard virtually no discussion of Vietnam, the city elections, or race. There was a single exception—an argument between Betty and myself over Song My—after which I had the feeling that something had been breached, that she would take particular care not to let it happen again.

This is not characteristic of the men's departments of the company where political discussion is commonplace, and I believe the women think that such heavy topics are properly the domain of men: they are not about to let foolish " politics " interfere with the commonsensical and harmonious adjustments they have made to their working lives. Race relations were governed by the same kind of neutrality and " common sense." The black women of the Commercial Department were of the same type as the whites: lower middle class and upwardly mobile. Among the Representatives, not an Afro was in sight. There were good and close relationships between the blacks and the whites—close enough for jokes about hair and the word " nigger "—and, as far as I could tell, the undercurrents of strain that existed were no greater (though certainly no less intense) than are character-

istic of such relations in the more educated and " liberal "
middle classes.

VI

Normally the question of unions is far from the interests of
the women in the Commercial Department. The women do
not see themselves as " workers " in anything like the class-
ical sense. The absence of this consciousness—deliberately
stunted by management personnel strategies—is a natural
and realistic response to the conditions of their work. Customer's Service Representative is the position from which
lower (female) management is recruited, and promotions are
frequent. Supervisors are always former Representatives and
their relations with the women they supervise are close and
friendly. The absence of rigid job definitions is an economic
boon to the company as well as a psychic advantage to the
employees. When a Supervisor is ill, for example, a " rep "
will take over and handle her functions, and reps as well as
Supervisors are occasionally asked to teach classes, coach
new employees, or take " acting " titles: a natural managerial flow which is unthinkable under most union rules.

This is not to say that the women think their working
conditions are good: they object to the salaries; they hate
the pressure; they dislike Observation; and they resent the
internalized time clocks which control their lunches and

breaks. But the women's trust remains with the company and their hopes for escape are mainly fixed on the individual's upward mobility into managerial ranks. " Worker solidarity "—the consciousness that all workers advance through collective action—is weak.

The Union of Telephone Workers, which " represents " the Commercial Department, reflects this condition. It is an " independent " union lineally descended from the company-sponsored employee organizations that existed in the Bell System before the Wagner Act. It belongs to an Alliance of Independent Telephone Unions composed of similar unions in Bell companies along the Eastern Seaboard. The UTW explicitly rejects the philosophy of " international " or " big " unionism in favor of a company-oriented approach " close to the problems " of workers and management. Its successes are precisely those modest concessions and policy changes which any remotely modern management would have had to make in recent years to maintain its work force.

The UTW's role is to stamp those concessions into the language and mold of " negotiated " agreements. It swings into action readily enough when it is attacked—a large part of the machinery of the Alliance exists for precisely this purpose—but it is generally a sleepy beast content to nuzzle in the bosom of Ma Bell. Numbers are irrelevant to its strength —only about 40 per cent of the women belong—and it does not seem interested in recruiting. As a new employee, I had to seek it out. Similar company unions represent the telephone operators in the Traffic Department (the serfs of the system) and the Accounting Department. The only AFL-CIO Union in New York Telephone is the Communications Workers of America, which represents the Plant bargaining unit—installers, repairmen, switchmen, and so forth. CWA has a reputation for company-mindedness elsewhere in the labor movement, but despite recent challenges it has long been the only " real " union with which New York Tel's management has had to deal.

This divided labor force (in addition to the four unions there are seven contracts, no two of which expire simultaneously) is crucial to management for three reasons. First of all, the work rules and sensitivities of the CWA would drive any rational management crazy. In the Plant department, a clerk will not answer a Foreman's telephone unless she is reclassified as a secretary; the men will not work " alongside " management even when—as now—a manpower shortage has created acute emergencies. And the men in the union not only obstruct a " rational " flow of work: they have interfered with management's efforts to expand its work force by hiring new employees at more generous starting salaries than those of the old employees. That—in addition to an undercurrent of racism—was a key issue in the telephone strike last fall. If that mentality were transferred to other departments, the company would be in far greater difficulty than it is now.

Second, it is precisely the absence of solidarity between

departments that gives management the leverage to break or control the frequent strikes the men provoke. When CWA strikes occur, they are usually ignored by the other unions, and lower-level management from the other departments is sent around to Plant to help with repairs, handle complaints, and so forth. If their departments were also on strike, these junior executives would have to attend to their own jobs: they could not be used as scabs against the CWA.

Third, though more remote, is a larger threat: the possibility of a single militant union of telephone workers, perhaps nationwide, actually stopping or, more fancifully, seizing, the network of telephone communications. For all these reasons, it is clear, management prefers the present arrangement to a more unified one.

In any event, the union question, normally static, uncharacteristically sprang to life during my stay at the telephone company because at the end of November the CWA opened a raid on the UTW. Its ultimate intention was to begin to assemble all company employees into a unified body. In this plan was a measure of wishful thinking, if not deception. CWA is not so popular within the company and though it recently won an election in the city Plant department (over a teamster-inspired challenge) it has also lost several others (against company unions) in upstate New York and in New England. Nevertheless, consolidation was its chief arguing point: in unity there will be strength.

CWA's problem was that members of the Commercial bargaining unit were spread out in small clusters in dozens of locations throughout New York. Their efforts, however, seemed particularly lackluster and should make New Left organizers take heart: the old dogs have no new tricks to teach.

They began their campaign in my area by calling an after-work meeting of Commercial Department women in a small working-class bar close by several of the Commercial offices downtown, attempting to lure people there by desultory leafleting the same morning. From my office—that is from among the one hundred Representatives who worked with me—no one came but me, though there was a handful of women from other Commercial units in the same building.

From another office, however, whose function was identical to mine, about forty women came, and in exploring why I discovered subtle differences between offices in the relations between managers and women. It seems that a manager at the other office had just held a meeting with his women in which he complained that they were stretching their breaks too long and cheating on their closed time. They found his remarks threatening and reacted with hostility. I later learned that this office is particularly understaffed and has an intracompany reputation of being one of the more tense places to work. I believe that the ethers of solidarity that float between our manager, Y, and the women in my office would have prevented such an exchange from taking place there.

352

THE TELEPHONE COMPANY

At the meeting the CWA was represented chiefly by shop stewards who had jobs as installers, switchmen, repairmen, and by one somewhat puffy and intellectualized bureaucrat from the International. The men were plain, decent, and serious, and had an intelligent point to make: if we stood together we would be the stronger for it. CWA dues were higher than UTW's, they admitted, but they paid for real union services: hard bargaining by trained negotiators, grievance procedures, fringe benefits, and so forth; most of the gains made by Commercial employees were the results of CWA pressures elsewhere in the Bell System.

The women's reaction to the sales pitch was pure Gomperism: what about free dental care, medical checkups, low cost car-purchasing programs? Some issues were raised that were more basic. They were women and they were being raided by men. They would be asked to walk out to support the men. Would the men walk out to support them? Why were there no women in top positions in the union when 45 per cent of the members were women? Why did women's salaries in the company start at $79.50 when the lowest amount paid to a man was $95.00?

Back at my office it developed that the women were not nearly so uninterested as their nonattendance had made it seem. Nor were they as anti-union as their lack of interest in the UTW suggested. It was more that they were not meeting-goers, on the one hand, and that they were disgusted by the UTW on the other. A group of women I talked to in the cafeteria one day told me that every time a UTW contract came up for approval, they and others they knew voted " no " but that somehow their votes didn't get counted. They were seriously interested in the CWA alternative, discussed it a great deal among themselves, and began filling out the cards required to petition the NLRB for an election.

The union issue stirred up the most serious conversation I had heard at the company, and, for a time, I had private fantasies about the possibilities involved in a CWA takeover: could the women be made to see their women's interests in some opposition to a male-dominated union, once they were in it, more clearly than they could see them opposed to the company, which was always holding out the carrot of personal advancement? Would the union, simply because it was in motion and in some way organized, because consciousness in it was more free-floating, be the right forum in which to raise war-related issues such as AT&T's involvement with the ABM? Could the racism inherent in the union's opposition to the company's new policies of hiring what it always referred to as the " hard core " possibly be overcome? For a time, these things seemed possible to me. Then management began its counterattack.

By early December management was calling private meetings of Supervisors to feed them anti-CWA propaganda, which they in turn would feed back to the women. Sally came back from such a meeting filled with grisly facts: " The President of CWA makes $35,000 a year," she said; the top

THE TELEPHONE COMPANY

officials recently voted themselves a $4-6,000 salary raise; top pay in New York is higher than top pay in places represented by CWA; it's true there's a dental plan but you have to use CWA dentists.

The main point of management's message was, if you're dissatisfied, reform the UTW. Is the President too old? Throw her out and get a more modern President. But don't throw away the union that has gotten you eleven paid holidays and all your other gains; don't throw out the baby with the bath. Later these arguments were repeated (almost word for word) in a similar chat which my floor supervisor, Laura, had with the women in her unit. The company also began to engage in all sorts of other activities, turning over the payroll lists to the UTW at an early date for propaganda mailings to the employees' homes, and at one point even circulating a UTW phone number which we were advised to call for " unbiased " information on what the raid was all about. The recorded message went like this:

This is a message to all Commercial Department employees. Your independent union and all of you are being raided by CWA. They are trying to mislead you into believing that the raid is for the sake of unity. Nothing could be farther from the truth. They want you only for your money. CWA dues run from $5.50 to $10.50 a month to support their Washington fat cat. The dues you pay to your independent union, the Union of Telephone Workers, are not wasted for Washington offices and fat cats. CWA claims to represent a lot of telephone workers in the United States but not a single contract for Commercial workers can meet your contract for wages. Your independent union, the UTW, has negotiated the highest wage rates for Commercial Department employees anywhere in the United States.

Your intelligence will caution you not to become a tool of CWA's misleading tactics.

Your desire for effective and orderly representation will caution you against buying CWA's walkout, wildcat strike sellout policies, and the constant loss of wages over ridiculous disputes.

Your experience and knowledge of human nature will keep you from getting fouled up in foolish frustrations and the hopeless fury of CWA's ineffective puppets.

A step toward CWA is a costly step downward: more dues, frequent assessments, loss of autonomy and less take-home pay.

This does not make good sense, does it?

Stay with your independent union, the Union of Telephone Workers.

This propaganda was later multiplied in individual mailings, and I believed it was likely to be effective, particularly when communicated to the women by Supervisors whom they trust. At least in my department (a small fraction of the overall bargaining unit) the women did not have enough class consciousness to suspect it merely because it was coming from the company. In addition, the CWA's rebuttal campaign—conducted through mailings—did not deal solidly with these concrete objections. In the election, held in mid-February, the CWA lost by about seven to two.

My ultimate conclusion about the CWA-UTW issue as I watched it struggling to its finale was that it simply did not matter. Images were left in my head: Dan, a fat CWA chief steward, driving me to an appointment uptown in a car decorated with American flags and an antique Veterans Poppy; a later meeting with him in which he described the company's new employees exclusively as tramps, pushers, and smelly apes; an interview with a union official after I quit in which he sighed and remarked, "The trouble with people today is that they want change for the sake of change." I thought: CWA does inspire something more closely akin to true "consciousness" than the company unions, but the consciousness it inspires is not close enough to what is needed. In view of the top-down control and inflexible ways of the CWA, and the marginal role of any union in the women's lives, the women's immediate interests probably are better represented by the UTW; and the CWA does not offer the compensation of initiating fights for larger political objectives, or even for objectives that have to do with the quality of life within the company. Thus the issues of dues, strike pay, and socialized dentistry become real.

VII

Perhaps the best way to think about the women of the telephone company is to ask the question: what reinforces company-minded behavior and what works against it? It is a difficult question. The reinforcement comes not from the work but from the externals of the job: the warmth of friendships, the mutual support, the opportunities for sharing and for gossip, the general atmosphere of company benevolence and paternalism; not to mention the need for money and the very human desire to do a good job.

I never heard any of the women mouth the company rhetoric about " service to the customer " but it was obvious to me that a well-handled contact could be satisfying in some way. You are the only person who has access to what the customer needs—namely, telephones—and if you can provide him with what he wants, on time and efficiently, you might reasonably feel satisfied about it. The mutual support—the sharing of closed time, helping one another out on commitments—is also very real. The continual raffles, sales contests, gimmicks, and parties are part of it, too. They simply make you feel part of a natural stream.

Working in that job one does not see oneself as a victim of " Capitalism." One is simply part of a busy little world which has its own pleasures and satisfactions as well as its own frustrations but, most important, it is a world, with a

358

THE TELEPHONE COMPANY

shape and an integrity all its own. The pattern of co-opta-
tion, in other words, rests on details: hundreds of trivial, but
human, details.

What is on the other side? Everyone's consciousness of
the iron fist, though what they usually see is the velvet glove;
the deadening nature of the work; the low pay; what is going
on in the outside world (to the extent that they are aware of
it); the malfunctioning of the company; the pressure of super-
vision and observation. There was a sign that sat on the desk
of one of the women while I was there, a Coney Island joke-
machine sign: " Due to Lack of Interest, Tomorrow Will be
Postponed." For a time I took it as an emblem and believed
that was how the woman really felt. But now I am not sure.

I think that for these women to move they would have to
have a sense of the possibility of change—not even to mention the desirability of change—which I am certain they do
not feel. They are more satisfied with their lives than not,
and to the extent that they are not, they cannot see even the
dimmest possibility of remedial action through collective
political effort. The reason they do not have " class-consciousness "—the magic ingredient—is that in fact they are
middle class. If they feel oppressed by their situation, and
I think many of them do, they certainly see it only as an
individual problem, not as something which it is their human
right to avoid or overcome.

How one would begin to change that, to free them to live
more human lives, is very hard to know. Clearly it would

require a total transformation of the way they think about the world and about themselves. What is impossible to know is whether the seeds of that transformation lie close beneath the surface and are accessible, or whether they are impossibly buried beyond rescue short of general social convulsion. It is hard to believe that the women are as untouched as they seem by the social pressures which seem so tangible to radicals. Yet I saw little evidence that would make any other conclusion possible.

I have a strong feeling of bad faith to have written this at all. I know the women will not recognize themselves in my account, but will nonetheless be hurt by it. They were, after all, warm and friendly: sympathetic about my troubles, my frustrations; helpful in the work; cheerful in a businesslike way. Betty, at least, was a friend. It is almost as if a breach of the paternalism of the company is involved. I fear a phone call asking " Was that a nice thing to do? " and I would say, perhaps not, perhaps the intellectual and political values of my life by which I was judging yours make equally little sense. Perhaps the skills which give me leverage to do it allow me only to express alienation and not to overcome it; perhaps I should merely be thankful that I was raised as an alpha and not a beta. Sometimes I am not sure. But I know that however it will seem to them, this piece is meant to be for the women of the telephone company, and that it is written for them with both love and hope.

A Note on the Authors

DOROTHY RICHARDSON published *The Long Day* anonymously, and little is known about her other than the information offered in that book. She apparently wrote no other books or articles.

ELINOR LANGER graduated from Swarthmore College in 1961 and worked briefly for the Washington Center for Foreign Policy Research and the *Washington Post*. For four years she reported on politics for *Science*, then became New York editor of *Ramparts*. Her articles have also appeared in the *Nation*, the *New York Review of Books*, and the *Atlantic*. Miss Langer now lives on a farm in southern Vermont, where she is working on a novel and teaching at Goddard College.

WILLIAM L. O'NEILL's most recent book is *Coming Apart: An Informal History of America in the 1960's*. He has also written *Divorce in the Progressive Era* and *Everyone Was Brave*, which has been widely acclaimed as the first important interpretation of the history of American feminism. He is now at work on a study of American attitudes toward sex since the Victorian era. Mr. O'Neill is Professor of History at Rutgers University and lives in Edison, New Jersey, with his wife, Carol, and their two daughters.